Praise for *Redefin*

"Fasten your seatbelt! This book brings clarity and insight to education priorities that prepare students for their futures, and pragmatic guidance for how schools can fulfill this promise. Grounded in decades of field expertise, the authors offer a powerful educational North Star of immense value to educators, parents, and concerned citizens around the globe."

—Ted Dintersmith, Founder
What School Could Be
Author, *What School Could Be*

"With the demands of the workplace never greater, and the need for effective citizenship never more urgent, the world demands a new generation of self-directed creative problem solvers. *Redefining Student Success* is the guide every leader needs to build an education system worthy of the students they serve."

—Daniel H. Pink, Author
When, Drive, and *To Sell Is Human*

"We must reconsider what we're working toward in education and reorient toward a purpose that's relevant for today's world, with all its challenges and opportunities. *Redefining Student Success* is an incredible gift—it's a road map for educators and other stakeholders seeking to develop a shared vision of the capabilities students (and educators) need to develop so they can shape a better future."

—Wendy Kopp, CEO and Co-founder
Teach For All
Founder, Teach For America

"Let's face it: most people know our schools can be better but they are not sure where to start. *Redefining Student Success* brings the steps for school transformation to life with sound advice, practical strategies, and rich stories sharing the whys and hows."

—Cindy Johanson, Executive Editor
Edutopia

"The global pandemic has created a cultural tipping point. Forced isolation has shone a spotlight on the critical need to accelerate our quest to improve the skills, knowledge, behaviors, and dispositions that will shape and prepare students for jobs, home, and societal responsibilities. With the imperative decisions school systems are making, Ken Kay and Suzie Boss provide a treasure trove of tools on behalf of district leaders who are working diligently to create bold, equity-focused, and futuristic initiatives in order to meet the growing demands of today's public education landscape. All children, no matter their zip codes, deserve every opportunity to turn their dreams into reality. *Redefining Student Success* can serve as a 'go-to' resource to help ensure that education for all learners becomes equitable, engaging, and authentic."

—Daniel A. Domenech, Executive Director
AASA, The School Superintendents Association

"Ken Kay has long been a significant thought leader and contributor to advancing 21st century education. In this new book, Kay and Suzie Boss offer powerful stories of school system leaders engaged in 21st century, deeper learning and how the changes made have positively impacted young people. Their amazing examples of real work in districts across the country are inspiring!"

—Karen K. Garza, President and CEO
Battelle for Kids

"What if you could design schools where students were passionately invested in the learning process and in the meaningful outcomes of that process? The good news is you can. With powerful examples, reflection, and action tools, Ken Kay and Suzie Boss show us how to engage parents, teachers, students, and leaders in a critically important conversation about what learning must look like now and for our future."

—Aaron Spence, Superintendent
Virginia Beach City Public Schools, Virginia

"Ken Kay and Suzie Boss bring home the point that leadership matters in promoting transformational change in school organizations. I love the 'ask yourself' sections of this book! They pose critical questions for reflection on the myriad ways in which education practitioners have worked to implement change in our nation's schools."

—David W. James, Superintendent
Akron Public Schools, Ohio

"*Redefining Student Success* makes the case for why every student deserves equal access to 21st century learning experiences and provides leaders with a set of tools and strategies to make this vision a reality."

—Steven Holmes, Superintendent
Sunnyside Unified School District, Arizona

"As we emerge from a global pandemic, we have the opportunity to 'reopen the schools of the future.' Ken Kay and Suzie Boss provide a clear path forward for educators to solidify the best we've learned about 21st century education. Brilliantly written and easy to navigate, let this book be your GPS for true educational transformation."

—Michael R. McCormick, Superintendent
Val Verde Unified School District, California

"Ken Kay and Suzie Boss have created a practical path that has the potential to transform American education. It includes an inspiring vision, vital components of change, and a realistic path forward. It is the long, overdue bridge from ideas to implementation. *Redefining Student Success* supports teachers and leaders in their journeys to create modern, personalized education for all students."

—Elizabeth Fagen, Superintendent
Humble ISD, Texas

"When two authorities on 21st century skills and project-based learning join forces, the whole can be greater than the parts—and that is the case with this book. Ken Kay and Suzie Boss bring their exceptional expertise together to offer a synthesized vision that can truly transform schooling. If you're ready to embark on the journey toward 'future proof' learning, this book is for you!"

—Jay McTighe, Co-author
Understanding by Design® framework
and *Leading Modern Learning*

"The vision of education needs to change and to make that happen, it must engage the community in a robust conversation about what our students really need for college, life, and career. Ken Kay and Suzie Boss's book takes the premise that our new vision of education needs to be rooted in our communities and shows us what is possible as we build that vision and allow it to take root deeply in every phase of education. It turns out when the community is engaged in developing the vision, they become co-owners and help light the path for students to obtain the skills, mindsets, and dispositions they need to be successful."

—Cheryl Carrier, Executive Director
Ford Next Generation Learning

"*Redefining Student Success* is an inspirational reminder that education is only limited by our vision, and teaching is first and foremost an act of leadership."

—John Wright, Senior Director for Strategy
National Education Association

"Ken Kay and Suzie Boss have both made so many helpful contributions to innovative learning and teaching. I love that they have teamed up. The strengths of this book are the specific strategies that help educators translate their visions for learning into concrete, actionable structures. The 'field trip' examples from schools across the country and the Portrait of a Graduate connections are fantastic!"

—Scott McLeod, Associate Professor of Educational Leadership
University of Colorado Denver
Founding Director, CASTLE

"For 20 years, Ken Kay has been the leading advocate for 21st century skills. Two decades into the century, Kay and Suzie Boss offer a timely update on what young people need to know and be able to do to thrive with a focus on creative problem solving and the addition of self-direction and civic engagement. This bold vision is a must read for any school or system reconsidering learning goals. We appreciate how the authors have incorporated sustainability, innovation, and entrepreneurship into a call for community-connected project-based learning."

—Tom Vander Ark, CEO
Getting Smart
Author, *Difference-Making at the Heart of Learning*

"Ken Kay and Suzie Boss are veteran edu-leaders in our march to transform K–12 learning. In *Redefining Student Success*, they give school leaders a powerful, detailed, and ready-to-use set of tools to move beyond the 'why' and on to the 'how' of school change. The book provides a cornucopia of examples from schools, leaders, and teams that are already well on the way."

—Grant Lichtman, Chief Provocateur
Author, *Thrive*

Redefining
Student Success

Redefining Student Success

Building a New Vision to Transform Leading, Teaching, and Learning

Ken Kay

Suzie Boss

Foreword by Tony Wagner

FOR INFORMATION:

Corwin
A SAGE Company
2455 Teller Road
Thousand Oaks, California 91320
(800) 233-9936
www.corwin.com

SAGE Publications Ltd.
1 Oliver's Yard
55 City Road
London EC1Y 1SP
United Kingdom

SAGE Publications India Pvt. Ltd.
B 1/I 1 Mohan Cooperative Industrial Area
Mathura Road, New Delhi 110 044
India

SAGE Publications Asia-Pacific Pte. Ltd.
18 Cross Street #10-10/11/12
China Square Central
Singapore 048423

Printed in the United States of America

Library of Congress Control Number: 2021939999

President: Mike Soules
Associate Vice President and
     Editorial Director: Monica Eckman
Senior Acquisitions Editor: Ariel Curry
Senior Content Development Editor: Desirée Bartlett
Senior Editorial Assistant: Caroline Timmings
Project Editor: Amy Schroller
Copy Editor: Karin Rathert
Typesetter: Hurix Digital
Proofreader: Dennis Webb
Cover Designer: Scott Van Atta
Marketing Manager: Morgan Fox

This book is printed on acid-free paper.

SUSTAINABLE
FORESTRY
INITIATIVE

Certified Chain of Custody
Promoting Sustainable Forestry
www.sfiprogram.org
SFI-01268

21 22 23 24 25 10 9 8 7 6 5 4 3 2 1

Contents

PART II: VISITING YOUR VISION

PART III: BUILDING YOUR VISION

For *The Student's Guide to 21st Century Learning, The Parent's Guide to 21st Century Learning* (both available in English and Spanish), and other materials, please visit the book's companion website at https://resources.corwin.com/redefiningstudentsuccess

Foreword

By Tony Wagner

Ken Kay and Suzie Boss make a bold assertion: We need to redefine student success—and in so doing redefine the goals of education. Why should educators even consider undertaking this work, you might well ask? The answer is staring us in the face, if we have the courage to look. As I write this in the winter of the pandemic, the many failures of our education system are now glaringly obvious.

After twenty-five years of school reform efforts in the United States, the inequities in learning opportunities and outcomes for young people from economically disadvantaged backgrounds have continued to grow. School reform efforts—the so-called Common Core State Standards, high-stakes testing, charter schools, and other such mandates and initiatives—have had zero impact on the problem. Test scores continue to be correlated with family income, thus creating a bell curve of tragic and inescapable proportions. And the fact that many disadvantaged students don't have internet access or a computer or a quiet place to study or even enough food to eat has made even more glaringly obvious the structural inequities in our education system.

The distance learning that the COVID-19 crisis necessitated has made visible to all the failure of the traditional "knowledge transmission" model of learning that has dominated education since the dawn of the Industrial Era. For the first time, parents and teachers could see for themselves how disengaged most kids are in classes where teachers did most of the talking. In some school districts, as many as 30 percent of students simply stopped attending their virtual classes. The number of course failures has skyrocketed as a result.

The costs of going to college have increased dramatically in the last thirty years, while wages have largely stagnated, resulting in spiraling student debt. The jobs that most college grads manage to find will not pay enough for them to get out from under this debt burden for many years, if ever. The nearly 50 percent of students who enter college but do not complete a degree are often in even greater financial peril.

Meanwhile, a growing number of employers are more interested in what skills students have mastered than in what degrees they may have earned. The list of well-known companies that no longer require a college diploma as a condition of employment includes Google, AT&T, Kaiser Permanente, McKinsey & Company, Microsoft, Walmart, and others. This has led an increasing number of families to question the value of a college degree.

The Fourth Industrial Revolution has changed the workplace forever. The World Economic Forum describes this latest transformation as "a digital revolution that has been occurring since the middle of the last century . . . a fusion of technologies that is blurring the lines between the physical, digital, and biological spheres" (Schwab, 2016). Increasingly, people will be required to work *with* technology, including artificial intelligence (AI), to perform their jobs. Rather than an Orwellian scenario of computers taking over, AI will push humans to do more of what they can do better than computers—such as critical thinking, creativity, communication, and collaboration.

The erosion of trust in government and many people's inability to distinguish facts from propaganda compel us to rethink what it means to educate for citizenship in the United States. Students need to spend less time listening to lectures on the U.S. Constitution and Bill of Rights—facts that most forget very quickly—and more time learning the skills of critical thinking, weighing evidence, reasoning, and media literacy. They also need opportunities to practice citizenship through involvement in local efforts to improve their communities.

This book is a clear and compelling road map to creating very different education goals and a system that provides genuine solutions to these challenges. It is filled with wonderful stories of educators doing this vital work—and of the students who are benefiting from these transformations of learning and teaching. Read it, study it with your colleagues, discuss it with your students' families, and act as if our children's and our country's futures depend on your bold leadership—because they do.

Preface

HIGHLIGHTS

American schools and districts are languishing in a model that does not match the moment. As a result, our students are not ready for the challenges ahead of them. This book provides leaders with tools for reimagining the goals of education to help today's students develop the skills they need to succeed. Backward design—starting with the end in mind—will help you chart the path forward. Having a shared Portrait of a Graduate (POG) provides you with a vision that will inform every aspect of your system while keeping the focus squarely on students. Co-creating a Portrait of an Educator (POE) with your instructional team will also ensure that teachers have a unified vision for their own professional growth to support student success. To show where this work can lead, we provide compelling examples of students already engaged in creative, self-directed problem solving around issues that matter to them and their communities. It's time to reset educational outcomes to be in sync with the demands of 21st century society.

By the time your current class of kindergartners reaches the end of high school, a third of this century will belong to history. Yet the promise of a 21st century education—one that equips students with the skills, knowledge, and mindsets they need to survive and thrive—continues to go unfulfilled for too many of our students.

This book provides you with tools and strategies to accelerate the transformation of your school system so that all students are prepared for the future they want to pursue. Insights from education leaders who are at different places on this journey, in diverse communities, will show you what's possible and, we hope, inspire a sense of urgency to join in the work. After two decades of advocating for 21st century learning, we are convinced that today's students can't afford to wait for schools to catch up with the moment.

The moment matters. The pandemic and social upheaval that began in 2020 are forcing school leaders to make hard decisions to resuscitate their systems. As you emerge from this crisis, will you fall back on outdated goals for education as the easiest way forward? Or will you take the courageous step to pursue the outcomes required by the realities of today? To reach the right decision for your community, you must be ready to lead a brave conversation with all your stakeholders.

This book articulates a clear path for reengaging your community in conversation about the future of education and then moving forward on that collective vision. Our message—informed by education leaders on the frontlines of change—is coming at a moment of real opportunity to provide our students with the education they need.

WHY US? WHY NOW?

Ken has been a leader of the 21st century education movement since its inception. He was the first president of the Partnership for 21st Century Skills, which synthesized the essential 4 Cs as communication, collaboration, creativity, and critical thinking. To support leaders in this movement, he and Valerie Greenhill co-authored *The Leader's Guide to 21st Century Education* (2012) and (with Alyson Nielson) co-founded EdLeader21 to build a national network of education leaders committed to redefining student success. He spent nearly a decade on the board of PBLWorks, an organization that has built global momentum for high-quality project-based learning.

Suzie has been a longtime advocate of project-based learning (PBL) to transform teaching and learning to align with 21st century goals. Her books have helped to define high-quality PBL (Larmer, Megendoller, & Boss, 2015; Boss & Krauss, 2018) and connect the dots between research and practice (Boss & Larmer, 2018). She has worked alongside teachers on nearly every continent who are designing projects that make learning more authentic and relevant. Their success depends on leaders who share their commitment to the hard work of school change.

From our different paths, we have reached the same conclusion: The time for debating the "why" of 21st century learning has long passed. What leaders and their teams want now is help with the "how." By our estimates, only 10 percent of U.S. school systems have started on this important journey by adopting a POG that redefines student success. This is not a problem confined to the United States. A recent international comparison found a scarcity of pedagogies to develop and assess students' 21st century competencies (Taylor, Fadel, Kim, & Care, 2020). Fewer than half of today's high school students think that what they learn in class helps them outside school (YouthTruth, 2017). This book is a response to the demand for practical strategies and tools to ensure that schools and districts meet the needs of every student. That was intended to be the laser focus of this book.

However, during our research, every leader we interviewed spoke about the historic events of COVID-19 and Black Lives Matter and their profound impact on education. Racial inequities that have gone unaddressed can no longer be ignored. "The bandage has been ripped off," one superintendent told us. These events are unfolding at a time when trust in political leadership is in steep decline (Winthrop, 2020) and communities are increasingly polarized. Amid these crises, teaching practices have come under the spotlight. Although some teachers have struggled to engage students in virtual settings, others have stepped into this moment with creativity and courage. One superintendent you will hear from in Chapter 4 described the events that began in 2020 as a turning point for schools everywhere.

These events should cause all of us to ask a hard question: When our students confront their own unprecedented challenges in the future, will they be ready? The need to develop creative problem solvers and engaged citizens has never been more clear or urgent.

OUR RESEARCH

Our research focuses on school systems that are already engaged in redefining student success. Within these parameters, we have cast a wide net, reaching out to district leaders from urban, suburban, and rural settings. We were eager to hear from women superintendents as well as men. (Of the forty-five state and district superintendents we interviewed, twenty are female.) We looked for racial diversity within our sample, both among the leaders and within the diverse populations they serve. Some leaders were familiar to us from their involvement in EdLeader21; others emerged from our review of the literature about school transformation. The overwhelming majority are public school educators; a handful are from independent and international schools.

Each conversation expanded our interview pool. Leaders often recommended others on their team who are deeply involved in rethinking professional development, instructional design, assessment, and other critical components of school systems. Suggestions also took us beyond school systems to talk with business and community partners who are taking on new roles to support student success.

By the time we started writing, we had interviewed more than 250 superintendents, state education leaders, principals, teachers, education professors, parents, union leaders, and thought leaders from education and other sectors. We spent a lot of time on Zoom.

One of the questions that proved most fruitful was, "What's the outcome of your work?" The replies underscore the importance of context. Each community must decide how to redesign instruction and assessment, how to measure and communicate growth, and how to manage the pace of change.

You will hear how school systems are creating new metrics to measure redefined student outcomes. For example, Val Verde Unified School District in California is expanding career pathways to reach all learners and developing new tools to measure and certify career-based competencies. In Pike County, Georgia, every student is building a digital portfolio to curate their best work toward mastery of competencies and participating in capstone experiences as they reach significant milestones in their education.

When leaders spoke about outcomes, they often described specific examples of students tackling meaningful challenges as evidence of learning. We followed up with many of these students, whose stories are woven throughout this book. These stories—of teachers teaching in new ways and students learning deeply by doing—became some of the most valuable contributions to this book. Storytelling is powerful. It should remind you as a leader of the kinds of stories you want to be able to share with your community to put a human face on your school transformation goals. Such examples not only demonstrate tangible results but remind us why this work is worth the effort.

Unless otherwise indicated, stories in the coming chapters were shared by sources personally interviewed by the authors. They have granted permission to be quoted in the book.

HOW TO USE THIS BOOK

This book unpacks the methodology to lead your school system and community through a change process that will produce tangible results. Transformation starts with a backward design process, informed by diverse stakeholders, to develop a POG. This becomes your community's North Star. With a clear vision, you will keep the focus squarely on student outcomes, even if you must make seismic shifts in your school systems to reach them.

You will tackle four bold challenges:

1. Create a community-based vision to ensure equity and close the readiness gap

2. Create a green light culture for teachers
3. Create a green light culture for students
4. Focus on creative problem solving that fits your context

In Part I: Embracing Your Vision, we focus on the importance of having a bold vision and bold conversations. You will be introduced to the concept of a green light culture and the role you can play in nurturing it. Chapters 1 and 2 highlight two important tools you can use to support your efforts to transform your school or district:

- **The Portrait of a Graduate,** a framework of student competencies intended to result from a broad community consensus on the outcomes necessary for student success. When the Portrait of a Graduate is based on this inclusive process, it can serve as the North Star for your system's transformation process.
- **The Portrait of an Educator**, a second tool some schools and districts are adopting to answer the question, "What competencies do educators need in order to enable students to attain the competencies identified in the Portrait of a Graduate?"

In Part II: Visiting Your Vision, we encourage you to imagine what schools of the future will look like by taking you on "field trips" to see creative problem solving underway in schools today. In Chapters 3 and 4, you will see that, when students and teachers have a green light to tackle meaningful challenges, contexts for student problem solving can include the following:

- Sustainability
- Innovation, invention, and entrepreneurship
- Civic engagement

If students are going to be intrinsically motivated to embrace these new and interdisciplinary contexts for learning, they must be driving their own education. Chapter 5 focuses on how to lead self-directed learners.

In Part III: Building Your Vision, you will be challenged to plan your next steps to address the leadership challenges you have set for yourself and your school system.

- Chapter 6 focuses on how to lead bold pedagogical and assessment challenges that move creative problem solving forward for *every* student.

- Chapter 7 describes strategies to engage your community in supporting problem-solving partnerships and explores how to maintain partnerships by reporting on progress toward your shared vision.
- Chapter 8 guides you to move this work forward with optimism and hope.

Special features to watch for include the following:

- **Chapter Highlights:** A succinct introduction to each chapter gives readers a heads up about what's ahead and why it matters.
- **Ask Yourself:** Reflection prompts and conversation starters throughout the book prompt your own thinking and spark discussions among your colleagues and stakeholders.
- **Final Reflections:** You'll find these at the end of each chapter to encourage you to connect the major themes of the book to your own context.
- **Resources for Implementation:** These are suggested readings and technology tools to support your work.
- **Action Steps:** The end of each chapter will list Action Steps to help you chart your way forward with your team.

Finally, the appendices include a reading guide to use with your leadership team and instructional staff, along with information for downloading free companion guides in both English and Spanish to engage students and parents in conversations about redefining student success.

SEIZE THE MOMENT

In the Foreword, Tony Wagner has done an outstanding job of explaining the urgency for the work we call for in this book. If school systems react to COVID-19 as a short-term crisis to be addressed with quick fixes, that urgency will likely dissipate. What we have learned from our discussions with dozens of bold educators is that crisis can create opportunity. We are more convinced than when we began this project that redefining student success is the urgent, essential work facing education today. We have the tools we need. Let's not wait another moment to begin.

Gratitudes

This section is usually called "Acknowledgments;" however, these aren't usual times. Writing this during the pandemic made life more complicated for everyone, and we want to do more than acknowledge those who assisted us. We thank you all deeply.

We have been particularly humbled by the outpouring of cooperation for writing this book at a time when education leaders and teachers have been overwhelmed by the impacts of COVID-19 on their jobs and lives and especially on the lives of their students. Somehow in the face of that reality, hundreds of educators took the time to talk with us. Each time you see a name in the book, realize that the person took time out of an extremely burdened schedule to help us tell their stories. To each of them, we are deeply grateful. In addition, there are dozens of others who spoke with us about the substantive underpinnings of this book. All the individuals we interviewed are listed in Appendix D. We thank each and every one of them for their perspectives and overall support.

In addition to the interviewees, several people spent time reviewing the initial outline as well as excerpts and chapters of the book. We are grateful to them for taking this time and for the cogent advice they gave us. Specifically, we offer deep gratitude to Tony Bent, Leondria Bryant, Cheryl Carrier, Stephanie Couch, Mike Duncan, Valerie Greenhill, Todd Hellman, Anisa Heming, David James, Braden Kay, Chip Kimball, Rick Lear, Kelly Lyman, Barry Sommer, Jay McTighe, Alyson Nielson, and Tony Wagner. Special thanks to Andre Daughty for being a critical friend for our work.

We also want to thank Ariel Curry, Desirée Bartlett, and the team at Corwin for their enthusiasm and support for this project. From our first interviews to the release of this book took about twelve months, an ambitious calendar that required an immense amount of collaboration and commitment. We so appreciate the professionalism and support provided by the Corwin team.

Finally, we are leaving this project more optimistic about the future of education than we were at the start because of the amazing students, educators, parents, and leaders we met along the way:

- Students leading the way as creative problem solvers who serve as role models for the future of education

- Educators demonstrating the future of pedagogy in classrooms today who are providing a challenging and rewarding vision for the teaching profession
- Education leaders serving as role models of public service for their communities as they lead thoughtful processes of groundbreaking consensus building

We not only owe them gratitude for the help they provided us, but we are deeply in awe of the pathways they are creating for all of us to follow. To all of these individuals, we are deeply grateful.

Gratitudes From Suzie

When Ken first approached me about collaborating on a book for 21st century education leaders, he was not quite retired but already looking ahead to his next challenge. I recall feeling flattered but not certain I was the right partner. After all, most of my professional work the past two decades has been with teachers rather than with education leaders. But as our conversations continued, I was drawn in by Ken's determination to speed up the pace of school change and to use storytelling as an accelerant. He didn't presume to have all the answers but instead was motivated by compelling questions. As a longtime advocate of inquiry and project-based learning, I realized I had found a fellow traveler. Thank you, Ken, for the invitation to join you on what has been an inspiring journey into the future of education.

Along with the dozens of people who generously shared their thinking with us for this book, I would also like to thank thought partners from the education community. In particular, thanks go to John Larmer and other colleagues from PBLWorks, Scott McLeod for his leadership on leadership, and Sam Seidel for keeping it real. Ron Berger's call for beautiful work continues to inspire. EL Education's advocacy for student-engaged assessment is transforming learning for thousands of young people. The urgency to unleash students' creativity and harness their passion for a better world has never been greater.

Finally, deep thanks to my husband, Bruce Rubin, for his patient listening, thoughtful questioning, and unfettered cheerleading, and to our sons Dan and Jay, who embody the best of 21st century citizens.

—Suzie Boss, Portland, Oregon, 2021

Gratitudes From Ken

I want to individually acknowledge a few people who have supported me personally on my twenty-five-year journey working on 21st century education.

Tony Wagner and Ted Dintersmith, colleagues and friends, have been wonderful supporters and beacons of light for this work.

I am so grateful for Karen Garza and her team at Battelle for Kids in their continuing work to carry the torch for 21st century education. Valerie Greenhill and Alyson Nielson have been my friends and "soulmates" on the work of 21st century education. They have both been a critical force behind much of the progress documented in this book.

My life-long friend Elaine Gurian has a special role in this book. She has been telling me for almost fifteen years that the 4 Cs weren't enough and we needed to add a 5th C: Civic Engagement. Elaine, Chapter 4 is dedicated to you.

My wife, Karen Christensen, has given me unflagging support over the entirety of my 21st century education journey. On this book, she has been a friend, thought partner, and confidant—and not so secretly happy I had a project to keep me busy during our quiet desert isolation due to COVID 19. Thank you, KC, for supporting me and this book in every imaginable way. For all of this, you have my love and deep gratitude.

Special thanks to my children Jeff, Braden, and Bergen, and grandson Ollie, for putting up with my passion for 21st century competencies and most importantly, for embracing and refining them in your own lives. And welcome to new grandson, Rye, who just arrived at a time of real transformation and will inherit the important work being done today.

And finally, deep gratitude to Suzie, who may be the world's best collaborator. What a joy to have partnered with you on this project. Even though we did this work during the most challenging of times, it has been a total pleasure to co-create this book with you.

—Ken Kay, Tucson, Arizona, 2021

PUBLISHER'S ACKNOWLEDGMENTS

Corwin would like to thank the following individuals for taking the time to provide their editorial insight and guidance:

Justin Gerald, doctoral candidate
CUNY Hunter College
New York City, New York

Teneshia A. Taylor, doctoral candidate
University of Northern Colorado
Greeley, Colorado

Terra Smith, consultant
TS Consulting Services, LLC
Sugar Land, Texas

About the Authors

Ken Kay is one of the founders of the 21st century education movement. He served as chief executive officer of EdLeader21, a professional learning community for education leaders committed to 21st century education. Prior to EdLeader21, he was the founding president of the Partnership for 21st Century Skills. He also served as executive director for the CEO Forum on Education and Technology. Along with Valerie Greenhill, Ken wrote *A Leader's Guide to 21st Century Education: 7 Steps for Schools and Districts*. For nearly a decade, Ken was a member of the board of PBLWorks (formerly the Buck Institute for Education). He is a graduate of Oberlin College and the University of Denver College of Law. Active on social media (@kenkay21), he maintains a website at kenkay21.com where he explains his ongoing role as "education provocateur."

Suzie Boss is a writer and educational consultant who focuses on the power of teaching and learning to improve lives and transform communities. She is the author of ten popular books for educators, most recently, *Project Based Teaching: How to Create Rigorous and Engaging Learning Experiences* and *Reinventing Project-Based Learning: Your Field Guide to Real-World Projects in the Digital Age*, 3rd ed. She collaborated with award-winning teacher Stephen Ritz to tell his inspiring story about classroom innovation in *The Power of a Plant*. A regular contributor to *Edutopia*, PBLWorks National Faculty emeritus, and frequent conference presenter, she consults with schools and nonprofit organizations around the world interested in shifting to a more student-centered, innovative approach to teaching and learning. Active on social media (@suzieboss), she maintains a website at suzieboss.com.

To bold leaders who are prepared to reimagine education with their communities and give their students the green light to chase their dreams and tackle the toughest challenges of our time

Introduction

A few years ago, Ken was asked to keynote a joint session of SXSW EDU and the Consortium for School Networking. He was interested in helping technology leaders see the importance of stressing 21st century skills in addition to technology competency. To put a face on what can seem like abstract goals, Ken began with a story about his young friend, Arijit, who was then in graduate school studying sustainability.

Arijit was diagnosed with colon cancer at the age of thirty. The chemotherapy treatments were expensive. Arijit realized that the university health insurance policy caps would be met after only a few treatments, leaving him facing medical bills over $100,000. Arijit and his wife didn't have those kinds of financial resources.

Arijit sprang into action with a two-pronged strategy. First, he built a website and assembled a team of artists and designers to help design tee-shirts and other products. He used those products to raise money for his treatments. Then he developed a sophisticated social media campaign to call out the insurance company CEO of the university's student health policy for providing a product that was clearly inadequate. He used his social media skills to garner online support for his complaint.

These strategies succeeded. Arijit raised $118,000 to cover his chemotherapy and medical expenses over the insurance cap amount. He was able to engage the CEO personally and ultimately had the caps waived for his expenses. The university also changed the policy terms for all students in future years. The money Arijit raised that was not needed for his medical care was donated to charities related to colon cancer treatment.

The story does not have a happy ending. Arijit died from his illness in 2013. He left, however, a legacy of self-advocacy that remains a powerful lesson today.

Let's consider a second example.

Mary Breslin went to college thinking she would spend her life working for the park service. After graduation, while working for park biologists in the Great Smoky Mountains National Park, she received a letter from her mom. The family owned several acres of land in Springfield, Virginia, just outside Washington, D.C. Her mother begged her to return home because the Virginia Department of Transportation (VDOT) had informed her parents that eminent domain would be used to build a road through the family property, a virtual nature preserve of native and endangered trees and plants.

Mary returned home and realized that nothing in her education thus far had prepared her to help her family win this fight. This realization completely shifted her education and life priorities. She enrolled in a graduate program in environmental policy to learn how to approach her family's challenge with VDOT. There she learned what she needed to be successful in the four-year battle to save her family's land. She further realized that she wanted to dedicate her life to equipping young people with the skills she had lacked.

Mary earned a graduate degree in education and became a middle school teacher in Alexandria, Virginia. One summer, she participated in a training program on how students can be engaged citizens and environmental problem solvers by using fact-finding to influence public policy. At the start of the new school year, when she asked her students to name issues they cared about, they responded with a question of their own: Do you know Winkler Botanical Preserve in Alexandria? Students had visited this nature preserve with their families and on school field trips as they were growing up. Now, Winkler was threatened by the same eminent domain Mary's family had experienced. Why? VDOT was planning a new road through it.

Mary recognized the irony. Her students were about to go on the same journey she had been on with her family's land. This time, though, she was prepared to help them learn how to tackle the challenge. "They were able to help save the Winkler Botanical Preserve in a mere six months," Mary reflected, "while it took me over four years to save my family's land. As middle schoolers, they now have the skills I didn't have by the time I graduated from college." We will hear more about Mary and her students in Chapter 3 when we focus on your role in leading creative problem solvers.

As you embark on this journey with us, pause and ask yourself the following questions.

ASK YOURSELF

- *How many of your students have the wide range of skills needed to meet the types of challenges that confronted Arijit and Mary?*
- *Is your school system intentionally developing these life skills?*
- *What challenges would you like your students to be able to tackle?*

PREPARING FOR CHALLENGES AND OPPORTUNITIES

Not every challenge facing your students will be as difficult as the circumstances that confronted Arijit or Mary. In fact, many of the challenges ahead can be reframed as positive opportunities—that is, if your students have the skills and confidence to not only survive but thrive.

Let's consider a few what-ifs:

What if the major employer in your hometown closes its doors? Will your students move away to chase brighter futures? Or will they lend their energy and talents to rebuild their local economy?

What if the drinking water in your community is contaminated or a natural disaster destroys vital infrastructure? Will your students have the knowledge and courage to advocate for what they and their families need to recover?

What if a new source of funding becomes available to support innovative ideas? Will your students know how to design and present prototypes or solutions that could garner grant money or seed funding?

What if students become passionate about saving a historic landmark from demolition, removing monuments that harken back to racist periods in history, or preserving significant habitat? Will they be able to build a network to support the causes they care about?

What if students research and recommend ways to save your school system thousands of dollars annually through energy efficiency retrofits and renewable energy projects? Will you trust them enough to invest school funds in their proposal?

In the coming chapters, you will meet young people who are tackling these very real what-ifs with their own creative solutions. Many have not yet graduated from high school or even middle school. Yet their stories provide irrefutable evidence that these students are prepared to survive and thrive. Together, they provide a compelling profile of a 21st century learner. They are prepared to ask hard questions, find important problems and solve them creatively, advocate for themselves and others, and engage others to partner with them. When circumstances call on them to step up, they are ready.

You may think it takes a superstar to achieve similar results. Dozens of interviews have convinced us otherwise. Any student who has passion and perseverance—and the benefit of an education that emphasizes creative problem solving—should be ready to tackle similar challenges. That's why this book is full of compelling stories that represent the new normal for schools that are redefining student success.

> You are not just redefining success for your students. You are also redefining success for yourself and your team as leaders and for your teachers as educators.

As you set forth on this journey, recognize that you are not just redefining success for your students. You are also redefining success for yourself and your team as leaders and for your teachers as educators. The relationship between these three is the central alignment that you will oversee in the work ahead.

HOW WE GOT HERE

For the past two decades, educators and academics have invested considerable energy in identifying the competencies students need to be prepared for 21st century success. The Partnership for 21st Century Skills (of which Ken was founding president) launched its work around the same time as the beginning of No Child Left Behind, legislation designed to increase accountability in education. The Partnership wasn't opposed to accountability, but it promoted a shift from accountability of outdated measures to metrics that truly matter for student success. Toward that end, in 2002 the organization introduced its colorful P21 "rainbow," which described eighteen essential skills across four broad domains. This framework was comprehensive but proved challenging for schools to grasp, let alone implement. Next came the 4 Cs. This was P21's effort to synthesize core competencies to a succinct list: communication, creativity, collaboration, and critical thinking. The shorter list quickly gained traction, but the conversation didn't stop there.

When Tony Wagner wrote *The Global Achievement Gap* (2010), he identified "Seven Survival Skills" that today's students need. Other thought leaders weighed in. Michael Fullan (Fullan, Quinn, & McEachen, 2017) and Bernie Trilling (Trilling & Fadel, 2012) identified their own lists of eight essential competencies. Fernando Reimers (Reimers & Chung, 2016) and Yong Zhao (2012) have advocated for global competency as the desired outcome of education in our increasingly interconnected world. ISTE (2016) has articulated the competencies needed for digital-age citizens.

Ken and Valerie Greenhill followed up in 2012 with *A Leader's Guide to 21st Century Education*, outlining a theory of change for transforming schools and districts. Innovative leaders responded to these provocations by attempting to build the 4 Cs (or more) into their core curriculum. They were addressing the question, "How do you embed critical thinking, communication, collaboration, and creativity into core subjects?" It was a good question at the time and one that has driven much of 21st century education implementation up to the present. These responses, however, have resulted in only an incremental approach to education system reform.

This book guides the next phase of development. It's not necessary to debate whether the correct number of competencies is 4, 6, 8, or greater. There is no one right answer. In the past, we proceeded as though there would be one definitive list. We recognize now that this discussion should be replaced by encouraging each community to come to consensus on its own as to which set of competencies makes the most sense for their particular circumstances. This book is rooted in the belief that local consensus building around the definition of student success is the best way to achieve meaningful long-term change in education.

> This book is rooted in the belief that local consensus building around the definition of student success is the best way to achieve meaningful long-term change in education.

Additionally, while building competencies into core curriculum was a reasonable incremental step in the early days of this movement, we want to push harder on bringing change more quickly and effectively. You need to find multiple contexts for self-directed problem solving. Siloed subjects don't offer enough or complete opportunities; only interdisciplinary challenges will be sufficient to give students real-world contexts for learning. The stories in the book are testaments to the power of interdisciplinary challenges. We urge you to embrace them.

REDEFINING STUDENT SUCCESS TO ADDRESS EQUITY

Much of the advice in the coming chapters was derived from interviews we conducted in the summer of 2020 with more than 250 thought leaders, educators, administrators, students, parents, and others who are committed to shaping the future of education. Every leader we spoke with was struggling with the pandemic. Recovery, for many, will mean rebuilding their systems to address racial inequities laid bare by these historic events.

These events are already having a profound impact on education. The pandemic and issues of racial justice elevate the need to develop creative problem solvers for every aspect of contemporary life. As you lead your school system out of these crises, your central challenge will be to ensure that every student develops the skills and knowledge essential to personal, economic, and civic survival in the 21st century. These competencies cannot be achievable only for students who meet a certain academic or socioeconomic profile.

There has never been a more critical time for bold leaders to transform our education system so that we meet the needs of every learner, in every community. This is what we mean by redefining student success.

THE TIME IS NOW

We hope this book will help you become the bold leader you need to be to address these current circumstances and those to come. We will support you by providing tools and strategies, inspiring you with stories about empowered students and engaged communities, and helping you recognize your strengths and identify your next steps for inspired action.

Your success will depend on your ability to listen to diverse voices in your community—including students, parents, teachers, and other stakeholders—and then engage them in partnering with you on meaningful transformation. It will also depend on your ability to join with other leaders in your region and around the country who can support and challenge you along the way. We hope you will consider us as guides, but like all courageous journeys, this challenge is ultimately for you and your community to master. While we will share a wide range of supports along the way, we cannot determine your final destination. Context matters, as you will see in many of the stories in the chapters ahead. Every community must arrive at its own vision of what education must become.

We are at a critical moment that cries out for bold leadership. Let's get started!

PART I

Embracing Your Vision

As we begin our journey, we invite you to act boldly:

- Embrace a bold vision focused on redefining student success to address equity.
- Embrace future-facing and bold conversations with your community.
- Embrace the adults in your system and co-create a culture that supports your vision.

Along the way, we will introduce you to concepts and tools that will help you make progress with these leadership challenges:

- Readiness gap
- Portrait of a Graduate
- Green light culture
- Portrait of an Educator

Taken as a whole, these tools can help you prepare your students for the challenges they may face in the next twenty to forty years. You will identify the competencies they will need and then develop a broad community consensus that will serve as the "Why" of your school or district transformation. You will engage with your administrators and teachers in creating the culture, professional development, and human resource policies that support them as they make the shifts necessary to realize your collective vision.

What to Look For

As you read Chapters 1 and 2, we encourage you to reflect on your own context as you consider the following:

- How will you redefine student success so it is focused on the real needs of your students and addresses inequities in your system?

7

"What would I tell the ninth-grade version of myself?"

"First, cultivating and maintaining positive and trusting relationships is the key to almost everything. Learn how to connect with people on a personal level, understand their perspectives and values, and then use the power of those relationships to get things done. Continuously work on building your own support team.

"Second, the ability to synthesize complex and often contradictory information is a skill you will use your entire life. Life is a constantly evolving "theory of change" to which we all add data continuously. If we pay attention and can open ourselves to reflecting on and reconstructing our views on a regular basis, we have a chance at gaining wisdom and seeing this amazing world and universe more clearly.

"Finally, identify those things you really love and are good at and work on them most of all. Don't spend all your time fretting and perseverating on what you don't do well. Sure, we all have areas where we need some basic skill and understanding, but the most successful people in this world find their gift and spend their life playing in that fountain."

~Jason E. Glass, commissioner and chief learner, Kentucky Department of Education

- How can you build a broad-based consensus with your community so the vision becomes a deep-seated commitment of the community?
- How will you build equity goals into your vision from the outset?
- How can you assure that your leadership team and teachers co-own the vision?
- How do you develop the culture your administrators and teachers need to be successful in this work?
- What leadership attributes will you need to be successful in this phase of your work?

This is a lot to think about . . . so let's get started by embracing a new vision for your system.

CHAPTER 1

Be the Leader of a Bold Vision

CHAPTER HIGHLIGHTS

Over the next decade, every education leader will need to take their community through a critical conversation. Is the current system of education truly serving the best interests of our students? Is the system focused on memorization, compliance, and test-taking, and if so, is that focus preparing students for the challenges they will face in 21st century life, citizenship, and work? What are the competencies your students really need to be prepared for the challenges they will face? This conversation will launch you and your community on the path to transforming your system and embracing important 21st century outcomes. The competencies your community articulates as essential to redefining student success will become the North Star for your system.

How will you help your school system find its North Star? Before anticipating your own way forward, let's hear how this journey has unfolded for leaders in three different contexts.

David James was the chief business officer for Akron Public Schools. In 2008, he decided to put his name in to serve as the district's superintendent. Many of us would think that he would be an unlikely candidate to lead a district transformation. His prior position conjures images of spreadsheets and "green eyeshades." However, as he tells it, his background in the private sector made him inherently customer oriented and used to asking tough questions. His basic orientation led him to constantly ask, "What is in the best interest of children?"

As David led his district, he became increasingly concerned that his students were graduating from high school without being prepared for the world beyond. He began talking to members of the community about this and searching for possible solutions. David heard about a series of high school academies in Nashville that he thought might be a helpful model for his district. In 2011, he organized a small delegation of education and business leaders to see the Nashville academies and their partner, Ford Next Generation Learning.

David was moved by what he saw in Nashville—a model of high school that truly prepared students for the next steps in their lives. When he got home, he went around the community trying to light a spark of enthusiasm for bringing such a model to Akron. But he wasn't able to create enough momentum. The timing wasn't right. David put the idea aside, intending to come back to it when he could.

About four years later, David began to sense an opportunity in Akron to bring up the career academies idea again. This time the business community was better organized, having formed a group called Akron Tomorrow. David sought out Bill Considine, head of Akron Children's Hospital and chair of Akron Tomorrow. Bill was enthusiastic about organizing another trip to Nashville with more business leaders able to see firsthand the work being done at the career academies.

This time the timing was right. Bill and David led a group of twenty education, business, and community leaders to Nashville. The group came back enthused and energetic. There was a solid core of support for bringing the career academy concept to Akron Public Schools and for partnering with Ford Motor Company Fund's Next Generation Learning to support the process. The initial work included a broad-based community engagement process to create a "Portrait of a Graduate" for Akron schools.

After some reflection, David determined the ideal location in his district for the first academy. He called Rachel Tecca, principal of North High School, to ask her if she would be interested. Rachel had been in the district since 1993, first as a special education teacher and administrator. In 2012, she took over as principal of North High School. As David and Rachel talked, she thought about the previous four years of graduation ceremonies at her high school. Each year, upon the stage, she shook every student's hand knowing they were graduating with a diploma that did not equip them to meet the challenges ahead of them. Rachel realized that there had to be a better way to help them prepare for their future lives. She told David that she was on board.

Shortly after that call, Bill Considine committed to David that Akron Children's Hospital (ACH) would be the first organizational sponsor of the North High School Health Academy. ACH made a commitment of $250,000 and devoted a full-time staff person to serving as a liaison between the high school and the hospital to ensure that the school and its students were fully supported by the hospital and its resources.

Today, there are fifteen career academies in the Akron Public School system. Rachel Tecca left her position as principal to oversee all of the academies districtwide. Each academy is supported by one or more organizational partners in the community. The Portrait of a Graduate (POG) developed by the community is embedded in the work of each of the academies. The district is now working to embed the same POG competencies in the work of their elementary and middle schools, including the "I Promise" school associated with basketball star LeBron James.

David James had a conviction about the high schools in his district better serving students. Initially, the schools were primarily focused on the traditions and practices of adults coming up through the system as well as compliance with state policies. David saw the genuine needs of his students being unmet by following that path. He pursued his conviction about student needs through a thirteen-year journey as superintendent, leading to a comprehensive transformation of Akron Public Schools.

***

In 2011, Brian Troop was hired as assistant superintendent of Ephrata Area School District because of his expertise in using educational data to improve student achievement. Ephrata is a small town in the middle of Pennsylvania Dutch country.

Two years later, when he became superintendent, Brian planned to spend his first six months on the job listening to district stakeholders. But barely three months in, the board asked Brian for a "100-day check-in" (an idea the board president had recently heard about at a conference).

When the entire school board met with Brian, they asked, "How are things going overall?" Brian thought for a moment and then responded: "We can proceed in one of two directions: We can continue to achieve incremental gains on standardized test scores each year, or we can set our sights on something greater, something more important for our students. We are positioned to do either. I just want to make sure I am taking the same path the board desires for the district."

Brian told the board, "I know you hired me as a numbers guy, but as I listened to folks during my first 100 days, I came to sense that we can do better than just what the numbers value. We can build a system that values the needs of our students. You hired me to bolster student achievement as we have known it. But I could take on student preparedness as it should be. In either event, I want your support. Which direction do you want me to go in?"

The board told Brian they wanted him to pursue the "student preparedness" route, and if he did, they would completely support him. That conversation was the fork in the road. Brian and the school board took the less traditional, more challenging route.

They began an extensive series of conversations with their community and in 2017, the board formally adopted their district profile of a "Life Ready Graduate." That model now permeates most aspects of the operation of the district. And seven years after their 100-day check-in, Brian and the board remain committed to their Life Ready Graduate strategy.

***

Karen Garza had a distinguished career as a school administrator in Texas when she was chosen as the next superintendent of the Fairfax County, Virginia, public schools, the tenth-largest school district in the country. Prior to arriving in Fairfax, Karen had worked as the chief academic officer in Houston Independent School District and in Lubbock, Texas, as superintendent. In both of those locations, she worked on implementing "fair and balanced" assessment systems, seeking to balance traditional state test scores with other attributes important for student success.

When Karen arrived in Fairfax in 2013, she came to a district that had already started conversations about 21st century skills. Kathy Smith, a Fairfax County school board member, had attended a National School Board Association panel on this subject and asked the then-superintendent, Jack Dale, to look more deeply into the work. Jack organized a meeting of his leadership team around the topic and convened a community meeting with parents. Some of the Fairfax regions began to hold professional development sessions for their teachers around 21st century skills.

Upon starting, Karen had to determine what would be the best next step for the entire district. She was impressed with the district's interest in the 4 Cs (critical thinking, communication, collaboration, and creativity). She thought, however, they needed to go much more deeply into the implementation of teaching these skills. Before that could happen, the new superintendent thought the district should first adopt a Portrait of a Graduate. After only six weeks in the district, she was already recommending a bold move for a district of 180,000 students. Karen had concluded that the complexity of the district required community buy-in for a common vision as the only way she could bring the entire group of 200 schools along.

Karen convened a large community advisory group consisting of seventy-five individuals from a broad and diverse set of backgrounds. This group went through a three-month process, concluding with the proposal to the Board of Education for Fairfax County to approve a countywide Portrait of a Graduate. Karen looks back at this process as one of her professional achievements that she is most proud of since it became the backbone of her work in Fairfax County.

Karen has long been convinced that the school district is the "unit of change" for much broader education transformation efforts. The Portrait of a Graduate process has changed her perspective on how to engage the community to garner broad-reaching community support grounded in the "why"—stakeholders' hopes, dreams, and aspirations for their children's education. From that shared why, districts can align educational outcomes to that vision. Today, she runs an educational nonprofit, Battelle for Kids, dedicated to helping school districts around the country create and implement their own Portrait of a Graduate. Under her leadership, her team has created many tools to help districts on this journey.

ASK YOURSELF

- *What were the leadership attributes of each of these leaders?*
- *What vision did each leader embrace?*
- *What relationships did each leader nurture?*
- *What helped them start the process of school transformation?*

Write down your own reflection of these through-lines—and when you share this book with your leadership team, have them reflect on the through-lines as well. Consider what these leaders had to focus on personally and what they needed to collaborate on with others in their communities.

We urge you to take seriously our invitation to reflect. Put the book down for a moment. Jot down what the significance of the stories is for you. Then, read on to compare your perspective to ours.

From our perspective, each story highlights bold leadership. These leaders were not just willing to go along with the current constructs of the system. They recognized the need to redefine student success for their systems, and they made the commitment to deeply implement the changes required to go in that new direction.

We also want you to consider the differences in each of these stories:

- David James had a long track record as a superintendent in the district, and it took until 2016 to get a second community delegation to Nashville to tour their academy structure.
- Rachel Tecca was a principal who began her education career as a special education teacher. She became a districtwide administrator in charge of fifteen career academies.
- Brian Troop was a first-time superintendent, just getting started in a new position.
- Karen Garza was a superintendent who was switching districts and inheriting a nascent 21st century skills initiative, which she decided to expand. She wanted to take the work more deeply into the community and into system-wide classroom implementation.

We hope you can find yourself in one of these leadership stories. We have designed this book to speak to experienced leaders, new leaders, and emerging leaders. Whether you are starting a Portrait of a Graduate or inheriting a transformation process, we want to help you on your journey.

In the coming decade, each of you will find yourself at the same crossroads these leaders faced: whether to focus on standardized test score improvement or to address a broader set of student needs. The goal of this book is to help you meet these challenges boldly.

We have organized the "bold vision" challenge of this chapter into two distinct pieces of advice for you:

- Construct a bold vision: Focus on the readiness gap.
- Facilitate a broad and bold conversation in your community.

These two steps will help to start a change process that will be true to your own vision and reflective of your community context and values. (See the Resources for Implementation box at the end of this chapter for additional tools and resources to help you on this journey.)

The most important observation we can make about embracing a vision for 21st century education is that the vision needs to be co-created with your community. However, before you engage your community, you must first reflect on your own beliefs and values.

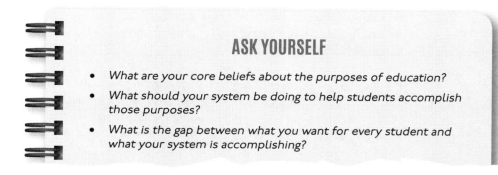

ASK YOURSELF

- *What are your core beliefs about the purposes of education?*
- *What should your system be doing to help students accomplish those purposes?*
- *What is the gap between what you want for every student and what your system is accomplishing?*

Record your answers to these questions, paying special attention to the final one. How would you describe the "gap" between where your education system is today and where you want it to be? This gap between what is in the "best interests of the kids" and what the current system focuses on today must become the core of your work. This should be a central component of your leadership going forward.

TO CONSTRUCT A BOLD VISION, FOCUS ON THE READINESS GAP

Today, much attention focuses on the "achievement gap" as the central problem facing education. We do not want to minimize the persistent disparities that subgroups of students continue to experience. Indeed, in many communities, the COVID-19 crisis has put a spotlight on longstanding racial and socioeconomic inequities that society—and our schools—must address.

But there's another gap we also must close if we want to create a more equitable education system. The achievement gap reflects academic measurement criteria that are more than fifty years old and are not central to student success today. It's time to shift the conversation to the gap between the competencies students are graduating with today and where they need to be if they are going to be ready for the challenges they will face in life, citizenship, and work. We call this the *readiness gap*.

The leaders highlighted at the beginning of this chapter were all focused on this readiness gap. They may not have used this phrase, but the gap in critical skills has driven all of their transformation work.

There is one more step you need to take by yourself: Determine your own ideas about the "North Star" for this work. It is not enough to define the readiness gap, which describes a system deficiency. You now must begin to define your own initial ideas for the system's destination before you gather your community to move forward with you in the process.

For Steve Holmes, superintendent in Sunnyside School District in Tucson, Arizona, the question leaders must answer for themselves is this: "What are your core beliefs around students and learning, and what do you want to head the organization toward?"

To define that destination, begin by articulating your own "first cut" of the student outcomes you want your students to have at the end of their time with you. You may be tempted to focus on familiar programs and strategies, such as competency-based education, project-based learning, performance tasks, capstones, portfolios, and so forth. Those may be part of your implementation, but strategies and tactics are not your destination. The destination will comprise the attributes you want your students to be able to acquire and demonstrate. Imagine, for example, a graduate who can

- Quickly master a new content area
- Utilize empathy and inquiry to consider the potential application of the content to practical problems
- Effectively communicate the importance of the content subject and its application
- Work creatively with others to pursue practical solutions using their content mastery and other skills
- Collaborate around creative problem solving

Spend some time constructing your own version of this list. Your version will serve as a helpful starting point as you describe to your community the kind of vision you want to co-create with them.

One question almost inevitably will arise: What is the name or label for the work ahead? We asked the forty-some superintendents we interviewed for this book, all of whom had pursued their own community's vision of a 21st century graduate, what name they gave to this work. We heard an incredible variety of responses:

- Portrait of a Graduate
- Profile of a Graduate
- Vision of a Graduate
- Life Ready Graduate
- The 4 Cs, or 5 Cs, or 7 Cs, or 10 Cs
- Deeper Learning
- Equity
- Student-Centered Instruction
- The Strategic Plan
- Inspire 2025

It is clear that leaders who have taken on this vision challenge have not been constrained by a one-size-fits-all term or title. In fact, they have customized their title to fit the specific context of their school or district. For the purposes of this book, we will call this vision the Portrait of a Graduate (POG). Hundreds of districts have adopted this overarching vision.

ADOPTING YOUR PORTRAIT OF A GRADUATE

We strongly recommend you adopt a POG because, in our experience, it is the single most powerful thing you can do to launch your school or district on its journey to redefine student success. Arriving at a POG involves a customized process by which a school or district adopts its own set of student outcomes to serve as the North Star for its transformation. If your community already has a POG, you will need to determine if it is time to do a review and refresh of it. Most communities with a POG update it every four to five years.

> Adopting a Portrait of a Graduate is the single most powerful thing you can do to launch your school or district on its journey to redefine student success.

You can see for yourself two examples of POGs from districts (Akron and Ephrata) we introduced at the beginning of the chapter in Figures 1.1–1.2.

Figure I.I   POG From Akron

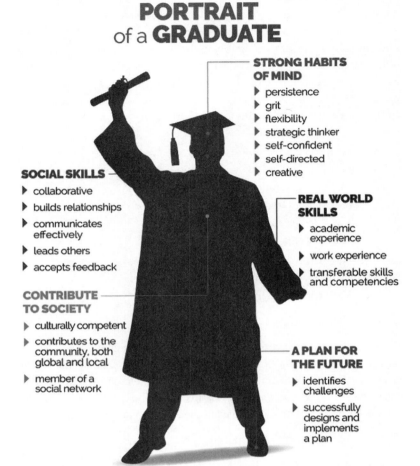

PORTRAIT of a GRADUATE

STRONG HABITS OF MIND
▶ persistence
▶ grit
▶ flexibility
▶ strategic thinker
▶ self-confident
▶ self-directed
▶ creative

SOCIAL SKILLS
▶ collaborative
▶ builds relationships
▶ communicates effectively
▶ leads others
▶ accepts feedback

REAL WORLD SKILLS
▶ academic experience
▶ work experience
▶ transferable skills and competencies

CONTRIBUTE TO SOCIETY
▶ culturally competent
▶ contributes to the community, both global and local
▶ member of a social network

A PLAN FOR THE FUTURE
▶ identifies challenges
▶ successfully designs and implements a plan

READY FOR COLLEGE. CAREER. LIFE.

You can explore additional POGs on the website, www .portraitofagraduate.org.

We hope you will appreciate the power of adopting a POG. It is not merely the adoption of a slogan, visual aid, or poster. Those schools and districts that seek to fully plum the value of a POG will see that the ramifications can be broad and profound.

We asked the superintendents we interviewed what they considered to be the biggest impact of their creation of a POG. Their responses clustered around four powerful impacts.

The first impact is unity of vision. Leaders noted that having the POG created the power of a common vision. There was now clarity around

Figure I.2   POG From Ephrata

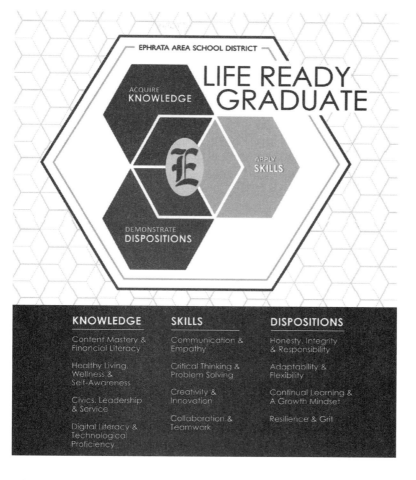

what they wanted for students. They were clear that, while content mastery remains important, standardized tests were no longer the single metric for student success. Readiness is broader than test scores. Several superintendents observed that the POG pushed them to define what we mean by success. Rich Fry, superintendent in Big Spring, Pennsylvania, worked on a POG with his board and community eight years ago and now notes, "We haven't talked about a test score in a board meeting in eight years."

An important second impact of the POG is better alignment within the system. This result is perhaps best captured by Mike McCormick, superintendent of the Val Verde School District in California, who observed:

> The POG seemed to verify a lot of complex ideas in education. For about six years, the dots weren't connecting. What is the point of performance assessment? Restorative justice? PLC? PBL? We had

a spiderweb of initiatives. The POG seemed to us to be a unifying force for people to build a mental model so each of the discrete initiatives could rise up and be part of one unified umbrella. It helps people determine where we are going and where they fit in.

Eric Eshbach, currently the assistant executive director of the Pennsylvania Principals Association, used the POG to guide his team when he was superintendent in Northern York County, Pennsylvania. "The POG was a target that showed us the direction to head in. We used it as the criteria by which all changes and initiatives would be judged. Everything needs to go through the POG lens. My administrators had to show me how their work is tied to our POG goals."

This alignment is powerfully reinforced when the POG is embedded into strategic planning and budgeting. Many districts have used the POG as the key objective of their strategic plan and then use the POG as a lens for their budget priorities.

The third impact is that of promoting student agency and self-direction. The attributes of the POG put students at the center of the educational model and emphasize the need for self-regulation and autonomy. The POG also pushes educators toward more personalization and self-assessment. We will explore these issues in detail in Chapter 5.

Finally, superintendents describe the impact of the POG on teaching. The POG shifts the focus of pedagogy toward more teacher facilitation and coaching and less direct instruction. Teachers are encouraged to embrace the challenge to experiment and are being given permission to occasionally fail. These issues will be discussed further in Chapter 6.

While on its face the POG is just a one-page document, the superintendents we interviewed describe significant impacts. These are the kinds of benefits you can reap if you are bold enough to embrace a big vision. However, you need to do it in a broadly collaborative way.

EMBRACE A BROAD AND BOLD CONVERSATION

Your deep personal reflection and your choice of a bold vision like a POG is just your starting point for the transformation process. That vision must be accompanied by a broad-based and rigorous process that assures you and your community are co-creators.

If you see the prospect of a POG solely as an exercise for your leadership team or your educators, it will never gain the deep traction required for real transformation. If you seize this opportunity to engage with your community in an invigorating conversation about the purpose of education, it can be the anchor for the profound and long-term transformation our current education system requires.

Ted Dintersmith, entrepreneur and author of *Most Likely to Succeed* (Wagner & Dintersmith, 2016) and *What School Could Be* (Dintersmith, 2019), has seen firsthand the value of bold community conversations. He shared this insight with us: "Andy Grove of Intel used to say if you don't know where you are going, any road will get you there. If you don't adopt a POG, you won't know where you are headed. We need each community to lean in and shape their own POG. Each time I have watched it happen, it stimulates truly constructive and creative discussions."

You will move next from your personal reflection to a period of outreach with your community. During this period, you will begin a genuine conversation about your initial concepts as you move forward in co-creating the community vision. This period will require you to

- Listen carefully
- Educate powerfully
- Collaborate deeply

Ideally, in the two to three months before you begin a formal visioning process, you should consider doing a "listening tour" of your community. You will want to include key individuals central to your success, including

- Your leadership team
- School board
- Teachers
- Students
- Parents
- Business community, including significant area employers and small businesses
- Youth development groups
- Local governments
- Community leaders reflective of the diversity of your community
- Religious leaders
- Workforce development organizations
- Higher education

Listen carefully to their hopes and dreams for your community's children. You will be surprised by their responses. Parents, in particular, will be grateful to be asked these questions. They likely have never been asked what competencies they would like their children to possess. It can be a positive and constructive conversation, one not likely to bring out the division and discord that many other topics around education tend to generate. You will find a large degree of consensus around competencies your community members think are valuable and important.

Lindsay Unified School District, serving a high-poverty community in California's agricultural Central Valley, began a dramatic transformation in 2007 by inviting families to describe future graduates of the school system. District leaders like Barry Sommer, director of advancement, listened as parents shared their hopes and dreams. "We're giving you our kids. Make their lives better than ours," Barry recalls hearing from families again and again, in both English and Spanish. That profound message shaped a vision of lifelong learning that continues to drive change, as you will hear in upcoming chapters.

Once you have listened carefully, you can begin the process of educating the community, helping them to see the powerful societal contexts that require a shift in the education model. You will want to share videos, books, speakers, and panels to build common language and understanding of these trends. (See Resources for Implementation section at the end of this chapter for suggestions.)

Now you are ready to begin a more formal process, whether you are formulating the community's first POG or updating one. Creating an advisory group is a helpful way to arrive at your community's unique vision of what it wants for students—your own customized POG. There are many ways to assemble this group. Depending on the size of your community, you can bring together a group of thirty to seventy-five members of the education and broader community in a three- to four-month process that will ultimately lead to broad-based support for this vision.

Your advisory group should include the broad base of individuals you met during your listening and education phases. Some of the people you met with may have expressed a willingness to participate in the group. We want to emphasize the importance of five key perspectives:

Students

Participation by students is one of the critical constituencies to have at the table. Middle and high school students have been very effective and active participants in these conversations.

In a district in a western state, known as a politically volatile community, a student was assigned to each table. When one of the POG sessions got contentious, a high school senior stood up and said, "I think the adults have brought their bickering into this room and it has no place here." She got a round of applause.

In the Schalmont School District in Schenectady, New York, an eighth grader, Mariana Riccio, was appointed to serve on the POG advisory committee. Mariana says that experience changed her life as it helped her to understand why she was really in school. Mariana now serves on a POG advisory group, helping the school district implement the POG.

Jason Glass, state education commissioner of Kentucky, underscored the importance of including students in the conversation: "If students and adults are in conversation together, transformation will emerge. When the conversation is rooted in the values of kids and community, it is hard to argue against."

Teachers

Getting teachers involved in the POG process is also critical. While some teachers may resist something new and different, most teachers want to teach in an environment that is less about "compliance culture" and more about giving teachers and students the freedom to explore their learning. In some districts, the teachers' union has been invited to participate in the POG advisory process, which has led to the union becoming a significant advocate for the work. The National Education Association (NEA, n.d.) was a founding member of the 21st century skills movement.

Future Workforce

Business leaders have an important perspective to share in this process. They know which skills and competencies are important in the 21st century workforce. Identify the major employers in your community and, if their CEOs can't join the process, invite their human resource directors to participate. Organizations can explain the kind of employees they are looking for and whether their current candidates—your graduates—meet those expectations or fall short.

Jim Philips, CEO of Azomite Mineral Products in Nephi, Utah, was asked to serve on the POG advisory group for the local school district in his rural community. Sixteen of Jim's twenty-one local employees graduated from Juab High School. Jim observes: "We tell our employees every day: 'We are paying you for your minds. We want you to be solving problems and finding new ways to do things.' We need our employees to have the basics of math, English, and communication skills, but after that, we need our schools to teach them how to solve problems. From a business perspective, that's what I want. That's why the POG makes a lot of sense to me as a business leader."

When Eric Eshbach was superintendent of Northern York County School District in Pennsylvania, he reached out to a wide range of regional employers to help shape the POG. "We had military recruiters sitting at the same table as university professors, lawyers, and small business owners. They all focused on the same question: What are you looking for in a worker?" An electrician who owned his own company brought the group to consensus when he said, "I can teach my employees what they need to know about electricity, but I can't teach them to be good workers. I need people who will show up." When the POG was finally adopted, it included the disposition of being conscientious.

Also, consider inviting the largest nonprofit organizations to share the kinds of employees they seek. While you will probably invite representatives from your Parent Teacher Association, also consider inviting parents who have "21st century jobs" or who run "21st century companies." They can give your process a helpful perspective on what competencies are or will be needed for successful workers. Consider which other business and governmental groups, including higher education institutions, have an interest in the workforce pipeline so you can include them in the process as well.

Diversity

You need to be certain that the members of your POG advisory group reflect the full diversity of your community. Only then will the consensus that emerges in the process include the commitment that *every* student will experience the impact of this work and that past inequities will be addressed in the new vision. Be relentless in pursuing broad and diverse participation in the group, identifying underserved communities, and assuring their representation. Invite individuals who are not "regulars" in your education conversations and be sure the 21st century competency discussions you have focus on the question: Will *every* student have access to these competencies? Often one group of students has access to engaged student learning, but not all students share in this. Karen Garza notes: "Our greatest challenge in this work is addressing the needs of underserved communities. The kids who need the richest, engaging instruction are often getting the least."

Youth Development Perspectives

Keep in mind that your work is designed to prepare young people not just for the workforce but also for their personal and citizenship challenges. Think about who else in your community is working on the physical, social, and emotional well-being of young people: church groups, YWCA/YMCA, Little League, 4-H Clubs, League of Women Voters, and so forth. These groups will be eager to participate because their work is to help young people attain the same competencies you will be working on. Perhaps you can consider adopting a regionwide POG for all youth-related activities once you have adopted one for your school or district.

These initial thoughts are intended to get your juices flowing. Be expansive and creative about the special and diverse perspectives you can invite to the table.

Cheryl Carrier, executive director of Ford Next Generation Learning, the group that helped Akron build their POG, observes: "The power of the POG is that you are bringing the community, business leaders, and educators together. It leads to a different kind of discussion. By bringing the community together you get more buy-in. And you then create the possibility of new partnerships to pursue the new opportunities." More than 200 businesses now participate in Akron's career academies program. (In Chapter 7, we will explore more strategies for building partnerships and regional networks.)

FOCUS ON EQUITY

As you build community consensus, equity is the one topic you must prioritize in your conversations. Every community faces inequities. Some districts have started to address equity issues; others have not. If you proceed to create your new definition of student success without focusing on equity, you will reinforce the current inequities. It will be even more difficult to address these issues moving forward.

Build equity into your own analysis of your Portrait of a Graduate. Have your advisory group address the equity implications of your POG work as it begins to work on the challenges in your district. Make sure you specifically ask the advisory group, "What are ways we can ensure that every child will have the resources they need to attain their competencies?" "How will we find additional resources for those who need them?"

As you lead this work, be inspired by other superintendents who are keeping the focus on equity.

Steve Holmes, superintendent of the Sunnyside School District in Arizona, oversees a predominately Hispanic, high-poverty district in Tucson. Steve describes their Portrait of a Graduate as their "equity work" for two reasons. First, the deeper learning that flows from a broader definition of student success is a form of engaged learning to which every student is entitled. Additionally, he knows that critical thinking, communication, collaboration, and creativity are necessary skills to address racism and equity.

Mike McCormick, superintendent of the Val Verde School District in California, describes a similar commitment: "The number-one goal from the Board of Education is solving the organizational challenges of diversity, equity, and inclusion in order for all students to gain access and opportunity to the educational programs and services offered by our school district. Our Portrait of a Graduate guides all aspects of our work."

McCormick recognizes that the district's POG and the competencies it describes are important tools to address diversity, equity, and inclusion. "Flexibility includes the ability to balance diverse views and beliefs to reach workable solutions in multicultural environments. Communication includes the ability to communicate effectively in diverse environments. Collaboration includes students demonstrating the ability to work effectively and responsibly with diverse teams."

Jim Montesano, superintendent in Nyack, New York, acknowledges the challenge of addressing equity. "Our data shows that our outcomes are not equitable. Getting people involved in the antiracism work has required open conversations on the topic of race on a monthly basis. We are working to solve institutional racism within the four walls of our buildings. Leaders need to understand what equity and institutional racism mean."

In the urban district of Akron, Ohio, equity is not an add-on to the POG process. "We apply the lens of diversity, equity, and inclusion to everything we do," explains Superintendent David James. That includes the POG. He adds, "We must ensure that we build a school and district culture that removes barriers based on race, ethnicity, religion, or identity so all students have equitable resources (both human and financial) to achieve what we outlined as our vision for success. The work is causing us to take a critical view on how we support our students and recognizing and acknowledging that we must do things differently."

RESOURCES FOR YOUR EQUITY WORK

Ensuring common language about equity will lead to more productive community conversations.

These resources provide clear definitions and guidelines for discussions with your stakeholders:

- "Equity vs. Equality and Other Racial Justice Definitions," published by the Annie E. Casey Foundation, offers a good starting point for ensuring shared language to "name it, frame it, and explain it" when it comes to discussing equity and racial justice. www.aecf.org/blog/racial-justice-definitions

- *Racial Justice in Education*, published by the NEA, provides resources for talking about racial equity, defining this goal as not just the absence of discrimination but also the presence of values and systems that ensure fairness and justice. neaedjustice.org/wp-content/uploads/2018/11/Racial-Justice-in-Education.pdf

- Districts Advancing Racial Equity (DARE) is an online tool published jointly by the Learning Policy Institute and Southern Education Foundation to help education leaders strengthen their capacity to advance racial equity in their school systems. It calls for ongoing cycles of improvement in partnership with school community members. Learn more and download the tool from learningpolicyinstitute.org/product/reln-districts-advancing-racial-equity-tool

Learn from other school systems that are making progress to remove barriers to equity. An excellent case study (Green, 2021) comes from an urban high school with a large population of English learners in Sudbury, Massachusetts. Leaders and staff first identified systemic inequities related to economics, English fluency, literacy, and social-emotional wellness. They adopted student-centered solutions, which have helped to close opportunity gaps even during the COVID crisis. Read the full case study at studentsatthecenterhub.org (search for "One School's Commitment to Equity Using Student-Centered Learning").

Many districts we interviewed have used outside facilitators who specialize in diversity, equity, and inclusion. You may want to consider bringing that expertise into your internal and external conversations.

Final Reflections

During your private reflection and community consensus-building phases, you will have relied deeply on your own mastery of the 4 Cs. Your personal reflection period was based on your own critical thinking capacities. The outreach and advisory board phases require collaboration and communication. Your ability to solve problems creatively will be important as you engage with your team to develop new programs and overcome challenges.

Some of the superintendents we interviewed used the term "transparent" collaboration to describe the idea that consensus building must not only be broad but also easily understood and accessible. If there is a future leadership transition, the vision will survive if it is perceived to be shared by the community and not the brainchild of the outgoing superintendent. Collaboration remains critical after the vision is developed because it leads to partnerships and alliances to do the actual work of implementation.

The superintendents we interviewed also emphasized that success in this work requires constant communication. When you think you have started to overcommunicate, you are likely just beginning to break through. Keep going. Keep the communications simple and clear. Early in the process, you will need to focus on the "why" of adopting a POG. As you progress further, you will focus on the "what" it will look like in practice. Make sure your communications engage the members of your community. Find new opportunities to keep them updated. Use social media to keep a constant flow of communication and feed the "buzz" around the work.

Greg Baker, superintendent in Bellingham, Washington, offers this observation: "You can boil the Superintendent Challenge down to its essence: There is one thing that matters, and that is your ability to talk to the public in a manner that compels action."

If your entire community owns the plan going forward, you will have a deep, long-term commitment to focus on the readiness gap and the outcomes for students that really matter. The community consensus around a bold vision and bold conversation will be a powerful platform on which you can build your school or district transformation.

Let's consider one final reflection:

Are you ready to go beyond standardized testing and challenge your school board and community to define a broader vision of student success for each and every student?

RESOURCES FOR IMPLEMENTATION

Two free resources from **Battelle for Kids** will help you get started on your Portrait of a Graduate:

- For inspiration, explore the **Portrait of a Graduate gallery** at www .portraitofagraduate.org.

- Download a copy of the **Getting Started Guide** (from the POG gallery website) to help you plan your next steps to engage your community in the POG process.

Community movie nights and book discussions are two strategies to foster rich stakeholder conversations about the future of education. Here are just a few examples of resources that leaders have used to catalyze community conversations:

- *Most Likely to Succeed*, produced by Ted Dintersmith, is available for public screenings by schools and districts. teddintersmith. com/mltsfilms

- **TEDx Talks** (www.ted.com) are popular for kicking off community conversations. For example, *The Myth of Average* features Harvey Rose, a high school dropout-turned-Harvard faculty member. Find it on YouTube.

- Combine a screening with a panel discussion or follow up with a reading group. Titles certain to provoke good conversations include *Most Likely to Succeed* by Tony Wagner and Ted Dintersmith or *What School Could Be* by Ted Dintersmith.

- Explore more resources in the **What School Could Be** community launched by Ted Dintersmith (community. whatschoolcouldbe.org).

Action Steps

As we close this first chapter, we want to raise a caution. Sometimes educators gloss over the "theoretical" or "strategic" and head straight for implementation. This is a big mistake.

If you try to undertake the ideas in the remainder of this book without devoting attention to the concepts in this chapter, your implementation will be floating around without a coherent anchor. The key elements in this chapter are central to your success on this journey. Take time to absorb and apply them.

We have asked you to take three action steps:

I.   **Redefine student success.** Take on the challenge of identifying the competencies that really matter for your student's success. Make a commitment to developing your Portrait of a Graduate (or whatever you decide to call it) and use this as your North Star.

2.   **Anchor the vision in your community.** Commit not only to creating a Portrait of a Graduate, but commit to co-creating it with your community. Some leaders are tempted to shorten the process by having a team of educators determine the competencies. That will not have staying power. POGs developed by a diverse cross-section of the community have a greater likelihood of being woven through the fabric of the district and not being tied to a single education leader. Make this your community's enduring vision of education.

3.   **Anchor the work in equity.** If you don't take on the challenge of developing your POG in the context of addressing the equity challenges of your district, you will simply exacerbate the inequities already present in your system. Focus on equity as an essential element of your redefinition of student success.

These action steps will launch your efforts. There is one additional essential step to take before you can begin the implementation of your POG: Work with the adults in your system to be certain they fully embrace the new direction. Developing that culture is a fourth essential step in the process, which we explain in Chapter 2.

CHAPTER 2

Be the Leader of a Green Light Culture

CHAPTER HIGHLIGHTS

While your new vision, the Portrait of a Graduate (POG), will help inform many aspects of your system, including transformed classroom practices, the essential next step is to attend to the adults in the system. Do you have in place a culture that will support the transformation you need? How will you co-create the expectations for the adults in the system? Nurture a green light culture in your school or district to give teachers the green light to innovate and experiment. You can work with your educators to co-create a Portrait of an Educator (POE), which includes the competencies they will need to fulfill the promise of the Portrait of a Graduate. You will use the Portrait of an Educator as the guide for transforming professional development and human resources.

If you are going to effectively redefine student success, it stands to reason that you will need to redefine educator success. You will need to co-create that new definition with your educators. This process will test your system's capacity to change.

It is a truism that culture may be the most important element in an organization's capacity to transform and grow. "Culture eats strategy for lunch" is just one version of that common organizational strategy theme. What this means for you is that if the right culture is not in place, you won't be able to achieve the transformation required by your vision. For example, if you want teachers to shift their pedagogy and the dominant culture is essentially, "We've always done it this way," you won't get very far. If you want your teachers to experiment and innovate, you can't have a culture that penalizes failure.

For our purposes, the easiest way to think about culture is to look at the elements of the POG and ask, "Are educator attitudes and predispositions likely to support the changes we will need to make?" "Which elements of the POG will educators need personally to be successful in teaching and assessing the POG?" "What other teacher attributes are needed to be successful in cultivating POG attributes in their students?" "Do teachers have the growth mindset to build upon their strengths and expand their capabilities?" These competencies and attributes taken as a whole will become the foundation of the culture of your school or district that you will build on.

In this chapter, we offer suggestions for concrete steps you can take to assure that you are at or can get to the place you need to be in the culture of your system. This includes taking a close look at the role of policies, procedures, and practices that influence culture.

CULTURE DURING CRISIS

When we started the interviews for this book in June 2020, we were generally interested in exploring culture issues with superintendents and other leaders. It soon became apparent that everyone we spoke to was now viewing their culture through a significant new lens—COVID-19.

We want to share with you two different organizational cultures that were tested by the pandemic.

Rob Bach was initially a high school assistant volleyball coach. He inherited a team with the motto, "Go for every ball." If you've ever watched a volleyball game, you know what that means. Every player on every play digs as deep as they can to go for every ball. A team that embraces this philosophy is gritty with a spirit of never giving up. Rob adopted this motto and worked to assure that it permeated the culture of his teams, which led to significant success.

In 2014, Rob became principal of Stillwater High School in Minnesota, which then served Grades 10 through 12. He realized that the culture of the high school needed to change. It had to focus more on the needs of the students than on the desires of the adults. But he knew he needed to wait for the right moment to initiate that change. A year later, that moment presented itself. The high school was expanded to a 9 through 12 school, and Rob realized this was the critical time to address the issue of the school's culture. He rejected the idea of merely "assimilating" the new students and teachers, deciding instead to model extra care in embracing each new student and teacher. Rephrasing his former motto, he focused on, "Go for Every Student." The goal was for each new student to be on-boarded in a way that helped them feel honored and that their voices were heard.

Rob felt the new slogan emphasized that the primary needs of each student—social and emotional learning and equity—were being met. He and his team utilized a social and emotional learning construct called Building Assets, Reducing Risks (www.barrcenter.org). BARR creates a scaffolded system for supporting students and their families. Initially, the system was used to support every ninth-grade student, family, and the new teachers. When the tenth- through twelfth-grade students and teachers saw the individualized support strategies for the ninth graders, they began to ask for the same individualized approach. Following this interest, BARR was extended to an additional grade each year so that at the end of four years, every student in the school was supported by the BARR system. This reinforced the school's "Go for Every Student" philosophy.

Rachel Larson, director of learning and student engagement for the district, observed, "The high school has successfully undertaken a change in culture. It has shifted from a staff-centered culture to a student-centered culture. The staff worked hard to incorporate student voice. Students now serve on the high school's continuous improvement committees."

When the COVID-19 pandemic began to affect school operations, Rob observed, "Our team hit it out of the park. We met as a team and discussed how our evolving culture and philosophy would embrace each student and their family during the crisis." The team made a set of decisions:

- Creation of a grid of every type of support students and families potentially would need, including food, health, internet connectivity, computers, transportation, books, curriculum, and so forth. One person in the central office was made responsible for each of these functions.

- Assignment of each teacher to be responsible for the thirty students in their fifth-period class, including calling each family on their list the day before school resumed and then on an ongoing basis. As the point of contact for those families, the teacher was responsible for determining whether the student or family needed any of the available supports. When support was needed, the teacher would contact the person in the district responsible for that support function and assure that the support was provided.

Rob commented, "Once this structure was in place, our COVID-19 response was a slam dunk. Every family knew we were there for them. We made good on our 'Go for Every Student' motto, and that culture created our platform for success. We received recognition statewide for our approach to COVID-19, but it was really our approach to personalization and social and emotional learning that made that possible."

Let's consider a second example.

Kim Abel was the relatively new head of her teachers' union when Jerry Hill became the superintendent of West Bloomfield School District in Michigan in 2012. Jerry had inherited a fractured relationship between the union and the district administration, describing the existing culture as "toxic." He recalls, "We were having problems with collaboration and problem solving in collective bargaining and were looking to find healthier ways of doing both."

Kim and Jerry agreed they were in need of help in reframing this relationship. They decided to use an interest-based bargaining (IBB) strategy in which the parties collaborate on designing a win–win solution to disputes (Klingel, 2003). The IBB process took root and led to a steady improvement in relations between the union and administration.

In the spring of 2018, Jerry approached Kim with the idea of the district undertaking a process to design its own POG. They formed a community advisory group to help create a broad-based consensus on the elements of the POG. Kim served on the advisory group along with a sizeable delegation of teachers from the district. That fall, they formed a new entity, the Learning Design Team (LDT), and charged it with overseeing the implementation of the POG. Kim and several teachers served on it. The level of collaboration on the LDT was high, and the district got off to a strong start in building the POG into the curriculum and instruction. Administration and teachers felt the POG gaining momentum.

Fast-forward to March 9, 2020, when the West Bloomfield cabinet met to discuss the possibility that schools might be closing due to COVID-19. They realized that the district should begin a planning process for that possibility and assigned that process to the LDT, which was to meet two days later. At the LDT meeting, the team quickly concluded that school closure in Michigan was imminent and there was a need to prepare teachers for this situation. Team members suggested that Jerry call a "non-snow snow" day two days later and use that day to get everyone on board with a COVID-19 strategy. The Learning Design Team spent the rest of the meeting planning the full day of teacher meetings on the upcoming non-snow day. On Thursday night, March 12, Governor Gretchen Whitmer announced the closure of all Michigan schools, effective March 16.

When teachers arrived at the planned Friday meeting, they all knew that there would be no further in-person classes for the foreseeable future. They spent the day doing detailed planning. The following Monday, the first day of school closure, was a logistics day, where staff made sure that all students had the materials they needed to begin online classes. The following day, classes began with relatively few bumps, and West Bloomfield had one of the easiest transitions of any district in the state to educating children during the COVID-19 closures. The district received accolades for its transition and performance.

It is interesting to listen to participants' perspectives on what transpired. Kim Abel, the union president, looks back on the district's performance and notes: "Teachers required support to make the needed transitions. COVID-19 shone a light on building leaders who fostered creativity and experimentation. They would say things like 'that was great' and 'glad you tried that.' Those comments made a big difference. On the other hand, there were a few leaders who did not nurture creativity and autonomy. These developments underscore the importance of a great principal who nurtures the right culture."

Superintendent Jerry Hill also had some helpful reflections on the district's performance during the first months of the pandemic: "The reason we were able to do what we did during COVID-19 was (1) we knew how to collaborate; (2) we had a vision; (3) we were ready for that moment. The culture of our district was, 'We can do this.' The POG was a concept, but in our district, it became a way of thinking. No problem is too big if we focus on the best interests of the kids and a collaborative culture."

These two stories are powerful reminders of the pivotal role leaders play in the culture of their districts. In both cases, the leaders recognized a cultural shift was needed. In one instance, the culture shift was necessary for a major design change in the school. In the other, the culture shift was undertaken to generally improve relations between administrators and teachers. In both, this cultural shift was in place when COVID-19 arrived, and both districts benefitted from the shifts in culture that had already been undertaken.

ASK YOURSELF

- *What has a recent crisis (such as COVID-19) revealed to you about the strengths of the culture of your district?*
- *If a recent crisis has revealed weakness in the culture, how might you use this as an opportunity to create a conversation around the culture?*

KNOW WHEN TO RESET YOUR ORGANIZATION'S CULTURE.

As you contemplate your system's capacity to transform, you can't overestimate the role that culture plays. Brian Greenberg, CEO of the Silicon Schools Fund, surveyed the more than fifty innovative schools in Northern California funded by his organization. He tried to determine which factors led to these schools adapting well in the COVID-19 circumstances. While technology acumen had some bearing on their capacity to handle the challenges of COVID-19, the existence of a culture of collaboration and flexibility was clearly the most important factor in assessing a school's ability to respond constructively to the pandemic (Greenberg, 2020).

This question deserves your attention: "Does your system have the culture necessary to reach your community's new vision for education?"

Chip Kimball, director of the International School of Prague and former superintendent of both Singapore American School and Lake Washington School District in Washington State, puts the challenge this way: "Determine what you want your culture to be and lead to it. Doing this work is all about organizational culture. This is your number-one job. Too often leaders accept the organizational culture as it is. The culture they are building, the DNA of the system, will have more to do with the successful transformation of their system than the direction in which they are heading. If your system needs it, you must hit 'reset' on your organizational culture."

If a culture reset is needed, be aware of events that could catalyze change. In Minnesota, Principal Rob Bach recognized that the conversion from a 10 through 12 school to a 9 through 12 high school was the right moment to begin a culture reset. In the Michigan district, frank discussion between the union leader and a new school superintendent opened the opportunity for a reset of culture. The right catalyst for transformation in your community will be unique to your context. Consider your POG process as a transition that could jumpstart significant shifts in your culture.

Is the culture required for redefining student success currently present in your system? Or do you need to change the culture to align with your community's vision? If your culture needs a reset, this must be your first priority. The best leaders realize that before they can take their Portrait of a Graduate into the classroom, they need to get their adults on board.

> The best leaders realize that before they can take their Portrait of a Graduate into the classroom, they need to get their adults on board.

Anthony Bent, leadership consultant and former superintendent of several Massachusetts school districts, puts it this way: "The quality of a district is not the printed documents, but who owns the printed documents. Whose documents are they? Do the documents reflect the collective will of the team?"

As you anticipate next steps, pay attention to when you will need to stay "tight" to focus on clear priorities and when it's better to loosen control to encourage creativity and autonomy. Good leaders do both. As the late Richard DuFour (2007) pointed out, "One of the most essential elements of loose–tight leadership is getting tight about the right things."

In your commitment to the vision, you want to be firm and clear (tight). You want people to know that the POG is not optional. However, the goals of the POG around specific competencies need to be co-created with your community (loose). Once the POG is adopted, you want every school and every classroom to embrace it (tight). However, the way to get there needs to be determined by each school leader and their team in the context of that school's specific context (loose).

Rachel Tecca, director of college and career academies in Akron, Ohio, appreciates the tight–loose leadership of Superintendent David James: "He lets you make sense of his vision in the context of your work. He is *tight* on his vision and *loose* in letting you make the vision your own."

There is one continuum of culture to which you should pay particular attention: *isolation versus collective efficacy.*

If you were in school in the 1990s or earlier, you know that the primary culture was "teachers rule" in the classroom. The culture was one of splendid isolation for both teachers and students. Each teacher was relied on to solve the problems of their classroom individually. That tradition has been slow to change. The shift to a Portrait of a Graduate requires a culture of collaboration. The culture of the adults needs to model the culture you want students to demonstrate. The challenges the adults take on require collaboration to accomplish.

Jim May, strategic advisor for the New Tech Network, underscores the importance of culture for student learning:

> Adult culture functions as a glass ceiling for student culture. I've never visited a school where the students are more intellectually engaged than the adults. I've never seen a school where the students collaborate at a higher level than the adults. One of the most important levers school and district leaders have available to them as it relates to shaping student learning and culture is their influence on shaping adult culture and the design of the adult learning system. I want school and district leaders to see themselves as environmental architects as it relates to the adult learning system.

Mike Duncan, superintendent in Pike County, Georgia, reinforces this message: "The systems and processes to support teachers have been the culture change. There is now recognition that one teacher cannot do this work alone. Collaboration is about working together. Collective efficacy is about the group taking responsibility for improving."

Working toward collective efficacy is just one of the cultural issues you need to consider. You and your team will identify other issues that are unique to your context. The key is to prioritize the ones that address your specific challenges.

Three more suggestions will keep your focus on creating the right culture to support student success.

Create a Green Light Culture

One helpful way to think about the culture of the adults in your system is whether you have or can create a green light culture. While you might at first think this refers to the sustainability or environmental awareness of your system, we mean the term more broadly. Do your teachers and administrators perceive they have the green light to experiment and innovate? Do they—and your board—also understand the necessary corollary, that it's OK to fail? These two questions are central to the green light culture, which is an essential underpinning of a culture that will support innovation and transformation.

Melissa Follin, a teacher in Virginia Beach, Virginia, teaches an engaging unit on the protection of oysters in the nearby Chesapeake Bay. More than 125 students in five different classes participate, along with more students who take part in an after-school club. When asked how she is able to do this innovative work, she responded, "Our principal, Dr. Kelly Hedrick, challenged us to *design to the edges*. She encouraged us to go above and beyond teaching at grade level. She wanted us to push hard to create authentic opportunities for students to experience the curriculum."

"Design to the edges" was the principal's way of empowering her teachers to innovate. It's also the theme of a TEDx talk called "The Myth of Average" (Rose, 2013) that the principal has shared with her staff as a culture builder. Kelly Hedrick elaborates on her key message: "A 'green light' for me is empowerment. Teachers who feel empowered and supported in their creative endeavors are more likely to do the same for kiddos. Nurturing the green light, for me, encompasses the entire mission, vision, and leadership I provide my staff. If they are going to take creative risks, they need to know they have more than just my support and permission. They need to feel empowered, and that begins with me. I have to create a safe environment where everyone feels valued and honored. They have to know that while I have incredibly high expectations, I am here to support them."

Julie (Wilson) Jungalwala, founder of the Institute for the Future of Learning, builds on this concept. As she points out, "There are so many yellow and red lights out there that stand in the way of innovation—federal policy, state policy, and sometimes even district policy. So it falls on the leader to stand up and offer a green light. But one suggestion: Don't assume just turning on the green light is enough. It may take some cajoling and convincing that you really mean it and won't change your mind. Folks will need to hear and see that message over and over again. You will need to make it public and prominent or folks won't believe the green light."

Anna Nolin, superintendent of Natick Public Schools in Massachusetts, nurtures a green light culture across her school system because it fosters "psychological safety." As she explains, "We make 'failure' not so scary and try to support staff to take risks without judgment. We call these ideas 'bright spots,' and we share them across the district. We try to find money for the bright spots to become full flames or to spread across the district."

Anna continually reinforces this culture with messages and practices. For example, she says, "I personally nurture it by trying to teach our principals to be evaluated without judgment and not worry over every little detail. We also make innovation teams at each level so people can get together and do post-mortems and share successes. This destigmatizes failure and just makes us all one set of colleagues working towards the best. We don't stand on hierarchy and we are creative with asking people to partner with us to share [the] financial load for creative ideas."

The following example from Jeffco Public Schools in Colorado illustrates how a green light culture affects everyone in the system—from students to the superintendent.

Alicia Asmus is a teacher in Arvada, Colorado, whose interdisciplinary science project we will feature in the next chapter. When we asked her how she knew she could take on the ambitious project she did, with students in the role of citizen scientists, she said, "Last year I tried a similar project that had some challenges. My principal was very encouraging, even in the face of some imperfection in the project. So I knew if I approached her on this new project, I would get a green light."

Alicia's principal, Brenda Fletcher, explains she was able to give such a clear green light because she knew her superintendent had her back on innovation. Then-Superintendent Jason Glass made it clear to his principals that innovation and experimentation were not only condoned but strongly encouraged.

The union president of Glass's district was John Ford, who concurred: "Jason opened this huge door, if teachers were willing to take the opportunity and had the courage to do something new. We had the right superintendent; he was willing to take risks. I welcome this approach, but the real green lights are at the building level, and not every principal is giving green lights."

Glass unpacked what the green light culture means for leaders:

> Creating a green light culture is an essential ingredient in transformation. There are three things you can do to support it: First, you need to put parameters on what you are green lighting. When I was in Jefferson County (Colorado),

we gave the green light specifically to authentic student learning experiences, problem- and project-based learning, and empowering site-based and classroom decision making. Second, once people take you up on the green light, you need to support them. You need to give them the authority they need and then showcase their work. Third, you need to defend what's been green lit from the rest of the status quo. The status quo system will be threatened and try to shut the green light down, and you need to create the safe space where the green lighters can operate.

So, my basic advice about green light culture is this:

—define it,

—support and nurture it, and

—protect it.

ASK YOURSELF

- *What are three examples where you have given your leadership team a green light?*
- *How can you determine whether your principals are developing a green light culture in their buildings?*
- *How can you showcase examples of teachers benefitting from a green light culture?*

Let's take a closer look at the components of green light culture. Mike Marks, former CEO of two very successful tech companies and adjunct professor at the Stanford Business School, is an international expert on innovation. He offers three pieces of advice that are helpful in this context.

Try stuff (and share): At one level, you simply want people to try new things. Mike recommends: "If you want innovation, you just have to be willing to try stuff and just move on." This goes to the heart of giving the green light when members of your team want to experiment with new approaches. It is also important to share these approaches, whether successful or not, so colleagues can benefit from the experiences as well.

Embrace failure (and learn from it): It isn't enough to simply "keep trying stuff." You have to be open to failure and to sharing the lessons of that failure. Maya Angelou has described failure as just a data point. In the context of education, you need to be certain all data points are shared so that you collaboratively learn from the failures. Mike Marks explains that failure is baked into the culture of Silicon Valley: "It is why I like it so much here. Often the first question one gets asked in a Silicon Valley job interview is, 'Where have you failed miserably?' If you can't answer that question, most often you won't get the job." He even encourages leaders to "celebrate failure," adding, "Maybe 'celebrate' is the wrong word, but I mean to let it be known that someone tried an innovation, it didn't work, but they learned from it and hope they will try again."

This is the opposite of the dominant culture of education. Most teachers succeeded as students by being the ones who failed the least. So they assiduously avoid failing, finding myriad ways to discourage failure. If we want generations of innovative and creative problem solvers, then we need adults to embrace failure and encourage risk-taking. This requires a major cultural shift. We need to help current teachers embrace risk-taking. We need to hire the next generation of teachers with an emphasis on their willingness to take risks and have an openness to the lessons of failure.

Park Ginder, principal of Homestead High School in Fort Wayne, Indiana, is emphatic on this point: "You have to create a culture in which it's OK for the adults to fail. Excellent work does not mean perfect. You have to demonstrate to your faculty that it is OK to not know the answer. It is our job as educators to break the rules for the betterment of kids. My superintendent has not told me 'no' once in eight years. I can preach failure because he lets me make mistakes."

Dave Sovine, superintendent in Frederick County, Virginia, relates the POG to breakthroughs in failure: "The biggest impact of the POG in our district is that our teachers are embracing the challenge to experiment. Failure can be our friend. Our most significant breakthroughs are teachers who began experimenting with student engagement as they work on more innovative pedagogy. We have seen tremendous growth by teachers in this realm." Jerry Putt, a principal in Frederick County, goes even further: "Don't just accept risk-taking—promote it. Risk-taking is empowerment. How do you engage in risk-taking so it is empowering?"

Be curious: Mike Marks's third piece of advice is to be curious. He goes so far as to say that in his experience with hiring or promoting leaders, the number-one determinant of an individual's likely leadership success is their inherent curiosity. If you are satisfied by what is, you will wallow in the current state, problems and all. If you are innately curious, you will not only want to find out how things work but how you can make things work better.

Many educators are inherently curious. Curiosity is so important in the 21st century that we need to shine a light on it. Look for opportunities for adults and students to share their curiosity with each other and showcase the benefits of being inquisitive.

A related piece of advice Mike offers is to look at what everyone else is doing. In an education context, this means looking at what other schools and districts in your region and state are doing in an area in which you want to improve. What are other schools or districts around the country doing with that challenge? This is why we flag this issue in Chapter 7 about joining networks that can serve as a professional learning community for you. It is also why we strongly recommend leaders taking their team leaders on site visits to see first-hand what others are doing. Chapters 3 through 5 are essentially mini-field trips to visit success stories in the realms of creative problem solving, civic engagement, and self-direction. These chapters are designed to show you current cutting-edge practices.

The desire to learn from others should also be directed outside the education community. Mike Marks explains that successful innovative businesses almost always look to see what is going on in industries other than their own. You should try that, too. Consider talking to two to three of the most innovative people in your community; you may have already identified them and included them on your POG advisory team. Perhaps they run a technology start-up company or have reinvented a community service organization. Meet with them to discuss their views on innovation. Bring them in to meet with your leadership team. Have them meet with your teachers. It will be helpful for your administrators and teachers to hear why experimentation and innovation are so important, why your students need those competencies, and how your adults need to model them.

We have described three potential elements of your green light culture:

- Try stuff
- Be open to failure
- Be curious

Now we want you to consider how you would define a green light culture for your school or district. Consider co-creating a rubric or descriptor of the elements of a green light culture you collectively want to embrace. It will help you, your leadership team, and your teachers to shift your current culture to an environment where experimentation and innovation are valued and modeled.

ASK YOURSELF

- *What next steps will you take to assess your system's green light culture?*
- *What next steps will you take to nurture your system's green light culture?*

Consider Creating a Portrait of an Educator

Creating a green light culture will help shift your system's openness to creative ideas that support your shared vision. Creativity among teachers and administrators is essential, but it's not the only attribute they need to help students thrive as 21st century learners. Another tool will help to build a culture more broadly while aligning with your POG. This tool is the Portrait of an Educator.

Begin by asking, "How does our Portrait of a Graduate, designed for students, apply to the adults in our system?" Then go deeper by asking, "For us to help our students attain the attributes of our Portrait of a Graduate, what competencies do we need, individually and collectively, as educators?"

That can be the starting point for working with your teachers to co-create a Portrait of an Educator.

The practice of creating a Portrait of an Educator is just getting started around the country and showing real promise. It is an easier process than co-creating the community-based Portrait of a Graduate because it involves only the internal participation of your own educators. Some of them will have already participated in the community visioning process; however, this is an opportunity for all teachers to be involved.

As the Portrait of an Educator is developed, an interesting question will need to be answered: Will our district adopt a Portrait of an Educator that uses the same competencies as the Portrait of a Graduate, or will the Portrait of an Educator have different competencies? Both strategies can work.

In Northern York County School District in Pennsylvania, the district adopted a Portrait of an Educator based on their Profile of a Graduate. According to their former superintendent, Eric Eshbach: "If this is important to expect of all students, then we must expect it of all who work with our students. Our POE uses the same language as our POG but adjusts the expectations to be appropriate to the educator level. While I left the district before realizing the full potential of the POE, I envisioned it being used to recraft our evaluation system for all educators." (See Figure 2.1: Northern York Portrait of a Graduate.)

A different approach was taken in Needles, California, where the teachers of the district thought the elements of their Portrait of an Educator should go beyond the Portrait of a Graduate competencies. They believed there were elements of a 21st century educator that fell outside the scope of their student-centered POG. Superintendent Mary McNeil commented: "During these turbulent times, our POE will help us frame the multitude of new skills and learning that is mandatory during the pandemic and allow us to focus on what we need to do to be supportive of our students as we move through these times" (see Figures 2.2–2.3).

In Natick, Massachusetts, the district began creating a Portrait of an Educator during teacher union negotiations, just after their Portrait of a Graduate was adopted. During those discussions, the union president, Jefferson Wood, suggested that it might be a good idea to adopt a Portrait of an Educator. He thought it would be powerful to have a unifying agreement on what makes a great teacher. "We want to use it to build a better evaluation model that focuses on what matters."

Natick Superintendent Anna Nolin responded positively: "I agreed with the idea because a vision for teacher practice inspires the heart and soul of educators. Having a Portrait of an Educator would also allow us to set practice goals and provide professional development to support core values and bring clarity and comfort to our teaching force."

Contemplate the multiple applications of the Portrait of an Educator. It can provide general direction for changing your culture by identifying the educator attributes that should be at the core of culture. It can also help transform components of your entire system.

Leverage Your Portraits

As you have heard, districts have taken different approaches to defining the desired competencies of adults. Some create a Portrait of an Educator; others use their POG to unpack the competencies adults need to support student success. What's important is to clarify your vision so that it applies to both students and adults, then leverage your portrait (or portraits) to drive culture change. Let's use POG/POE as shorthand for whatever you decide to create.

Figure 2.1   Northern York Portrait of a Graduate and Portrait of an Educator

Northern York County School District
Profile of a Graduate

Civically Engaged ... Personally Responsible ... Intellectually Prepared ...

CREATIVITY
COMPETENT
COURAGEOUS
CRITICAL THINKING
COLLABORATION
CONTRIBUTING
COMMUNICATION
CONSCIENTIOUS

Northern York County School District's

Profile of an Educator

Educators of the NYCSD have learned and understand the importance of **Creativity** in the learning process. They show this through their: • Flexibility and openness to learning with, from, about and for students and peers. • Ability to be solution oriented, using inquiry to solve problems. • Willingness to seek, encourage, and provide meaningful learning opportunities for students. • Innovation through risk taking, problem solving, and exploring.	Educators of NYCSD are **Contributing** members of the community, the nation, and the world. They: • Model and support a service mindset. • Seek opportunities to be generous with their time, resources and talents. • Intentionally build positive, appropriate relationships with students and colleagues. • Cultivate an environment that promotes empathy toward others. • Demonstrate respect for all viewpoints. • Recognize and appreciate student and staff differences.
Educators s of the NYCSD have strong skills in **Communication** as demonstrated by their keen capacity to: • Speak openly, respectfully, clearly, and in a timely manner. • Engage successfully by listening in a non-judgmental manner. • Relate positively through non-verbal, written and spoken interactions. • Collaborate constructively with all stakeholders. • Utilize multiple platforms and resources to enhance communication	Educators of NYCSD are **Courageous** and demonstrate their ability to exhibit a problem-olving approach by: • Being able to consider perspectives different from their own. • Having a willingness to try new and possibly, uncomfortable things while trusting in the process and the team. • Embracing the opportunity for personal and professional growth through, a positive growth mindset. • Modeling "extreme ownership". • Having the professional courage to do what is right for kids.

Educator s of the NYCSD have honed the skill of **Critical Thinking**. This is evident in their ability to:
• Gather information relating to all members of our community, in order to consider and develop successful outcomes.
• Synthesize information, identify available resources, and enact viable, student-centered solutions.
• Reflect on the effectiveness of decisions and the impact they have on our community, particularly our students.
• Adapt and adjust accordingly, including:
  • Adopting a growth mindset,
  • Implementing changes when necessary,
  • Supporting the team.
	Educators of NYCSD are **Competent** in a wide range of professional skills and are able to demonstrate that competency through:
	• Mastery in his/her content area of expertise and the essential functions of the assigned position, along with a willingness to his/her expand knowledge in that area
	• Mastery of technology related to job expectations.
	• Ethical behavior, including behavior that is honest, empathetic, and respectful.
	• Contributing to a positive culture and climate.
	• Understanding the social and emotional needs of students.
	• Personal wellness (physical, emotional, social, financial, etc).

Educators of NYCSD use **Collaboration** effectively and persistently and value: • Building positive and respectful relationships with students, parents, colleagues. • Accepting and giving constructive feedback from students, parents, colleagues, • Participating in PLC's, department/grade level meetings, and professional development. • Engaging others in thoughtful discussion, centered on mutual respect to improve teaching and learning.	Educators of NYCSD are **Conscientious**, which is evident because they are: • Self-Directed, • Reliable, • Responsible, • Self-Disciplined, • Self-Motivated, • Lifelong Learners, and • Hard Workers.

Figure 2.2   Needles Portrait of a Graduate

Figure 2.3   Needles Portrait of an Educator

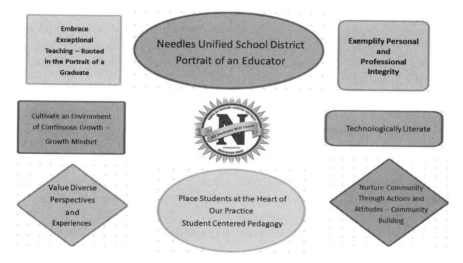

One of the best aspects of creating your POG/POE is that it can drive major changes in areas you might not have initially imagined.

In many districts, one of the first areas impacted by the POG/POE is professional development. Teachers need to be supported in making the necessary transitions to help their students develop the desired competencies.

Liz Fagen, superintendent in Humble Independent School District in Texas, talks about the transition this way: "If you look at our Portrait of a Graduate, we want our students on a continuum of improvement for the elements of the Portrait. For that to happen, our teachers need to be on a continuum of improvement, too. This transformation work requires a growth mindset for all adults and students in our system. Our professional development has to help our teachers develop their own growth mindset and work on the growth in the areas that require change in our approach to teaching. The specific shift in approach to teaching is often characterized as moving from the front of the classroom to a 'guide on the side' model."

Royd Darrington, assistant superintendent of the Juab School District in Utah, describes the shift this way: "Our job as educators is changing from being the gatekeepers of what education is to being the facilitators of what education should be. Those are two very different roles, and our teachers need support for how to become great facilitators."

Jerry Hill, superintendent in the West Bloomfield, Michigan, district featured at the beginning of this chapter, observes that professional development in his district has gone through a complete transformation: "Our PD has totally changed. The teachers now informally network with each other. Our PD for next year will be focused on competency-based education that is personalized and job-embedded for teachers. Our professional learning communities are taking responsibility for individuals. A lot of this work has become a way of thinking and doing and less about creating free-standing courses of PD."

David Larson, superintendent of the Glenbard High School District in Illinois, also sees professional development as a culture shift. "We have 550 teachers, with probably fifty to 100 innovators. How do we move along our other 400 or so teachers? We've redesigned our PD to integrate our Portrait of a Graduate competencies into student-directed, project-based tasks. We want all 550 teachers to have the capacity to guide those students in accomplishing those tasks. This is an essential component of their professional capabilities."

Everyone in K–12 education knows that PD needs dramatic transformation. Fortunately, POG/POE provides a clear and concrete direction for that needed change. The student and educator competencies need to be a key component of revitalized professional development.

At the same time, these are not the only components of a transformed PD strategy. In Chapter 6, we will explore pedagogical and assessment strategies to enable student attainment of the POG competencies. These strategies will become essential elements of your new PD, as well.

Another area that can be deeply impacted by the POG/POE is human resource policy. Many administrators don't immediately see the tie-in between the POG/POE and HR policy, even though the relationship is profound. Bill Considine, former CEO of Akron's Children's Hospital, points out his hospital used these competencies to evaluate him and his team. "The 4 Cs (critical thinking, communication, collaboration, and creativity) are in our staff evaluation at Children's Hospital, and they also were included at the CEO level for my evaluation."

Many companies and nonprofits use POG-like competencies to evaluate their employees. It's also critical to do so in K–12 education. If we are going to help students develop those attributes, we need educators to be able to model those attributes. Imagine the power of your school board members embracing the POG/POE as principles for how they conduct themselves individually and as a group.

Farmington, Connecticut, is a district that has had its POG for many years. As their experience with it deepened, they applied it to more and more areas of their human resources policy and operation. Their recruitment and hiring of teachers are aligned to their vision of a graduate. They look for "learners" to become members of their learning organization. They want individuals who have a "learner's mindset." Their vision of a graduate defines the kind of teacher they want to hire.

Kim Wynne, assistant superintendent in Farmington, is emphatic: "I love the teacher prospect who can spontaneously articulate how students are collaborative, creative problem solvers. Our vision of a graduate is now front and center on the recruitment table. We want teachers who are teaching students, not content."

Similarly, Danielle Prohaska, superintendent in the small, rural district in Ohio's Mechanicsburg Exempted Village Schools, tells the story of using the POG to hire a new principal during the pandemic. "We asked each candidate to review our POG, explain how their prior experiences prepare them to lead this work, and what each would do to move it forward. The successful applicant made the best impression on those criteria and is now moving the high school forward on the POG during the pandemic."

Farmington not only uses their POG for hiring but also designs their orientation for new teachers, with their "vision of a graduate" as a prominent feature. They hold five to six sessions for new teachers in the first two years with the vision of a graduate at the core of that training. Kim Wynne goes further: "We want to give them a sense of districtwide coherence. They leave the orientation sessions understanding our district's 'theory of action' in which our vision of a graduate is a central feature."

Finally, in Farmington, teachers set their own benchmarks for the vision of a graduate. They are asked each year: "What are your action research goals for the vision of a graduate for the year?" This work is now a formal component of teacher evaluation.

Farmington is a good example of a district that started with a vision of a graduate and each year embedded it more deeply in their system. It demonstrates how your POG/POE is likely to have applications to your work that you might not have anticipated when you first adopted it.

ASK YOURSELF

- *How will you co-create your POE with your educators?*
- *How will you use your POE?*
- *How will you assess your own progress on the competencies in your POG/POE?*
- *How will you encourage your leadership team to do the same self-assessment?*
- *What can we do individually and collectively to improve performance as adults on one of the elements of our POG/POE in the coming year?*

Final Reflections

In this chapter, we have asked you to focus on the adults in the system before starting to make changes in your classrooms. Your administrators and teachers need support for the shift you are asking them to make. How will you provide that support for transformation? Rob at Stillwater High School began with a culture of adult-oriented priorities, and he put in place structures that redirected the new culture to be student oriented and personalized. Jerry and Kim in West

Bloomfield inherited a history of deep mistrust between the administration and teachers. They put in place structures to encourage a dialogue building upon trust and mutual support for differing perspectives. Now's the time to consider leadership moves you want to make to better align your culture with your vision.

You may have found that the COVID-19 crisis has put issues of culture front and center. Listen to Aaron Spence, superintendent in Virginia Beach, Virginia, describe how he has guided conversations about culture with his team, with a specific focus on equity:

> At the heart of this work, if you want to change, you have to ask, why are we doing business the way we are? COVID-19 threw down the gauntlet. Will people really want to go back to what is super comfortable?
>
> During COVID-19, I asked my team three sets of questions: (1) In this moment, what are we doing that we must keep doing? Have we caught lightning in a bottle? How do we keep it? (2) What are we doing now that we know we need to stop? This has really brought equity to the surface. Kids who don't have relationships with teachers and families are in an untenable position. We must change our practices for them. We have to stop behaving as though it's OK for some kids not to be engaged. (3) What are we not doing that we should be doing? What are the new challenges and opportunities? For example, how do we address post-traumatic stress disorder (PTSD) for kids, families, and teachers?

These are important leadership questions not only for coping with the pandemic with equitable solutions but during any unexpected crisis or change in circumstances:

- What are we doing that we must keep doing?
- What are we doing that we know we need to cease?
- What are we not doing that we should be?

You may discover that unanticipated events will not necessarily interfere with transformation but rather underscore the need for change.

Finally, take time to reflect on questions related to the big topics covered in this chapter. When it comes to being the leader of a green light culture,

- Where does a green light culture exist in your district? How can you expand its impact?
- How will the shifting culture of the district help to close the readiness gap for all students?

RESOURCES FOR IMPLEMENTATION

To help you develop your Portrait of an Educator, **Battelle for Kids** offers helpful resources. www.battelleforkids.org/portraitofaneducator/landing

For Your Bookshelf

- *The Human Side of Changing Education* by Julie (Wilson) Jungalwala, founder of the Institute for the Future of Learning

- *Leadership for Deeper Learning* by Jayson W. Richardson, Justin Bathon, and Scott McLeod

Action Steps

Just as we cautioned at the end of Chapter I not to skip over the need to set a vision, anchor it in your community, and focus on equity, here we caution you not to underestimate the importance of addressing your system's culture. You can't create aspirations for students and teachers to innovate and experiment if your culture can't support these changes. Many good and great ideas for educational change have fallen victim to dysfunctional culture. Three action steps will ensure that culture is given the appropriate priority as you move forward with your new definition of student success.

I.   **Commit to a green light culture.** Analyze the degree to which you currently have a green light culture. Don't gloss over deficiencies. Does your team really believe it is getting a green light from you? Do your teachers believe they are getting a green light from their principals? Focus the green light on those next steps that truly matter.

2. **Adopt a Portrait of an Educator**. To complement your POG, co-create a Portrait of an Educator with your teachers. Together, you will identify the competencies they need to fully implement the POG and reach a collective decision: Will you adopt the same POG for adults and students, or will you identify a different combination of competencies that fully define the Portrait of an Educator in the 21st century?

3. **Leverage your POG/POE**. Use the POG and POE to define your adult culture. Specifically, consider using the portraits to define your approach to professional development; hiring practices; orientation; and evaluation policies and procedures. This is not an exhaustive list of what can be done with the POG/POE. The further you examine your system, the more applications you will find for using the POG/POE.

Up to this point, we have been discussing vision, community, and educator consensus building. As you continue on this journey, you and your stakeholders need a sharply focused mental picture of the tangible work that students will be doing to achieve the POG competencies. To bring this picture into focus, we have arranged a series of "field trips" to bring to life the full potential of 21st century teaching and learning. Part III of the book will guide you on this inspirational portion of the journey.

PART II

Visiting Your Vision

Coming to a consensus on a vision like the Portrait of a Graduate (POG) can be exhilarating, but it also can be viewed as somewhat esoteric—more aspirational concepts than real or concrete activities. It can be helpful to literally see the vision in action. Many leaders organize field trips to classrooms or programs where a vision has come to life, and we strongly recommend doing that.

To anchor our discussion of vision in reality, we have organized this section as a three-chapter "field trip" intended to give you a real sense of what the commitment to your Portrait of a Graduate looks like in practice. Your own POG may highlight different competencies, but these field trips focus on the critical competency of creative problem solving. You will read about students engaged in creative problem solving in several challenging, 21st century contexts.

If not aligned to your vision, these compelling topics could be taught in a traditional "top-down" lecture style. Instead, focus on the need for self-direction as part of your transformation. We will share examples of students and teachers actively engaged in self-directed learning. We hope these "visits" to sites across the country will anchor your own vision and give you and your team a deeper understanding of what the educational experience encouraged by a POG will look like in real life.

Some words of caution: The POG can't be a simple matter of "shoehorning" skills into the existing curriculum. If creative problem solving is the goal, you need to offer students robust interdisciplinary problems to tackle. You also need to help them learn how to identify worthy problems themselves. We will challenge you to

- Offer your students opportunities to take on challenges and produce results in the realms of sustainability, innovation, invention, and entrepreneurship

- Ensure that each of your students, at every level of their education, is given an opportunity to take on a civic engagement challenge so that they will have at least three significant artifacts of their civic accomplishments in their portfolio at the end of their K–12 education
- Be certain that the goal of self-directed learning is clearly defined and adopted so that all students are intrinsically motivated and in charge of choosing and managing the challenges they take on

We offer the challenges of Part II to encourage you and your team to move from an occasional problem-solving task in a sea of content mastery to a set of robust challenges that excite and engage your students on their education journey to becoming self-directed and creative problem finders and solvers.

What to Look For

As you read Chapters 3, 4, and 5, consider the following:

> "What would I tell the ninth-grade version of myself?
>
> "Trust that if you leave high school with the confidence to take on big challenges as a creative problem solver, you'll be ready to move forward in life with a sense of purpose and mission. Use these precious years to explore, to learn how to learn, to seek out opportunities full of ambiguity and challenge, and to get to know yourself and what you find fulfilling. You will be on your way to the success and happiness that otherwise may prove quite elusive."
>
> ~Ted Dintersmith, education advocate and venture capitalist

- What leadership do you need to provide to move your team to a place where creative problem solving is a hallmark of your school or district?
- How do you ensure that creative problem-solving experiences are available to each and every student, not just to those in advanced classes or after-school experiences? What additional resources or support is necessary to bring creative problem solving to those students farthest from opportunity?
- How can you highlight the creative problem-solving work already taking place in your school or district? How can you do this for the work of other schools and districts?
- How do you move from students aspiring to high grades or merely doing what they are told to do, to students who are intrinsically motivated and self-directed?

These are important questions. As you explore the concrete examples in this section, imagine your own aspirations for creative problem solving coming to life for your students. Buckle up—the field trip is beginning!

CHAPTER 3

Be the Leader of Creative Problem Solvers

CHAPTER HIGHLIGHTS

If you prioritize one competency over all others, it should be "creative problem finding and solving." We predict that schools of the future will have students spending 30 percent to 50 percent of their time identifying and solving real-life problems that exist in their schools, neighborhoods, towns and cities, regions, and beyond. You need to start making that shift now. Don't just focus on embedding creative problem solving in core subjects. Look for interdisciplinary challenges that will excite your students and unleash their problem-solving potential.

After two chapters extolling the necessity of co-creating your vision with your community, it may surprise you to hear us devote special attention to one competency. Here's why we feel compelled to do so.

If we had to reduce all the lists of competencies from all the Portrait of a Graduates (POG) we've seen to a single critical competency, it would be (drumroll!) creative problem solving. Before you nod in agreement or begin to muster your counter-arguments, keep in mind that several competencies (including the 4 Cs) could be subsumed under creative problem solving. If you are a creative problem solver, you will need to know how to critically think, communicate, and collaborate to fully solve a problem.

We nominate creative problem solving as the first among equals. It represents the fundamental shift underway in education from a system that requires and produces compliant knowledge workers to a system that produces self-directed problem seekers and solution finders.

We're not the only ones who think this is true. Peter Sanchioni, superintendent in Tiverton, Rhode Island, maintains, "Creative problem solving is the holy grail." Mike Duncan, superintendent in Pike County, Georgia, declares, "It's not what students know, it's what they can do with what they know. Can they take their knowledge and apply it to a problem they have never seen before?" Being able to apply knowledge to novel situations is perhaps the strongest evidence of deep learning (Hewlett Foundation, 2013; NRC, 2012).

> Creative problem solving represents the fundamental shift underway in education from a system that requires and produces compliant knowledge workers to a system that produces self-directed problem seekers and solution finders.

Phil Downs, superintendent in Southwest Allen, Indiana, argues, "The future of schools is all about problem solving. To prepare kids for what is ahead, you have to get them to attack the problem, identify the right questions, and develop the networks to solve them." Karen Garza, CEO of Battelle for Kids, supports this view, saying, "Our young people can solve the problems of our communities, but we need to prepare them the right way." The North Salem Central School District in New York has this concise and compelling mission statement: "Engage students to continuously learn, question, define and solve problems through critical and creative thinking."

It's hard to argue with the proposition that creative problem solving is an essential 21st century competency. In this chapter, we will spend significant time unpacking what this means for you as a leader. In this and the following two chapters, we explore specific contexts that can captivate your students with engagement and refine their creative problem-solving skills at the same time.

Which problems will your students be most interested in tackling? Which contexts for problem solving will be the best fit for your community? To help you consider these questions, we share concrete examples that showcase the power of creative problem solving. In this and the following two chapters, we highlight creative problem solving in the contexts of the following:

- **Sustainability (Chapter 3):** Management of human, natural, and financial resources to meet current needs while ensuring that resources are available for future generations
- **Innovation, Invention, and Entrepreneurship (Chapter 3):** Development of breakthrough solutions or original products, combined with business and marketing strategies to bring them to scale
- **Civic Engagement (Chapter 4):** Informed participation in civic life for the betterment of society
- **Self-Direction (Chapter 5):** Ability to set goals, make choices, and manage one's own actions

By the time you have completed these three chapters, you will have a much clearer image of the future of education. You will see fewer attempts to squeeze problem solving into a memorization agenda and more emphasis on creating a problem-solving landscape infused with deep content.

RECOGNIZE OPPORTUNITIES FOR CREATIVE PROBLEM SOLVING

Before we get fully into that problem-solving landscape, let's explore six distinct steps you can take now to emphasize creative problem solving:

- Focus on problem finding *and* problem solving. Develop strategies that help students identify worthy problems.
- Emphasize creativity broadly throughout the school day. Don't curtail activities, such as art and music classes.
- Shine a light on current problem-solving accomplishments of students and teachers.
- Consider systemwide approaches, such as a creative problem-solving challenge each year for elementary and middle school students and a creative problem-solving course each year for high school students.
- Consider the role that constraints play in spurring or crushing creativity.
- Focus on interdisciplinary approaches to problem solving.

What's the source for your students' creativity? We often tell students to nurture their creativity wherever they can find it—music, dance, pottery, poetry, creative writing, and so forth. At a moment when we should be expanding those opportunities in a school day, many schools and districts are cutting them back.

Daniel Pink, with his highly regarded book *A Whole New Mind* (2006), launched a major discussion of the importance of creativity in a variety of realms, including education. We checked back with him to see what the results were. He told us: "Long-term commitments to creativity often lose out to short-term metric hitting. As a result, even given all the discussions we've had as a society, we probably aren't any better at creativity. The U.S., for example, has applied very little creativity to our most vexing problems."

Pink confessed that he didn't emphasize problem *seeking* in his book. He explained how his thinking has shifted over the past decade and a half: "Today, problem seeking is more important than problem solving. With the advent of machine learning and artificial intelligence, the really important question is: 'What is the right problem to solve?' We have all of this data, so what is an interesting question we can ask of it? This suggests you need to be emphasizing problem identification as much as problem solving."

Ted Dintersmith, an entrepreneur-turned-education advocate, expands on this approach: "Find the moments of creative problem solving already going on in your school or district and build upon them. If you want your kids to be creative problem solvers, shine a light on the creative problem solving already going on and explain, 'This is what we are already doing.' This can create real momentum for creative problem solving."

Consider giving awards to students and teachers each year for creative problem solving. Organize a day of professional development led by teachers bringing their best examples of creative problem-solving pedagogy. This is a good way to shine a light on creative best practices for cultivating problem solving and create momentum for expanding the universe of educators who embrace them.

You may also consider systemwide goals for students taking on creative problem-solving challenges. In Chapter 6, we emphasize the importance of setting bold instructional goals for your school or district. Peter Sanchioni, the Rhode Island superintendent quoted earlier in this chapter, suggests that you set an annual goal of one major creative problem-solving challenge in elementary and middle school and one entire creative problem-solving course in high school.

Also, think about the power of constraints in their relation to problem solving. Too often, educators think of constraints as an impediment to creativity. In fact, the opposite can be true. Daniel Pink notes, "Constraints are not always helpful, but done right, constraints can be liberating."

For example, Chris Wang, a student at Homestead High School in Southwest Allen, Indiana, was asked to help find a solution that would allow the football and basketball scores from the scoreboard to be directly communicated to the school's digital broadcasts. A commercial technology solution would have cost the district $3,000, which was not feasible. Chris used his ingenuity and a $20 microcomputer interface with the scoreboard that worked to accomplish the desired result, at a fraction of the cost.

Depending on the circumstances, deadlines can enhance as well as crush creativity. Think back on your experiences under COVID-19. Which constraints spurred creativity and which crushed creativity? What are good examples of creative problem solving in your school or district during COVID-19 by both teachers and students?

Finally, consider the importance of interdisciplinary studies to promote problem solving. Most problem solving doesn't exist in a single subject area. For example, many challenges involve technical issues (science, technology, engineering, and mathematics or STEM) with policy implications (social studies) and skillful writing (ELA). Daniel Pink suggests: "We need to have our students look at the world through a wide aperture. We don't want them stuck in silos. We want them to look for the connections between things: physics and poetry, dance and chemistry. Don't start the challenge with the silos in mind—start with the project in mind. This is the power of project-based learning. Then you can bring in the disciplines as you need them."

This leads us to the main topic of this chapter. The bold move is not to "shoehorn" problem solving into the current disciplines. Instead, it is to find the problems in the contexts in which students are inherently interested, which inevitably will be interdisciplinary. These contexts will lead to student engagement as well as rich acquisition of content knowledge and competencies aligned with your POGs.

> The bold move is not to "shoehorn" problem solving into the current disciplines. Instead, it is to find the problems in the contexts in which students are inherently interested, which inevitably will be interdisciplinary.

To help you imagine the possibilities, let's embark on "field trips" to visit specific contexts we commend to you and your team as potential platforms for your students' creative problem-solving endeavors.

RESOURCES FOR CREATIVE PROBLEM FINDING AND PROBLEM SOLVING

d school K12 Lab, part of the Hasso Plattner Institute of Design at Stanford University, offers professional development, special events, experiments, and courses to build creative confidence in students (and teachers) from elementary through secondary. dschool.stanford.edu/programs/k12-lab-network

Project Zero at Harvard Graduate School of education has curated a wealth of resources about creativity. pz.harvard.edu/50th/creativity

Essential Creativity Guide from Common Sense Media features recommended apps, games, and websites with the potential to unleash students' creativity. www.commonsensemedia.org/guide/essential-creativity-guide

Thinking It Through: Coaching Students to Be Problem-Solvers by veteran educators K. Michael Hibbard and Patricia Cyganovich (2021) offers practical, classroom-tested strategies to teach authentic problem solving by integrating creative and critical thinking.

SUSTAINABILITY IN ACTION

Let's focus first on the topic of sustainability to show you how schools are introducing creative problem solving in this context that has global significance and attracts strong student interest. We will take you on three field trips to demonstrate concrete and inspiring examples of students doing meaningful and impactful work in this area.

We hope these next field trips will help you see that students find problem solving in the context of sustainability to be compelling. They are learning deeply by working on challenges in areas that they care about personally and intellectually.

Field Trip

Contributing as Citizen Scientists in Arvada, Colorado

Zach Ford was about to begin sixth grade at Moore Middle School in the summer of 2019. On a walk around Lake Arbor near his home in Arvada, Colorado, he noticed new signs closing the lake due to blue-green algae. He asked his dad, "What is causing the blue-green algae in the lake?" He also wanted to know if there was anything they could do about it. Zach's father, John Ford, was the local teachers' union president (you may remember meeting him in Chapter 2). John said he didn't know the answer and suggested they ask his science teacher the same questions. John and Zach went to see Alicia Asmus, his sixth-grade science teacher (who you also met in Chapter 2).

Alicia wasn't sure but hypothesized that the algae were the symptom of excessive nutrients coming into the lake upstream from runoff of fertilizers (containing phosphorus and nitrates and causing "eutrophication"). Alicia did know that the lake was important to the community, and she decided that her sixth-grade science class should spend time investigating the problem. She mentioned to John that she didn't know anyone at the city of Arvada who was in charge of the lake. Fortunately, John had good contacts with city officials and put Alicia in touch with people at the Arvada Water Department.

When Alicia asked Water Department staff if they would be open to student scientists investigating the problems with the lake, they welcomed the help. Alicia enlisted the two other sixth-grade science teachers to engage all 203 students in the project. When Alicia approached Principal Brenda Fletcher about the idea, Brenda immediately asked, "What can I do to help?" Alicia responded, "Just give us the green light." Brenda did.

On a cold and windy November day, busloads of students arrived at Lake Arbor. Teachers and city scientists had set up ten stations for scientific data gathering. Students and teachers worked with city employees and learned how to collect samples. By the end of their time at the lake, each group of students had collected a variety of water samples for analysis by the city. Back in the classroom, students also conducted their own tests for pH, phosphate levels, and nitrate levels. The results of both the classroom testing and the city's spectrophotometry test showed that there was a high level of phosphates in Lake Arbor.

The teachers then turned the data collection into an analytical writing assignment, with each student preparing a "Lake Arbor Scientific Paper" (complete with

(Continued)

(Continued)

introduction, abstract highlighting the findings, explanation of research methods, results, and discussion of the problem of high phosphorous levels). Classes put together a summary of their reports to present to the Arvada City Council. Five students were selected to make oral presentations. City council members were pleased to better understand the water quality data and open to receiving student recommendations on how to address the problem. When a video of the council meeting was shown to the entire sixth grade the next day, students and teachers alike were impressed with what their representatives had accomplished.

After the winter holidays, classes began the solution phase of their work. Teachers asked, "Now that we know the phosphorous level is high, what do we do about it?" Students developed ideas for solutions and presented them to each other. They narrowed the list to two: develop floating gardens for the lake where the plants would consume the phosphorous; create a public education campaign for the community, informing people of the causes of the problem and what individuals could do about it. When COVID-19 curtailed the construction activities around the floating gardens, Zach and his dad kept the momentum going by building a prototype of the floating garden structure.

We asked several of the participants for their thoughts on the project. Zach commented: "This was a good way to learn about the environment, lakes, and plants. I learned a lot of geometry building the floating garden. I'm glad others got so interested in the project. I felt like a leader. If education was like this more often, kids would be more interested and involved in their education."

Alicia notes that the development and presentation of the city council testimony were key: "The most important thing was for the kids to see their peers presenting to the city council because they saw that they could have a real impact. They could see that what they do in sixth grade can matter. This is where education should be heading—kids should have a big project like this every year. This is what they will remember about sixth-grade science."

Principal Brenda Fletcher reflects on how students changed their perception of themselves, as well: "You may be twelve, but you are a scientist, a mathematician, a writer." She also comments on her role as a leader: "My teachers took off, and all I needed to do was to give them a green light and get out of the way. Sometimes that's the most important thing I can do. And look what happened. The students are happy, the parents are happy, and the city of Arvada is thrilled. That's a pretty good result!"

Field Trip

Removing Mushrooms (and Mold) in Alexandria, Virginia

You met Mary Breslin in the introduction. She is the person who came home to help her parents fight the road proposed to go through their property and then later supported her students when they also fought a Virginia Department of Transportation road proposed to go through a local nature preserve. That project spanned the 2009 through 2010 academic year. Now let's fast forward to fall of 2018, when Mary is working with students at the beginning of the school year to find a project they can be passionate about.

As students worked on the assignment, the teacher heard two boys at the back of the room singing a song about mushrooms. Her first impression was that they were off task, but then one of the best-behaved students told her that the boys were serenading real mushrooms growing in the back of the classroom.

Mary was stunned to see mushrooms growing along the walls. She quickly realized the health challenges that she and many of her students had been experiencing over the past several weeks were likely allergic reactions to the mushrooms. Students began to ask questions: "What's causing the mushrooms to grow here?" "Are there other places in school with mushrooms?" "Are these good for us?" "What can we do about them?"

Mary had been training her class in the methods of an organization called Earth Force that uses fact-finding to influence public policy. She focused a group of six students on fact-finding. They were charged with thoroughly investigating the problems of mushrooms and mold in the school, with the intent to present their findings during the science fair in December.

At the science fair, the mushroom team presented the results of their investigation, including evidence of mold throughout the building. Students received pushback to their advocacy from a central office administrator. (Those interactions eventually led to a cultural shift in how the district manages its facilities challenges—a place where the students have had an impact.)

In the second semester, the focus shifted to public policy. One of Mary's classes decided to seek a resolution from the school board supporting their attempts to pass a policy to test the school for mold. Students met with members of the school board and the school board policy director. Both offered their assistance to the students in pursuing appropriate responses.

(*Continued*)

(Continued)

The students met with the legislative director for the city along with several elected officials. They testified before the school board and also organized a tour of the school building for board members. The obvious evidence of mold made a compelling argument, although students' claims were not believed by all individuals in power until mold testing finally conducted in spring 2020 confirmed the accuracy of the students' investigation.

Another class focused on possible changes in policy at the state level. Their research revealed Virginia did not have a state statute covering mold in schools as a health hazard. Students set out to pursue legislation to remedy this omission.

The state legislative journey was predictably longer. Students testified in Richmond in favor of legislation, SB 845, introduced by Senator Adam Ebbin, who was working with them on the problem. The bill required school boards to create mold testing and remediation plans for submission to the Department of Health for approval. Eventually, the legislation passed and was signed into law by Governor Northam in the spring of 2020, eighteen months after the students first found the mushrooms.

Bridget, one of six students still involved in the work (the group calls itself "Standing for Tomorrow"), shared this reflection: "Just from a life-outside-of-school standpoint, this kind of advocacy is a skill everyone should have. 'Persistence' and 'courage' were so key to our success until we got the adults around us not just to listen but to act."

Benjamin, another student, agreed: "You shouldn't graduate high school without an experience like this. I will remember this experience all of my life. Also, I think students should have a major voice about issues involved in the building they spend their day in."

Vince Meldrum is the head of Earth Force, the organization that trained Mary in its approach to teaching science and environmental public policy. He commented: "After you see what these kids accomplished as seventh graders, you wonder why adults don't give kids enough responsibilities to take on. Adults underestimate what kids can do, and they are afraid of giving away control and letting kids take charge. We need our education leaders to help their educators give up control. It's amazing what kids are capable of."

Field Trip

Advocating for Climate Justice in Portland, Oregon

In her last two years of high school in Portland, Oregon, Sriya Chinnam became a climate justice activist. As a junior, she participated in the school Climate Justice Club. She learned that three years earlier, in 2016, students had rallied at the Board of Education office and asked for a K–12 climate justice curriculum. As a result, the Portland School Board passed a resolution calling for "a plan so that there is curriculum and educational opportunities that address climate change and climate justice in all Portland Public Schools." But Sriya realized that nothing like that had happened—yet.

When the global climate demonstrations occurred in 2019, Sriya recognized an opportunity. After one of the local gatherings, almost two hundred students from her high school followed Sriya to the Board of Education where they asked for a climate justice coordinator who would oversee the development of the promised climate justice curriculum. A few months later, students engaged in a sit-in at the board meeting, bringing a petition signed by 2,000 students in support of their request. The Board of Education agreed to hire a coordinator for environmental justice who would be charged with developing the environmental justice curriculum.

It's worth noting that Portland Public Schools had adopted both a POG and POE (Portrait of an Educator) in 2019 after extensive community outreach. Among the nine competencies highlighted in the graduate portrait are "influential and informed global stewards" and "transformative racial equity leaders" (Portland Public Schools, 2019).

When Sriya reflects on her experience, her words touch on additional POG competencies (such as "inclusive and collaborative problem solvers" and "resilient and adaptable learners"). She explains, "Even though the board passed a resolution in 2016, nothing happened. We had to tie our latest activism to concrete steps we wanted the board to take. It took perseverance and persistence."

Nichole Berg was hired to coordinate environmental justice efforts in Portland. Her new role, climate change and climate justice programs manager, is thought to be the first of its kind in any school system in the United States. She has convened a districtwide group to help develop the curriculum for the high school course on environmental justice, grounded in the district POG. Students and adults

(Continued)

(Continued)

together determined scope and sequence, which standards to prioritize, essential understandings, and recommendations for projects. They also constructed a student-inspired capstone for the end of the course. Yena Perice, Class of 2021, was one of five students appointed to this group. She comments: "We ended up with something pretty great. We defined environmental justice as the intersection of climate justice and racial justice. We also included things students can do to have an impact and to design solutions."

All three of the previous examples show how real-world learning happens at the intersection of disciplines. For example, students in Arvada and Alexandria collected extensive data and performed wide-ranging analyses rooted in STEM topics. In all three scenarios, students had to draw on a wide array of 21st century competencies. You saw vivid examples of critical thinking and analysis, creative problem solving, and leadership skills. Students were also refining their self-direction and project management skills while being challenged to improve their communication and advocacy abilities.

We will focus on civic engagement in Chapter 4, but you can see that each sustainability field trip involved a public policy component, turning a theoretical question into a real-life challenge with real-life significance. Each field trip includes a component of empowerment where students gained self-confidence in their ability to have a real impact on issues important to them and to their community.

As significant as the impact of these projects was for the students, you should also note the critical role adults played. The teachers and administrators exhibited powerful pedagogical strategies and observed the efficacy of empowering their students to tackle important challenges.

The context of sustainability can serve as a particularly meaningful one for developing your students' creative problem-solving skills. As you reflect on the previous field trips, consider steps you can take in the context of sustainability in your school or district. One first step is to shine a light on the sustainability activities your students and teachers are engaged in currently. Use them as a base to extend your sustainability work even further.

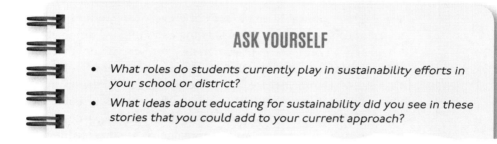

ASK YOURSELF

- *What roles do students currently play in sustainability efforts in your school or district?*
- *What ideas about educating for sustainability did you see in these stories that you could add to your current approach?*

We're certain that you have your own sustainability success stories in your school or district. You can shine a light on those and build on them.

For example, in Val Verde Unified School District in California, Superintendent Mike McCormick describes two systemwide exposures for all students in the area of sustainability. "First, we have gardens at all of our schools and continue to push enough production so that vegetables grown in our school gardens are used in our school salad bars. We are in the process of building a million-dollar greenhouse at one of our high schools to really solidify this effort. Second, we also have solar at all of our schools. Each school has a display that is accessible to teachers and students that reports the number of kilowatts that the panels are producing. This allows for teachers and students to monitor energy production on a daily basis and have conversations and lessons on green energy and sustainability."

Beyond highlighting your current work, we also want you to consider systemwide sustainability challenges.

Consider this challenge: Every student, before leaving elementary, middle, and high school will have made significant and age-level appropriate contributions to sustainability in their school and community through authentic project-based learning. Imagine if every elementary student graduates from fifth or sixth grade having participated in a sustainability project that becomes part of their student portfolio. Imagine similarly each student at the end of eighth or ninth grade and again at the completion of eleventh or twelfth grade.

With interdisciplinary design, your team can integrate STEM skills as well as language arts, social studies, and civic engagement into these projects, similar to those shown in the examples described in Arvada and Alexandria. (See Resources for Sustainability Education later in this chapter to learn more about benchmarks for effective project design.)

There is an even more ambitious challenge, an opportunity which educators often overlook in considering educating for sustainability. The major physical assets in your system are your school buildings. Your buildings visibly communicate the values of your school system; they also use resources (water and power sources) that are instrumental in keeping students and teachers healthy. These are assets that in most cases are in substantial need of a sustainability strategy—not only to increase energy efficiency but also to demonstrate preparedness and hope for the future. With renewed commitment to climate action at the national level, having a sustainability strategy for school buildings should be considered a "must have" rather than just a "nice to have."

For example, consider whether every building in your district could have a plan for a zero-carbon footprint by 2030 and how you and your students can co-create and co-implement plans to achieve that result. Whether you are responsible for one building as a site leader or for an entire system, this is a challenge worth tackling.

Engaging students to assess your physical plant not only has the potential to reduce carbon emissions (and save money) but can also help to close an often-overlooked equity issue in education. Laura Cole, assistant professor in the department of architectural studies at the University of Missouri, suggests, "Access to a high-quality built environment is an equity issue. Healthy, green school buildings are especially important in under-resourced communities. Through green building education, youth [such as the students in Alexandria, Virginia, who tackled the mold and mushroom issue] can be empowered to become change agents for improving poor quality facilities."

We suggest that, in the next two to three years, you adopt such a plan for every building in your district and involve the students in each school to participate in the development of those plans. Work with your students to organize a systemwide effort to implement the plan by 2030. Imagine the deep learning that can occur in the development and implementation of those plans. Imagine further that a network of leaders around the country (dare we suggest the globe?) would work collaboratively on these plans along with networks of students.

We know students are passionate and sometimes overwhelmed about climate challenges. Imagine what would happen if educators gave students the opportunity and power to own the sustainability of their own school buildings. This is a good opportunity to tap into the passions and interests of students and for students to co-own solutions to these problems, developing a sense of efficacy in the face of our climate challenges.

Answer the questions in the following box as you consider the sustainability field trips in this chapter.

ASK YOURSELF

- *How can you expand on current sustainability plans and goals for your school or system?*
- *How can you give your students a more significant role in analyzing, designing, and implementing the sustainability plans and goals of your school or system?*

RESOURCES FOR SUSTAINABILITY EDUCATION

Arc, a free sustainability benchmarking tool, was created by the U.S. Green Building Council and can help illustrate for students what their building's eco footprint is—and then improve it. The Center for Green Schools offers the Building Learners program to assist schools in using the Arc platform for this purpose. learninglab.usgbc.org/building-learners

Learning Lab, a project of the U.S. Green Building Council, offers curriculum and resources for sustainability education, such as an exploration of green careers and climate action projects. learninglab.usgbc.org

Green Schools National Network connects educators who use sustainability to drive innovation in classrooms, schools, and districts. The network offers online resources and hosts an annual conference showcase of best practices. greenschoolsnationalnetwork.org

(Continued)

(Continued)

Cloud Institute for Sustainability Education, founded by Jaimie Cloud, provides resources, coaching, and leadership to build the field of educating for sustainability. cloudinstitute.org

The Education for Sustainability Collective has developed **EFS Benchmarks for Individual and Social Learning**, identifying essential elements for designing and assessing place-based projects to emphasize systems thinking, the science of sustainability, sustained impact, and perseverance. www.efscollective.org

Earth Force is a nonprofit organization that engages young people in problem solving by teaching them to identify and investigate environmental issues, gather data, and advocate for civic action. Offerings include professional development for teachers. earthforce.org

INNOVATION, INVENTION, AND ENTREPRENEURSHIP IN ACTION

We hope you felt, as we did, the power of creative problem solving in the context of sustainability. Let's explore another big context for creative problem solving: innovation, invention, and entrepreneurship. Many students have a natural interest in becoming entrepreneurs— perhaps imagining themselves pitching on the popular "Shark Tank" television show or becoming the next Elon Musk. Nearly half of all students from Grades 5 through 12 aspire to invent something that will make the world a better place (Gallup, 2016). The following field trips will give you a feel for the dynamic challenges that are possible in this arena.

Field Trip

Charity Shark Tank in Mansfield, Connecticut

In 2018, three teachers in Mansfield, Connecticut, began brainstorming a project for their fourth graders. The teachers intended to integrate their POG into the project, along with building business literacy into a unit on changemaking. They wanted students to feel what it would be like to make a difference by raising funds for a local charity. They set out a plan for the students to (1) choose a group of kids to work with; (2) choose a local charity to raise money for; (3) survey other students and parents to find a product that they would be willing to purchase; (4) develop a business plan to produce the product; (5) make the case that the business plan is worth an investment of school funds; (6) manufacture or produce the product; (7) market and sell the product; and (8) donate the proceeds to the charity.

The teachers completed this design phase, wondering whether their principal would not only give them a green light for the project but also participate in the project. They suggested that each team of students would pitch their business plan to him using the "Shark Tank" process, and he could allot the funds to move forward. He gave them the green light.

To find out how the strategy had been received by the students, we were able to get some "inside" information by interviewing Ken's grandson, Ollie, now a sixth grader. Ollie had participated in the fourth-grade project and had vivid memories of the experience. He recalls: "We had to make a 'Shark Tank' pitch to Mr. Seal [the principal]. We had to pitch our idea, what it would cost to make and what we would sell it for. He told us how much money we would get out of his fund to make it."

Ollie's team had surveyed students and decided to make bracelets out of cotton loom bands. His group chose as their charity the local hospital, where one of them had been a patient. Ollie learned about unit costs and profitability. He found that helpful. "I now had the tools to figure out how to run a lemonade stand in my neighborhood and price it so I could make money."

When we asked Ollie how he reacted to this type of instruction, he said, "I think this style of teaching is great. It allows the students to choose their own path. You have to stay in the lane, but within that lane, you have real freedom."

Field Trip
Fashioning Braille Labels in Frederick County, Virginia

Jerry Putt is principal at Frederick County Middle School in Frederick County, Virginia. In the 2016 through 2017 school year, he and his colleagues instituted an Innovation Hour once a week in Grades 6 through 8. Students were challenged to investigate a local problem or challenge they thought they might be able to influence. This aligned with POG competencies and reflected the principal's belief that "middle school is the perfect place to double-down on the POG."

One of the innovations that resulted came from two girls who designed a project with a visually impaired classmate as a client. Daylyn, their classmate, explained that she had to have someone pick out her clothes for her each day because she could not identify colors. Together, they prototyped and tested a solution to design braille tags for each clothing article so that visually impaired students could determine colors and patterns that might go together well. The principal reports: "The girls coordinated their work with the vision teacher, the ed tech teacher, and the family and consumer science teacher. They developed a pattern for colors with the braille printer. They used Tinkercad to create a 3-D model, and they tested the result with the classmate before learning how to sew the labels onto her clothes." Their client loved the innovation, and her classmates built empathy along with technical skills. FCPS Media Network (2019) has produced a video about the project, including interviews with the three girls.

That's not the end of the story. Jerry continues: "The students felt so empowered. They wanted more Innovation Hours, and they wanted this kind of learning in their regular classes. Somehow, we find ways to zap the curiosity out of kids. This is a way for them to rediscover their love of learning. We need activities like the Innovation Hour in middle school, but we also need to nurture problem solving in all of our core subjects."

Innovation Hour now happens every other school day for each student, alternating with physical education. Teachers in core subjects are noticing how motivated the students are with the innovation activities, and as a result, teachers are now embedding more interdisciplinary creative problem-solving approaches in their courses.

Field Trip

Inventing a Breathalyzer Bracelet in Lancaster, California

Rachel Thibault describes "growing up in the back of my mom's classroom." Her mother was a teacher and single parent, and they didn't have much money. Rachel recalls that beginning in the third grade, she told everyone that she wanted to be a doctor when she grew up because she didn't want to be poor anymore.

After her first year of college, Rachel realized that teaching children was her real passion. She switched her major to education. The first few years of teaching weren't as fulfilling as she had hoped; Rachel felt like she was just reciting STEM facts all day long. She began to watch another teacher, one who was connecting to his students, and she recognized the critical importance of forming real relationships with students. In fact, Rachel was so impressed with this teacher that he is now her husband!

Another critical moment in her career came a number of years later, just after Rachel started a new job at SOAR High School in Lancaster, California. As she was about to leave on spring break, a group of students asked for her help. The students wanted to apply for a grant to create an invention and needed a faculty member to sponsor them. Rachel agreed. She wrote a paragraph for them to include in their application without even reading the rest of it, which had to do with a proposal for a water treatment product for people in sub-Saharan Africa.

Several months later, Rachel received a call from the Lemelson-MIT Program in Massachusetts. Her students had won one of the thirty-five semi-finalist slots in the invention grants initiative. As a result, Rachel was being invited to a week of professional development in Cambridge to be trained in supporting her students as they finalized their proposal. If selected to be one of the fifteen grantees, the students would be invited to present a working prototype of their invention at MIT at the end of the school year. Rachel was stunned. She knew nothing about invention or patents.

When Rachel finally read the entire student proposal, she was disappointed to see it wasn't very strong. She called Lemelson-MIT to find out how this proposal had been selected. She was told that the product description itself was only one aspect of the selection process. The rest of the application, explaining the personal backgrounds of the student applicants as well as community and school support for their efforts, had been viewed as exceptionally well-qualified. Rachel also learned that the team could start all over on the invention they would propose to build.

(Continued)

(Continued)

Rachel traveled to MIT and had "the best week of professional development of my life. I was trained on how to support my students in the invention process." When she returned to California, she devoted the entire summer to working with her students on the final proposal. It was due in early September, and they spent many twelve-hour days in her classroom, including time on the weekends. By mid-August, she and her students had considered and rejected almost thirty distinct ideas. As the September deadline approached, they were all starting to get anxious.

Rachel took a break for lunch with a favorite teacher colleague who, sensing Rachel's concerns, generated a list of fifteen new ideas for the team. When Rachel shared the list with students, one idea seemed to captivate all of them. The suggestion was to develop a breathalyzer that young people could wear as a bracelet, so they could check their own blood alcohol level before they started to drive a car. The team thought it was a cool idea and began research to determine whether anything like it had been invented. They had two weeks to develop a rigorous case for the invention. They met the deadline and soon learned that they were selected as one of fifteen teams and awarded $9,200 to support their development efforts during the coming school year, culminating in a presentation of their prototype at MIT the following June.

The nature of the project changed dramatically about a month later due to a tragedy in their community. A college student, who was driving drunk, lost control of his car. It hurtled into a house where a local sixteen-year-old high school student, asleep on the couch in the living room, was killed instantly. Rachel notes: "The team realized from that point forward that their product was not just a STEM assignment but something that could save lives and make a difference. The accident changed the impact of what they were doing."

Rachel and her students spent the following months working to build their invention. They also had to raise almost $20,000 in additional funds. The grant only covered expenses for six students to showcase their working prototype in Massachusetts, and there were fourteen members of the team. They were all determined to make the trip to Cambridge. The team did public speaking to groups across the region soliciting contributions from the community. They managed to raise the needed funds and traveled to Boston where there was another challenge to overcome: TSA had opened the box with the components of the project, failing to close it carefully, and the contents spilled all over the baggage conveyor belt.

Once they arrived in Cambridge, the students split into two groups: one to reassemble the exhibit and put the components back together and the other to polish the final details of a provisional patent application in order to file it prior to their presentation the next day. They hit "send" to submit their patent application at 3 a.m. on the day of the presentation.

Rachel recalls: "For all of the students and me, this was one of the highlights of our lives. You have to understand this was the most unlikely of student teams. Although exceptional students, they did not have extensive STEM backgrounds. We had only one student who could code passably. We had no engineers. This was a group of kids who made the invention come to life out of sheer willpower and commitment to succeed. It is the best example I know of consummate perseverance. Today, several of the students have careers in the sciences, which was not even on their radar prior to this project. Another student was so affected by the presentation activities for the trip fundraising that she chose communications as her college major."

Rachel remains involved in this work and has since coached another group for the Lemelson-MIT Program. They, too, ended up with a successful grant application. Both of the products that Rachel's students built over a school year were awarded U.S. patents with the assistance of pro bono legal support. Rachel comments: "Kids are the perfect inventors. They aren't hampered by 'I can't' or lack of confidence."

Invention education has become a major focus of Rachel's work. She convinced her administration to include invention as a course in the curriculum under the title, STEM Research. Rachel has forty students working on inventions and robotics each year. The school plans to expand the course to accommodate a second group of forty students.

Field Trip

Building Entrepreneurs in Fort Thomas, Kentucky

When Karen Cheser became the superintendent in Fort Thomas School District in Kentucky, she wanted to do a POG. But before starting the process, she knew she needed to do a lot of listening. She reached out specifically to the business community in northern Kentucky and the broader Cincinnati area. Karen created a listening session for twenty-two corporate executives and innovation experts from the region.

(Continued)

(Continued)

They gave her input on the need for specific 4 Cs skills, along with their perceived need for entrepreneurial skills.

As a result, she got strong community support not only for creating the district's POG but also for building entrepreneurship more deeply into the district's work. The district uses several programs as building blocks of an entrepreneurial mindset, including the Kidprenuer program from the University of Virginia; Junior Achievement; makerspaces; and a multi-course pathway in entrepreneurship, including courses for a dual credit for undergraduate studies at a local college.

Consider the following questions to help you think about introducing or expanding similar opportunities with your students.

ASK YOURSELF

- *What are examples of your students demonstrating creative problem solving in the context of innovation, invention, and entrepreneurship?*
- *How will you develop creative problem-solving contexts for those students furthest from opportunity?*

In these field trips to see invention, entrepreneurship, and innovation education, you can sense the excitement and energy of the students as they work to solve the challenges before them. Equally important, the projects activate serious content challenges, including

- Budgeting and pricing math questions
- Use of technology in the production of an end product
- STEM challenges of analyzing, designing, and producing a patentable product

At the same time, other skills are being developed. Serious team building and collaboration resulted in the first three examples along with advocacy and communication in the fundraising pitch and campaign to raise funds for travel. As in the sustainability examples, the evidence of powerful pedagogy is also apparent. In the case of Fort Thomas, administrators demonstrated their leadership skills in using the POG to institute a comprehensive approach to entrepreneurship across the curriculum.

As you can see, the contexts of invention, entrepreneurship, and innovation are vibrant and engaging. They offer opportunities for developing knowledge across multiple disciplines and the development of technical and collaboration skills that are exciting and relevant for young people. They are also interrelated and support each other.

Don Wettrick, founder and CEO of the StartEdUp Foundation, has a way of connecting creativity, innovation, and invention. Don calls it the "Innovation Continuum." He suggests:

- Elementary school students focus on creativity
- Middle school students focus on innovation
- High school students focus on entrepreneurship

This may be a helpful way to see these skillsets building on one another, although you can see from the stories we have shared that the lines between these areas are not absolute. For example, there was value to the "Shark Tank" type of entrepreneurship presentation in Ollie's fourth-grade class.

It does help to identify creativity as a core competency. Emphasizing it from elementary school onward makes sense. We don't believe, however, that de-emphasizing creativity in middle and high school is a good idea.

The concept of the Innovation Hour—also called Genius Hour—seems to be a good theme for middle school students who are capable of designing and creating improvements for their homes, the school, or their community. The Innovation Hour that Jerry Putt and his team are nurturing in Frederick County, Virginia, is based on Wettrick's experiences as described in his book, *Pure Genius: Building a Culture of Innovation and Taking 20% Time to the Next Level.*

There's no need to wait for middle school to give students opportunities to be innovative—and for the adults in your system to witness the results. Big Springs School District in Pennsylvania offers Genius Hour once a week for ninety minutes in Grades 3 through 5. Students present twice a year on their Genius Hour activities, with board members in attendance. The same program is now being expanded to Grades 6 through 8, according to Superintendent Rich Fry.

Rachel Thibault's story and her teaching journey have been deeply impacted by the work of the Lemelson-MIT Program in the field of invention education. The "invention education" movement has been around for almost twenty-five years but is just now coalescing into the K–12 curriculum. Materials for middle and high school levels produced by Lemelson-MIT and other programs are accessible through the organization's website and through the InventEd website supported by The Lemelson Foundation. (See Resources for Invention, Innovation, and Entrepreneurship Education later in this chapter.)

The challenge of entrepreneurship can build on the work of invention. It can tie the skill of problem finding to ascertaining customers with analysis of their needs and solutions to their problems. Entrepreneurship can be pursued in for-profit as well as nonprofit circumstances. The burgeoning field of social entrepreneurship applies strategies from the business world to tackle social and environmental challenges with sustainable solutions.

Ayele Shakur is the CEO of Build.org, an organization that promotes entrepreneurship to students in urban school settings and assists schools in offering elective courses in that subject. Ayele comments: "Entrepreneurship is a skill for the future. It can help students reinvent, pivot, and problem solve, not just in the context of a product or service but also in the context of their own lives and career trajectory. We believe it should be a requirement for every high school student across the country."

Tom Vander Ark, CEO of Getting Smart, underscores this point, saying, "99 percent of support for students in high school focuses on 'finding' a job. Less than 1 percent of high school attention is focused on how you *make* a job. We need to put our focus on the new expectation that you are entrepreneurial no matter what you are doing. Each student needs an entrepreneurial mindset and skillset so they can reinvent a product, service, company, or their own career. This must be a required experience in high school."

RESOURCES FOR INNOVATION, INVENTION, AND ENTREPRENEURSHIP EDUCATION

BUILD teaches students to engage in entrepreneurship to ignite the potential of youth from under-resourced communities. build.org

InventEd resources on invention education are accessible at inventioneducation.org/resources

Lemelson-MIT materials and competitions should be useful to schools and districts who want to expand their invention offerings. www.lemelson.mit.edu/resources

Ewing Marion Kauffman Foundation shares stories and resources that focus on education, entrepreneurship, and equity. www.kauffman.org

STARTedUP Foundation, founded by educator Don Wettrick, teaches students to be innovators and entrepreneurs and provides opportunities for them to pitch ideas and attract investors for their original ideas. startedupfoundation.org

For Your Bookshelf

Creating Innovators: The Making of Young People Who Will Change the World by Tony Wagner

Difference Making at the Heart of Learning by Tom Vander Ark and Emily Liebtag

Invent to Learn: Making, Tinkering, and Engineering in the Classroom by Sylvia Martinez and Gary Stager

Pure Genius: Building a Culture of Innovation and Taking 20% Time to the Next Level by Don Wettrick

Consider the questions in the following box as you and your team reflect on the elements of Don Wettrick's Innovation Continuum (creativity, innovation, invention, entrepreneurship).

ASK YOURSELF

- *What could you and your team do to expand dramatically the use of innovation, invention, and entrepreneurship as contexts for creative problem solving?*
- *Which of these will you prioritize?*

Clearly, there is a range of ways to implement these contexts. You can highlight them in clubs or afterschool activities or offer them as an elective class. It is critical that you address equity issues in this effort. If every student needs creativity, innovation, invention, and entrepreneurship, can clubs and electives accomplish that goal? Those approaches make it likely that the more affluent students will be able to take advantage of the opportunities while other students may not be able to follow suit.

You may decide to launch your involvement in one of these areas with a club or elective as a starting point, but we believe you need a bolder vision of your work on creative problem solving.

THE CREATIVITY, INNOVATION, INVENTION, AND ENTREPRENEURSHIP CHALLENGE

Consider a bold and broad challenge for creativity, invention, entrepreneurship, and innovation, specifically in the context of a student portfolio that we hope you will develop. (The portfolio concept is discussed in more detail in Chapter 6.) Imagining the projects in this domain as part of a student portfolio may give you a clearer image of the goals you set out:

- By the end of elementary school, students will have developed an ability to be empathetic and understand problems faced by others and have artifacts of their creativity and innovation for their portfolio.

- By the end of middle school, students will have developed the ability to reduce their creative ideas to practice, giving rise to artifacts of their innovation and entrepreneurship activities that can be compiled in their portfolio.
- By the end of high school, students will be confident in engaging with others to find and define problems; have the technical skills and ability to work with others to produce prototypes of their creations; will be able to determine if they are both useful and unique and will know how to protect their intellectual property; and will know how to bring their work to intended audiences through commercialization or social entrepreneurship activities.

Along this pathway, students will develop their capacity for reflecting on their growth as creative problem solvers.

These are not meant to be rigid requirements. We are suggesting a flexible framework to assure that *every* student has the creative problem-solving skills needed in a variety of societal settings. You and your leadership team can use this as a starting point in structuring a set of problem-solving contexts that work best for your students and community.

We hope these stories and resources help you envision the wide range of exciting contexts for inspiring and enabling student problem solving. These kinds of student-led learning activities are happening around the country, and most likely, you will find examples already occurring in your own school or district that you can showcase. Our advice is to support and advance these specific contexts more intentionally and pervasively.

CREATIVE PROBLEM SOLVING AND YOUR POG

It is also critical that your POG be visible to students while they are engaged in these areas. There is a serious need for alignment between worthwhile context areas and the student competencies of the POG. Sustainability, innovation, invention, and entrepreneurship educators must embed the 21st century skills in the learning activities of each project. Teachers need to be purposeful and intentional about teaching, scaffolding, and assessing the 21st century competencies. Help students see their growth as they tackle problem-solving challenges. Using the competencies as self-assessment tools for the projects is one way to do that.

This point was made directly by Ollie, Ken's grandson, who noted: "I had another class where the teacher gave us the 4 Cs and asked us to write how a project she assigned to us helped with our 4 Cs skills. I think that would have helped with the entrepreneur project. I would have understood better how the project helped me with those skills."

Final Reflections

Leaders who promote the POG often think it is adequate to extend POG competencies into core subjects. That isn't enough. The traditional emphasis on core subjects has not succeeded in closing either the achievement gap or the readiness gap, particularly for students of color and those growing up in economically challenged communities. For the POG competencies to truly thrive in the interdisciplinary contexts described in this chapter and the ones to follow, you need to create opportunities for all your students.

Let's close this chapter with these questions:

- How will you lead your district toward interdisciplinary problem solving?
- How will you ensure the problem-solving challenges you embrace are available to each and every student in your school and district?

Action Steps

We hope these field trips have convinced you that, by identifying compelling challenges, you can find dynamic contexts to help your students develop creative problem-solving skills. There is little doubt that these skills are essential. The issue is that these are not self-executing skills in the current system. You and your team will have to work hard to be certain robust creative problem-solving opportunities are present for every student. Four action steps will move you from aspiration to implementation:

I. **Showcase your current best practices.** Identify examples of sustainability, innovation, invention, and entrepreneurship that already exist in your district. Make these examples more visible by highlighting the work of the students and teachers with the school board and the broader community.

2. **Create systemwide challenges.** Go beyond your current practices to ask your educators to create challenges in sustainability, innovation, invention, and entrepreneurship at appropriate grade levels. For example, consider asking students to help design and implement a zero-carbon footprint for every building in your system. You don't need to prioritize all of these topics at one time. Select the challenges that work best for your community and its particular needs and interests.

3. **Give the green light to interdisciplinary problem solving.** Consider ways to incentivize educator proposals for interdisciplinary creative problem-solving. Some schools and districts have innovation funds or education foundations that focus on innovative educators with compelling proposals. Harness those resources to support worthy ideas that align with your POG. You need to be willing to push back against the propensity of some educators who want to operate in "silos." Give the green light to interdisciplinary creative problem solving in as many ways as you can.

4. **Use your POG competencies for assessment.** You must use these creative problem-solving experiences to foster the competencies identified in the POG. At the outset of the project, have your students choose which competencies they will be focused on in their work. Then have those students self-assess themselves on those competencies. Make the POG competencies visible throughout the progress of the project.

We hope you are inspired and find the examples of sustainability, innovation, invention, and entrepreneurship in this chapter useful. We turn next to a fourth context where creative problem-solving skills can and must flourish: civic engagement.

CHAPTER 4

Be the Leader of Engaged Citizens

CHAPTER HIGHLIGHTS

We are at a moment that calls out for renewing our commitment to civic education. In the previous chapter, you heard examples of problem solving around sustainability, entrepreneurship, invention, and innovation. You might choose to focus on any of these contexts as a bold move for your school system. Civic engagement, in contrast, should not be treated as an elective or an optional focus; it must be addressed for every student. Deciding what civic engagement looks like in your school system will also depend on local context but should create opportunities for students to build knowledge and take informed action. The journey for students to become engaged citizens requires both knowing *and* doing.

Civic engagement is another context for student problem solving that demands your attention. Preparing students to be engaged, informed citizens is not a new mission for schools, but the pandemic and recent political upheaval have brought renewed attention to this responsibility. Let's start by visiting a community where civic education has become an opportunity for deep learning and problem solving.

Field Trip

Students Using Their Voices for Change in
Anaheim, California

Nearly a decade before the Black Lives Matter movement, a series of police shootings triggered protests over racial justice in Orange County, California. Leaders from the Anaheim Union High School District, attending a summer conference, watched from afar as television coverage showed young people facing off with police.

Michael Matsuda, a district administrator who would later become superintendent, rushed home to consult with key teacher leaders. Matsuda and teachers then met with students and encouraged them to turn their anger into civic action. Hundreds of students marched to city hall. Two students spoke for the group, describing their shared dreams of fair treatment and good jobs. Their message resonated with city officials, who later formed a partnership with the district that has led to expanded opportunities for career education.

"With the right leadership, our kids went from rioting in the streets to making thoughtful presentations at city hall," recalled Jackie Counts, another longtime district administrator. "Students are hungry for the opportunity to find their voice, find their passion, and unleash it in a positive way."

Under Matsuda's direction, civic engagement has become embedded in this diverse district, serving 30,000 students in Grades 7–12 who collectively speak nearly fifty different languages. Poverty is pervasive; 20 percent of students are homeless. Despite socioeconomic challenges, the district has earned the highest award in the state for outstanding civic learning.

Two initiatives reflect the district's deep commitment to civic education:

Project Soapbox, a civic action program of the Mikva Foundation, has been embraced across Anaheim schools. Students identify an issue they're passionate about and create a two-minute speech that includes research-backed evidence and a call to action for listeners. Although interest in the program began with just a handful of enthusiastic Anaheim educators, some 300 teachers—a quarter of the district's faculty, across all content areas—have volunteered to be trained in the program. The speeches address the district's Portrait of a Graduate (POG) competencies, which expand the 4 Cs with a "5th C," namely compassion/character. "Students learn how to engage in tough issues, but in a civil manner. They're demonstrating democracy in action," Counts said.

To go even deeper with its 5th C, the district has joined the **California Democracy School** project, which advocates for all students across a school system to participate in civic inquiry. Professional development for teachers is core to Democracy School so that teachers have the instructional strategies they need to engage every student. "This isn't just for honors kids," emphasized Superintendent Matsuda. "Every student has to have the opportunity to deal with a controversial issue." Anaheim's participation has grown from two high schools to fifteen, the most of any district in the state. (In the next chapter about self-direction, you will hear how this program prepared students to navigate a controversial issue as a deep learning experience.)

Matsuda credits the district's focus on redefining student success as the catalyst for this transformation to civic engagement. "That's where it all started," he said.

ENDING THE CIVICS SLIDE

What's happening in Anaheim is a powerful example of where we need to head. Nationally, we know that civic knowledge is limited, even among adults, and trust in political leadership is in steep decline (Winthrop, 2020). Although a healthy democracy depends on informed and engaged citizens, the amount of time schools devote to teaching civics has dropped significantly over the past twenty years. The Campaign for the Civic Mission of Schools describes the current situation as nothing less than "a slide into civic illiteracy" (CivXNow, 2019, p. 4). An estimated 60 percent of rural youth and 30 percent of their urban and suburban peers are growing up in civic deserts, with few or no opportunities to discuss issues and address problems (Kawashima-Ginsberg & Sullivan, 2017). In a 2018 national survey, only one in three high school principals cited promoting informed participation in civic life as one of their school's top three goals (Rogers & Kahne, 2021).

Global education is not faring any better. Richard Haass, president of the Council on Foreign Relations and author of *The World: A Brief Introduction* (2020), underscores a basic understanding that too many students (and adults) are missing: "Most people don't see the connection between the world and their lives. In the last couple of decades, we've had 9/11; COVID-19 beginning in Wuhan, China; climate change, fires, and floods—all these manifestations of how the world matters. Only a negligible percentage of young Americans is at all literate about the world that will affect their lives in all sorts of ways."

At the same time, school leaders are having to navigate everything from racial inequities exacerbated by a global pandemic to increasingly polarized communities and social media that's anything but civil. As an education leader, events beyond your control may pull you into situations that are fraught with challenges. It takes political savvy to negotiate conversations in polarized communities. If you can manage the tensions, you may be able to help your community find a better way forward.

In Houston, Texas, the devastation of Hurricane Harvey in 2017—including flooded schools and damaged homes—forced even resistant members of the community to confront the reality of climate change. In Humble Independent School District, a cohort of teachers designed projects that engaged students in learning about the science of watersheds and what they could do to restore them. For Superintendent Liz Fagen, the community's collective response to the disaster stands out as "our best example of citizenship."

Bella Wong, superintendent of Lincoln-Sudbury Regional School District in Massachusetts, cited the death of George Floyd at the hands of Minneapolis police in 2020 as a turning point for schools everywhere. "Before George Floyd, citizenship was important. After George Floyd," she said, "you need to take your place and participate." To inform your next steps as a leader, Wong offered three insightful questions: "What kind of world do we have? What kind of world do we want? How do we educate our students to build that world?"

This chapter will suggest how to turn those questions into three leadership moves: get your community on board; commit to tackling society's biggest challenges; set a bold civics challenge. They add up to making a major commitment to civic engagement.

GET YOUR COMMUNITY ON BOARD

In the previous chapter, you took field trips to visualize students solving problems around sustainability, entrepreneurship, invention, and innovation. We suggested that you might choose to focus on any of these contexts as a bold move for your school system. But when it comes to civic engagement, you can't afford to opt out.

> When it comes to civic engagement, you can't afford to opt out.

Jason Glass, state education commissioner for Kentucky, offers this timely reminder: "One of the central purposes of education is to prepare young people to be citizens in our democracy."

Although citizenship was once a primary focus of K–12 schooling, many communities have drifted away from this noble mission over the past twenty years. Experts point to a number of factors, particularly the focus on math and reading achievement with less time and attention for social studies, civics, and global education. When it comes to what should be taught in social studies, political posturing can get in the way of thoughtful decisions about curriculum.

Some schools try to fill the civics gap by requiring community service *hours*, without the advantage of genuine service *learning* that increases students' civic engagement and social responsibility (Carnegie Corporation of New York & CIRCLE, 2003). "Requiring service is not going to get the outcomes we want for students," argues Amy Meuers, CEO of the National Youth Leadership Council. "It can feel like just one more thing to check off to graduate." Well-designed service learning gives students choice and voice, connects to academics, and challenges them to think critically about their role in society. Poorly designed service experiences—like being told to pick up litter—can feel punitive. The Center for Information and Research on Civic Learning and Engagement has identified a "civic opportunity gap," with students in struggling schools and those not headed to college less likely to experience the benefits of quality civic education (Kahne & Middaugh, 2008). This gap leaves historically marginalized students at a disadvantage when it comes to leading change.

If you are just developing your POG, this is a good time to invite your stakeholders to get serious about civics. What are your shared aspirations for preparing students to be informed, engaged citizens? What will success look like? How comfortable is your community with students investigating controversial issues, having a voice in decision making, or taking action on local, national, or even global issues? If your goals for civic education are indeed about strengthening democracy and advancing equity, then your efforts to get your community on board must be inclusive of community members whose voices have not been heard in the past. (You may want to revisit the advice in Chapter 1 for engaging diverse stakeholders.)

If you already have a graduate profile, you may need to have deeper conversations to reach consensus about these questions. If your school system has just focused on the 4 Cs, consider adding a fifth for civic engagement. This will ensure that students focus not only on themselves but also on how they will give back to their community.

Even if your vision does not explicitly name civic engagement, stakeholders may have similar goals in mind if they talk about students developing empathy, learning to appreciate other perspectives, developing media literacy, advancing social justice, or contributing to the community through service learning. Help your stakeholders see how these goals will be well served by a commitment to civic engagement for all students.

Becoming an engaged citizen requires students to build knowledge and apply that understanding to solve problems. This coherence— *knowing and doing*—is reflected in the College, Career and Civic Life (C3) Framework for Social Studies State Standards (National Council for the Social Studies, 2013). The combination of understanding and action is also the emphasis of CivXNow, a national coalition focused on improving K–12 civic education. When school is an incubator for democracy, young people emerge knowledgeable about the history and mechanisms of government and are prepared to volunteer, vote, and engage with their communities and the wider world on important issues.

"If you only know the facts, you will drown in the facts and do nothing," asserts Fernando Reimers, Ford Foundation Professor of Practice in International Education, Harvard University. "Facts alone produce worry. You need to combine worry and hope. Hope comes from seeing clear pathways to improvement. For example, around climate change, knowledge alone will not give students the efficacy they need. You need a scaffolding of active engagement to create efficacy."

Embracing civic engagement as central to student success does not mean that you will be mired in controversies. As you will see in upcoming examples and field trips, students can have powerful civic experiences by engaging in less polarizing but still important issues: advocating for sidewalks and crosswalks, testifying about broadband access, proposing public housing, or conducting voter registration drives.

Even the youngest students are capable of both *knowing and doing* when it comes to civics. In Big Spring School District, Pennsylvania, children who were approaching the end of kindergarten admitted that they felt scared when they first started school. To ease the way for next year's incoming students—and demonstrate what they had learned about empathy and citizenship—kindergarteners planned an orientation for the pre-kinders. They produced everything from a picture book to help orient the newcomers to hands-on activities that the "older" students facilitated with the newcomers. That's school citizenship in action.

Field Trip

Educating for Democracy in Oakland, California

Let's see how the Oakland Unified School District in California took concrete steps to commit to its vision of civic learning for secondary students. A catalyst for change was the district's participation in a multi-year project called Educating for Democracy in the Digital Age, a collaboration with the University of California, Riverside, and the National Writing Project. Across ten high schools, students applied their academic knowledge to work on community issues that mattered to them. In the process, they learned to research, analyze, and act on civic issues, using digital media to amplify their voices (Hodgin & Choi, 2016).

This is the kind of learning experience that prepares young people to play a more active role in their communities. Young Whan Choi, manager of performance assessments for the district, described one student's dramatic transformation from being homeless to becoming an effective advocate for food justice (2019): "The student had to work with peers and adults to advocate for a complicated piece of policy that expects the district to purchase food based on factors like transportation, treatment of animals, labor practices, and nutrition. This experience sparked a passion for politics."

Since implementing the civic education project, Oakland has revised its graduate profile to include "Community Ready" along with "College and Career Ready" goals. Community Ready students are prepared to draw on their civic and digital learning experiences to identify and analyze issues that matter to them and their community; to take informed, thoughtful action in collaboration with others; to analyze the effectiveness of their action and reflect on what they learned.

These specific descriptors move the vision of a "community ready" graduate from aspirational to actionable. They bridge the gap between civic knowledge and civic engagement. They demonstrate a commitment to citizenship education as the right of every student.

The leadership skills that supported your visioning work with stakeholders will prove essential as you build consensus around civics goals. To support students on their citizenship journeys, leaders must be willing to understand diverse perspectives and practice active listening—in other words, to model the very skills that students need to acquire.

Of course, your vision must reflect your community values. Encouraging students to focus on local issues—like improving pedestrian safety or access to fresh, affordable food—might be a better starting point for your school system than tackling hot-button issues like gun control. Veteran school leader Jason Glass offers advice to help you navigate challenging issues. "Often, finding the 'right' answer doesn't mean finding the correct one. Instead, it means the right one for your community and context, and the only way we can know that is to wade into what the community is talking about when it comes to the most difficult issues" (Glass, 2020, p. 37).

At times, your recommitment to civics will demand courageous leadership. Student activism can stir up controversies you might prefer to sidestep. To be successful in this work, you will need to back up your students and teachers even if you get pushback or strong reactions from parents and other community members. Ultimately, as Steve Laatsch, superintendent in Saline, Michigan, told us, "This is the right work."

ASK YOURSELF

- *Does your POG reflect your community's commitment to raising young citizens?*
- *Do your stakeholders understand that effective civic education includes both building knowledge and applying understanding (knowing and doing)?*

COMMIT TO TACKLING SOCIETY'S BIGGEST CHALLENGES

"Education is much more than an entry to the job market. It has the power to shape a sustainable future and better world."

This insight from Ban Ki-moon (2012), former secretary-general of the United Nations, reminds us of the awesome responsibility of educating young citizens. Are your students making the connection between what they are learning and the world they are inheriting? Do you empower your teachers and instructional leaders to help students identify problems worth solving, build the knowledge and skills to tackle them, and engage others in working toward solutions? These are the big questions facing leaders who are committed to meaningful civics education across content areas and grade levels.

As you make a major commitment to civics education, the strategies you pursue can take many forms. It's easy to get caught up in the logistics of implementation or the challenges of scaling pilot projects. We encourage you to keep the big picture in mind. Brandon Wiley, a longtime advocate of global education and currently chief academic officer at the Alexander Dawson School in Las Vegas, Nevada, sums up the challenge this way: "We want students to answer the question: How do we make the world a better place?"

Your commitment to tackling society's biggest challenges as a school system will open the door for both students and teachers to be contributors to a better future. Around the world, hundreds of educators are aligning learning with the United Nations Sustainable Development Goals and creating a community of practice that crosses geographic boundaries. The global goals outline seventeen major agenda items for the planet, from ending hunger and poverty to making cities safe and resilient. Help your students and teachers see how even small, local actions can help to move the needle on these ambitious challenges. In 2019, students in more than 1,600 classrooms around the world participated in projects aligned to the global goals.

Field Trip

Literacy as a Civil Right in Detroit, Michigan

When fifth graders in Detroit, Michigan, learned that their local community is a "book desert" with a dearth of public libraries, they were motivated to take action. Partnering with artists and local activists, they built, painted, and stocked miniature lending libraries with hundreds of books they had gathered in a community book drive.

This was a major accomplishment, but learning went much deeper, guided by a language arts curriculum developed by EL Education and adopted by Detroit Public Schools Community District. By studying the Universal Declaration of Human Rights and other texts, students came to recognize literacy as a civil right. Their local actions contributed to UN Sustainable Development Goal #4: Quality Education. Learning experiences like this prepare students "for success as readers, writers, thinkers, and leaders ready to meet the challenges of our future," according to Beth Miller, chief knowledge officer for EL Education (EL Education, 2020).

Similar stories are emerging around the world as young people apply their civic learning in inspiring ways. Across India, dozens of examples of youth-led social change are emerging through an initiative of Teach For India called Kids Education Revolution. Projects range from efforts to enroll uneducated children in school to micro-learning centers where peers tutor children who are unable to access formal education. Sandeep Rai with Teach For India said these projects reflect his organization's mission to prepare "students who can solve problems and lead for change." To be effective partners in this work, Teach For India fellows receive leadership training in the organization's "8 Cs" (courage, compassion, curiosity, critical thinking, creativity, collaboration, consciousness, and communication), so that they can help students tackle real-world challenges. "Kids and adults need the same skills," Rai added, "to build a movement."

Wendy Kopp, founder of Teach For America, has been CEO of Teach For All for the past twelve years. She and her global organization have been working to develop young education leaders around the world. From the beginning, Teach For All's network partners have been focused on working with local communities to ensure that their efforts are anchored in the hopes and aspirations of those communities. Wendy explained, "Our network partners center their work around a definition for student success that is locally contextualized and co-created by each community. We have seen beautiful examples of this across our global network."

Examples like these are too transformative to confine to occasional projects or electives that reach only a select population of students. Instead, encourage your team to look across content areas and grade levels for entry points to worthy problems. The possibilities are endless—from science students reducing their family's carbon footprint to language arts students sharing their writing about racial identity to journalism students interviewing medical experts about the COVID-19 pandemic in order to educate their peers.

Experiences like these also help students and teachers reimagine community service. By focusing on service learning and not service hours, "that's how we get not only citizenship skills but also growth in math, science, English, social and emotional learning, 21st century skills—all at the same time," said Amy Meuers of the National Youth Leadership Council. When service learning leads to informed action, she added, "students get to make change now—not some distant time when they become adults."

As a leader, look for examples of civic participation to highlight in your own school systems. Showcase the contributions of your teachers and students, and encourage them to share their strategies to build momentum.

ASK YOURSELF

- *How do you celebrate and showcase students' efforts to make the world a better place?*
- *How can you use your influence as a leader to give teachers the green light to tackle society's biggest challenges as core to instruction?*

SET A BOLD CIVICS CHALLENGE

Once you have committed to citizenship as central to your vision, you need to make sure you have programs and resources in place to engage every student. Use your influence as a leader to set a bold civic engagement challenge for your students and community. Talk up the challenge with stakeholders and on social media, and celebrate progress when you see it. Imagine the value of students reflecting on civic action as they progress from elementary through secondary grades. By the time they graduate from high school, they will have developed a set of skills and the mindset to contribute to their community as informed, engaged citizens. They will also have compelling evidence of learning to share in a portfolio.

There is no one approach to civic engagement that fits every school system. The right challenge for your community might be

- Capstone experiences at the end of elementary, middle, and high school
- A commitment to service learning, global education, or world languages that extends across content areas and grade levels
- Adoption of existing civic education programs, including a commitment to professional development for teachers
- Development of your own curriculum in-house

What's important for you, as a leader, is to set a bold challenge for your school community and then ensure that your team has all the support needed to pursue it.

If your stakeholders need help imagining what a bold civics challenge could lead to, or if you are wondering how other leaders are making progress in this arena, let's take four more field trips to see civic engagement in action at different grade levels. As you read, look for ideas to catalyze your civic engagement efforts.

Field Trip

Starting Early in Andover, Massachusetts

In Andover, Massachusetts, elementary students are building literacy skills along with a strong foundation as citizens with an interdisciplinary framework called One Community, One Nation.

Superintendent Sheldon Berman, a longtime advocate of civic education and one of the founders of Educators for Social Responsibility, says One Community, One Nation, represents a developmentally appropriate citizenship challenge for students in K–5. It builds students' understanding of American history through case studies while also building their civic dispositions—how to negotiate and compromise, think critically, and listen to other perspectives with an open mind.

"Children come to political understanding at a much earlier age than we anticipate," Berman said. His own research and writing underscore that message, along with the insight that children decide at a relatively young age "either to back away or see themselves as empowered" as members of the larger society.

Berman began shepherding the development of One Community, One Nation in his prior leadership roles in Hudson, Massachusetts, and Louisville, Kentucky. It started as a social studies curriculum. When he came to Andover, he was inspired by the work of two gifted educators who were integrating literacy and the arts. Seeing the opportunity to think bigger, he recruited them to be part of a design team to transform One Community, One Nation into an interdisciplinary, open-source framework that any community can adopt and help to expand. So far, a dozen districts across Massachusetts have expressed interest and sent their own teachers to institutes hosted by Andover.

That's the kind of groundswell that a bold citizenship challenge can create.

Field Trip

Capstone Experiences in Nyack, New York, and Saline, Michigan

As students move into the secondary grades, capstone experiences that emphasize informed civic action offer a powerful way to help students reflect on their growth as engaged citizens. Let's take field trips to two communities that bring their POGs to life with capstones.

At Nyack Middle School in New York, Principal David Johnson is on a mission to help his 640 students become "world changers." His message to parents and teachers is that students must develop the skills to "sift through information, analyze it, and apply it to real-world situations. That's what will make our students productive citizens in our new world."

The principal's vision aligns with the district's POG, which includes cultural awareness and compassion along with the 4 Cs and content mastery. It also reflects community values. Nyack has a long civic engagement history and is diverse both racially and economically. The middle school is minority majority and includes students who live in public housing as well as those from expensive homes overlooking the Hudson River.

To bring the world-changing vision to life, Johnson advocates for learning experiences that enable students to engage with issues of racial justice and equity "that our curriculum does not always bring out." Given opportunities to explore issues that matter to them, students have become passionate about everything from addressing hunger to disrupting the school-to-prison pipeline. It's the school leader's job, he said, "to empower your students to tackle topics that mean something to them and empower your staff to create an environment where they can be successful."

A good example is the eighth-grade capstone project. Although many school systems wait until high school for such ambitious efforts, Johnson saw a perfect fit at the end of middle school. "It's a dynamic age. Students come in as shy babies. They leave us as confident young adults—but only if they learn how to self-advocate, make connections, and reach out to their community. We often forget," he added, "that our students are citizens, too. Citizenship doesn't start when you turn eighteen."

The principal envisioned a capstone project focused on community issues that students were passionate about, with connections across the curriculum. Whatever topic students chose, he wanted them to do more than research. The goal was civic action. As Johnson explained, "keeping the focus on our own community would move students from just having an idea to developing a *realistic* action plan with local impact."

Johnson teamed up with Tom DiLeo, assistant principal, to figure out how to move from vision to implementation. A former high school social studies teacher, DiLeo appreciated the value of a project that would put citizenship front and center. He was also inspired by a recent visit to High Tech High in San Diego, California, where he had seen interdisciplinary project-based learning in action. An eighth-grade capstone to engage Nyack students in community action, he thought, "will give our students the opportunity to fly."

It turns out that students themselves have become the best ambassadors for the capstone. The first year, staff buy-in was a challenge; some teachers worried about

(Continued)

(Continued)

finding time. When the first group of students were ready to present their local action projects—focused on everything from supporting local food banks to challenging racial profiling—the principal made sure the faculty attended. His message was clear: "Isn't this what education is all about?"

Teachers came away convinced. "The kids proved to the staff that this project was worth it," DiLeo observed.

Once on board, teachers took part in a summer workshop to fine-tune the capstone, creating rubrics for assessment and calendars to make sure there was time in every content area devoted to the project. They also planned a presentation to parents about the capstone for back-to-school night. "I call it the magic triangle of success: students, teachers, and parents all moving in the same direction," Johnson said. "They all have to believe in the vision."

Now let's consider how capstones build students' competencies in high school, when students are fast approaching voting age and making decisions about college and careers. This may be your last chance as a school leader to ensure that students have meaningful experiences as community contributors and problem solvers.

Next, let's visit the Saline Area Schools in Michigan, which have designed a senior-year elective with a strong civic engagement focus. The year-long interdisciplinary course, taught by a trio of teachers from social studies, English, and science, focuses on the essential question, "What are a student's local, state, national, and world responsibilities?"

Students begin by choosing service-learning experiences that connect them with local issues (for example, volunteering to work with community partners on homelessness, animal abuse, or emergency preparedness). Then they move into regional problem solving, such as investigating the impacts of poverty on nearby Detroit or providing access to clean drinking water in Flint, Michigan. Finally, students choose a global issue to pursue in depth as a capstone.

The next challenge is scaling the experience so that every student builds the skills of engaged citizenship. About a quarter of Saline High School seniors (roughly 100 students) take the Senior Capstone Experience course currently. As next steps, Superintendent Steve Laatsch said the district aspires to create capstones across grade levels. In Grade 10, the focus would be on local issues; Grade 11, regional problem solving; Grade 12, global citizenship tied to the United Nations Sustainable Development Goals. "How do we make this not an elective," Laatsch said, "but just what we do? That's where we want to go."

That's the kind of civics challenge that has the potential to transform your school system by aligning curriculum with your shared definition of student success.

Consider what it would mean for students to have capstone experiences like these to mark the end of elementary, middle, and high school. Over time, students would be building portfolios to document their community contributions and reflect on their growth as engaged citizens. Consider, too, the added value of having students present their work to civic engagement panels made up of local government and nonprofit leaders, along with other interested community members. These rites of passage would be opportunities for spirited discussions, student reflections, and celebrations with your young citizens.

Field Trip

Scaffold Knowledge Building Before Taking Action in Tucson, Arizona

The summer before starting high school, a student was watching the news with her parents. Coverage of Black Lives Matter rallies in their hometown of Tucson, Arizona, prompted her parents to ask, "Why are people going out to protest?" She responded, "It's our duty as citizens to stand up if we see something that's not right."

The student credits a civic education program called We the People with awakening her to her responsibilities as a citizen. The program educates students in middle school and high school about their Constitutional rights. Regional events lead up to a national competition in Washington, D.C., modeled on Congressional hearings, where students field questions about topical issues from expert panels. After that well-scaffolded learning experience, students are primed to apply their understanding by taking informed action.

"This program takes you seriously," the Tucson student said. "I know that I can do things as a citizen," she added, because she has already done so. After competing in We the People, she continued working on social justice projects in her own community.

"Unless we have a program like this," said teacher Norma Higuera-Trask, "kids are slumbering with their civic knowledge." She encourages school leaders to not just endorse the program but commit to seeing it in action. "Once leaders see students cite *Marbury v. Madison*, that changes conversations." After coaching students through the program for fifteen years at Challenger Middle School in Tucson and also training other teachers to implement We the People, Higuera-Trask is convinced that every student should have access to similar experiences by the time they complete high school. The results can be transformative.

(Continued)

(Continued)

Another alumnus of the program is Patrick Robles, currently a student at the University of Arizona.

After taking part in We the People during middle school, he became student body president at Sunnyside High School in Tucson. He worked on a variety of issues, but his biggest success as school leader was advocating for a major crosswalk renovation near his school. According to District Superintendent Steve Holmes, the school had been trying for years to fix the problem, but red tape and bureaucratic roadblocks kept getting in the way.

At the beginning of Patrick's senior year, he took on this challenge. After reaching out to fellow students, teachers, his principal, and the superintendent, Patrick got the green light to approach the Tucson City Council. By the end of January, the Tucson Department of Transportation had installed a Rectangular Rapid Flashing Beacon crosswalk, a new technology being piloted in another Tucson location.

When asked why he thought he had succeeded when adults had failed at the same project, Patrick said, "Young people bring a unique perspective and tone to the conversation." What other skills and competencies did he develop through the process of advocating for a crosswalk? "I am now able to be in a conversation with adults and get my point across. My writing has improved, and I also improved my empathy skills."

Participating in student government, Patrick added, requires "a great deal of agency. We need to put that agency in the classroom. More agency in the curriculum will help students build a sense of ownership in their work, in the classroom, and in the school."

As a college student, Patrick continues putting his civic education to work. "I'm kind of a small guy, but when I speak, people say, 'I didn't expect that to come out of him!' I owe that to the [We the People] program. Once you've been in settings where you have to speak with confidence and get your points across, that stays with you. People look at you differently."

Field Trip

Civic Engagement for All in Utah

In Utah, state leaders have set a bold challenge with 2020 legislation calling for students to participate in civic engagement as a high school graduation requirement. Even at the pilot stage of implementation, educators are recognizing that they now have the green light to pursue citizenship programs that give students a real-world context for learning.

At West High School in Salt Lake City, geography teacher Suzanne Arthur uses resources from the National Geographic Society to engage her students in geo-inquiry projects about their community. For one project, students investigated and mapped the walking routes that students take to school. They interviewed transportation experts, including city planners. Once students documented safety concerns—such as train tracks that some students have to cross on foot and inadequate access to bus services—they developed recommendations to the school district, supported by the evidence they had gathered. They not only learned about geography but also how to work within the system to make a meaningful difference in their community.

Meanwhile, another teacher at the same school uses a program called Generation Citizen to engage students in studies of U.S. history and government. The rigorous program, aligned to academic standards, emphasizes student participation in the political process. To participate effectively, students have to understand how government works and how it got that way. "They're getting content," said teacher Holly Reynolds, "just not in the traditional format." Instead of following a scripted curriculum, students build understanding of government and history by asking and answering their own questions.

Both Reynolds and Arthur credit school leadership, especially social studies coordinator Dessie Olson, with giving them time for the professional learning they need and the green light to experiment with new teaching approaches. "What we need most as teachers is ongoing support—not cheerleading," said Reynolds. "That looks like meaningful professional development, time to plan and troubleshoot with colleagues, and room to make mistakes. It's a learning curve for us as teachers."

By now, you have read about a variety of approaches for building your students' knowledge and skills as engaged citizens. Pause and ask yourself the following questions.

ASK YOURSELF

- *Which of the field trips stands out to you as most applicable to your school system? Why? How might you need to modify this idea to suit your context and develop the competencies called for in your POG?*

- *How will you ensure that your commitment to civic education is developmentally appropriate and scaffolded across grade levels?*

Final Reflections

Your leadership challenge when it comes to civic engagement involves both listening and leading. Community members need to see that civics programs align with the POG goals that they have helped to shape and that you have listened to their input. At times, you may also need to bring your stakeholders along to appreciate the benefits of students taking a more active role as citizens and raising issues that have gone unaddressed in the past. Remind them that the K–12 years can be a time for young people to connect to their communities in positive ways or to disengage. Remember Sheldon Berman's insight that children decide at a relatively young age "either to back away or see themselves as empowered" as members of the larger society.

If you're going to give students and teachers the green light to tackle meaningful and perhaps controversial challenges, they need to know that you will have their backs. That's part of bold leadership, too.

Here are three questions to consider:

- How are you sharing students' stories with your stakeholders to show them the benefits of engaged citizenship?
- How will you use your influence as a leader to set a bold citizenship challenge that reflects community values and reaches all students?
- How will you ensure that civic education programs align with the goals of your POG?

RESOURCES FOR IMPLEMENTATION

Composer is an online resource providing access to civic education resources—including games, simulations, and discussion guides—created by leading organizations in citizenship education. composereducation.org

Kids Education Revolution, an initiative of Teach For India, showcases students as community problem solvers. kidseducationrevolution.org

Project Citizen, a program of the Center for Civic Education, teaches students to identify and research community problems and then develop and present policy solutions. civiced.org/project-citizen

Teach SDGs is a global community of educators who design learning experiences in which students address the UN Sustainable Development Goals. http://www.teachsdgs.org/

World 101, produced by the Council on Foreign Relations, is an interactive resource for learning about international relations and global issues such as climate change, global health, and human migration. world101.cfr.org

For Your Bookshelf

Empowering Global Citizens: A World Course, by Fernando Reimers and colleagues from the Harvard Graduate School of Education, is a research-based global education curriculum for K–12. Available at no charge on Kindle

Teaching for a Living Democracy, by Joshua Block, offers a veteran high school teacher's insights on designing learning experiences that inspire students to be active citizens.

The World: A Brief Introduction by Richard Haass offers an invaluable primer on global history and global issues.

Action Steps

Your challenge when it comes to civics is making sure that every student has the opportunity to participate fully. Don't adopt programs only for honors or college-bound students. Don't let academic achievement be a barrier to participation. Every student deserves opportunities to become an engaged citizen.

Three action steps will help you move from shared vision to empowered learning as you lead your students to engage with the issues that matter to them and their communities.

I.   **Get your community on board.** Advocate for a renewed commitment to the civic mission of schools as central to your

(Continued)

(Continued)

shared vision for student success. Emphasizing civic engagement may test your leadership at times, but preparing all students with the knowledge and skills they need to be informed, engaged citizens is at the heart of redefining student success to emphasize equity.

2. **Commit to big issues.** Make sure teachers have the green light to design learning experiences that connect to the local and global challenges your students care most about tackling.

3. **Set a bold civics challenge.** Challenge your instructional team to make a major commitment to civic engagement that addresses your POG competencies. Commit the resources and time needed for professional development to help teachers adopt or develop new programs that are developmentally appropriate. Encourage students to reflect on how these challenges help them to develop POG competencies, and encourage them to build portfolios that show evidence of their growth.

Fostering civic engagement will, by design, strengthen your students' self-direction. In the next chapter, we explore strategies to promote self-direction across the curriculum and beyond.

CHAPTER 5

Be the Leader of Self-Directed Young People

CHAPTER HIGHLIGHTS

We do our students a disservice if we continue to reward them for compliance. How often do you hear students ask, "What do I need to do for an A?" If this is their most pressing question, it's a signal that we are not encouraging curious learners who set their own goals. The jobs of the present and certainly those of the future depend on self-starters who are intrinsically motivated. Our civic and personal challenges also require self-directed young people. Being able to identify a problem and knowing what to do next to solve it is a 21st century survival skill. Instead of rewarding compliance, we must cultivate a green light culture for students that gives them more ownership of their learning. That's how we will prepare our students to become self-directed people and partners in school transformation.

In the previous chapter, you heard how civic engagement has been embraced as a goal for all students across Anaheim Union High School District. What happens when the focus on civics is coupled with a deep commitment to self-directed learning? Let's pick up the Anaheim story to find out.

Field Trip

Confronting the Past in Anaheim, California

Carlos Hernandez was in his second year as principal of Savanna High School in Anaheim when he faced a crisis. One of his favorite parents, a local pastor and African American father of two students, arrived at his office "fired up and frustrated" about the school mascot. He demanded to know why, in 2017, the school was still honoring Johnny Rebel, a racist symbol of the Confederacy.

Hernandez listened and then asked, "Do you believe we love and value our students and their families?" The parent agreed, and the principal invited him to continue working together on a solution. The two of them met again, this time with Superintendent Michael Matsuda.

The superintendent recognized a teachable moment, completely aligned with the district's vision. Why not empower students to determine the best recommendation for the school board?

That was the start of a powerful experience of students leading their entire community through a controversy. "We wanted students to really own this, and we wanted every student to have a voice in the decision," Hernandez recalled. (He has since moved into a district leadership role as director of curriculum and instruction.)

Here was a chance to apply all 5 Cs from the district's graduate profile (critical thinking, creativity, communication, collaboration, and character/compassion), but not for an assignment that only teachers would see. This was about connecting learning with real life.

Trusting students didn't mean leaving them on their own to wrestle with controversy. The principal enlisted his social studies teachers as facilitators. "They were primed for this," Hernandez said, from having undergone training with the California Democracy School program (described in Chapter 4). "Teachers saw this as an historic opportunity, a chance for students to leave a legacy."

Teachers quickly designed a five-day lesson plan for all classes that would take students through a process of understanding the issue, conducting research, engaging in respectful dialogue, reaching a conclusion, and taking action.

On day three of that schoolwide lesson, Principal Hernandez walked into a classroom accompanied by the same father who had first raised the mascot issue. They found students sitting in a circle, engaging in a Socratic seminar to debate the question, "Should Savanna High School keep, replace, or rebrand its mascot, Johnny Rebel?" Passions ran high, but students thoughtfully backed up their arguments with research and evidence. If they disagreed, they did so with respect. The teacher charted the discussion to make sure every student spoke, but otherwise let the conversation flow.

Even before the controversy was resolved, the principal knew that students were gaining an invaluable life lesson. "They were learning a process they can use in any environment where there are disagreements. They can have respectful discourse so that everyone is heard, everyone listens." By trusting his students, Hernandez reflected later, "They taught us what's possible in this divided country."

The next step was a public forum, open to the media, where student representatives made the case for each of the three options: keep, replace, or rebrand the mascot? Principals from across the district, school board members, and other interested community members gathered in the packed Savanna High School gym alongside students.

"This was not a day for adults to speak," Hernandez recalled. "It was a chance for our students to model to the community how to address a controversial issue. It was a day to show that by giving students a voice, they will reach the right decision. We can trust in their humanity, even if they are 15 or 16 years old."

In the end, a majority of students voted to rebrand the rebel, honoring the school's history but stripping the mascot of Confederate symbolism. At the next school board meeting, over the dissenting and sometimes loud voices of adults, board members voted unanimously to accept the students' recommendation.

It takes courage, as a school leader, to trust your students to lead on problem solving while capitalizing on the learning potential of such experiences. This chapter will prompt you to consider a number of questions when it comes to cultivating self-direction in your students. For starters, think about how your system currently encourages self-direction.

ASK YOURSELF

- Do all students have a voice in your school system or only those who fit a certain profile? How can you engage students you are not hearing from?
- How do you and your team intentionally build every student's capacity to take ownership of their learning?
- How do you encourage students to take advantage of opportunities outside the classroom to develop their skills as self-directed people?

The three moves described in this chapter—take it seriously; take it deep; take it wide—will get your students on the path to being more self-directed; in learning and in life.

As you consider the many examples ahead, keep in mind our starting point: Self-directed people are intrinsically motivated to identify problems and figure out what to do next to solve them. We can't afford to wait until students launch careers to develop these skills. That's too late. Instead, K–12 education is the ideal environment for students to practice and hone the skill of self-direction.

> Self-directed people are intrinsically motivated to identify problems and figure out what to do next to solve them.

TAKE IT SERIOUSLY

A vendor of digital curriculum was making a sales pitch to Shelby County Public Schools in Kentucky. The Zoom call included students alongside adult decision makers. When it was time for questions, one of the students took the microphone and introduced himself as a lifelong learner—one of six competencies in the district's Portrait of a Graduate (POG). He wanted to know, how would this product help him manage his own learning?

For Chief Academic Officer Susan Dugle, what was notable about the conversation wasn't that students literally had a seat at the table. Student participation in decision making is common practice in this district that walks the talk when it comes to empowering students. Rather, it was hearing the student, unprompted, use indicators from the district's Portrait of a Graduate. "There's the proof in the pudding," she reflected later, that the district's vision is coming to life.

Empowering students to take more ownership of their learning is a common goal in schools that are undergoing transformation. Many school systems already prioritize students as active participants in their own education. POGs and vision statements commonly include terms like lifelong learner and agency.

The emphasis on self-direction reflects a broader economic trend, which author Ted Dintersmith sums up this way: "In the fifties and sixties, the economy didn't ask for self-direction. The jobs of that era are now gone."

In practice, however, the path to self-direction can be challenging for school systems to navigate. Language in your POG may not easily translate to what happens in the classroom. Giving students more choice and voice about when, where, how, what, and with whom they learn means that educators have to relinquish control. Empowering students to make decisions means adults have to be willing to share power with them. Students themselves may need help shifting from being passive recipients to more active questioners and knowledge creators. They need opportunities to practice advocating for themselves. This is especially important for students whose voices have not been heard, including students with disabilities who may not have had opportunities to make decisions about their own education (National Center for Learning Disabilities, 2018).

In your community visioning process, we're almost certain that self-direction emerged as a shared goal. It may not be explicitly named in your POG, but every other 21st century competency depends on students becoming more active, engaged participants in learning. Now you need to be serious about making this a reality.

For starters, enlist your stakeholders to help you take a self-direction snapshot. What questions will parents, teachers, business and community leaders, and students themselves ask to gauge the degree of self-direction among learners in your system right now? What evidence will they look for? The data they gather—however informal or anecdotal—will help you recognize where you are and where you need to go next.

If there's confusion about what your system means by self-direction, that's a signal that more work is needed to define terms and create common understanding.

Let's consider a few of the competing terms that come up in education discussions around this topic.

Agency: Students who develop a sense of agency are active participants in their education. They set goals, take action to reach them, and reflect on their progress. They have the capacity to leverage resources to navigate obstacles and create positive change in their life (Kundu, 2020). They are buoyed by the belief that they can be successful—what experts call self-efficacy (Poon, 2018). Students who develop agency "are far more likely to find purpose in learning, be motivated to persist through challenges, and be able to manage their progress in learning," according to James Niehof, retired superintendent of Shelby County Public Schools in Kentucky (Niehof, 2020).

Self-direction: The Institute for Self-Directed Learning offers this definition, which shows benefits extending far beyond the traditional classroom:

The cognitive, developmental, and sociocultural mechanisms that facilitate one's ability to self-identify their passions, interests, and goals, in service of finding their life's purpose and therefore uniquely contributing to their community and society as a whole. (www.selfdirect.school)

Personalization: Personalization is the opposite of a one-size-fits-all pedagogy. It means tailoring learning for each student's strengths, needs, and interests (Slocum, 2016). What's more, a personalized approach to education "breaks down the walls that separate subject areas into silos, the school world from the outside world, and individual achievement from community growth. Students learn from and are influenced by the adults, peers, and experts with whom they work as they socially construct knowledge" (Kallick & Zmuda, 2017, p. 8).

Student-centered: Students at the Center, a project of Jobs for the Future, has developed a framework for learning that starts with the student's experience and identity. From there, students advance at their own pace toward proficiency, harnessing the full range of learning experiences, both within and outside school (studentsatthecenterhub.org/framework).

Which of these terms shows up in your POG? Which terms describe instructional strategies your district is considering? Do you need to be clearer about what you mean? Think about who in your system you can enlist to unpack a definition so that it's more useful for setting goals and assessing progress.

To move its Portrait of a Graduate (see Fig. 5.1) from vision to practice, teachers and district administrators in Mansfield Public Schools in Connecticut collaborated to clarify its definition of student-centered learning.

The district has identified these specific "look-fors" when learning is student centered and students are constructing knowledge through rich, authentic tasks:

- The student takes ownership of learning and builds understanding through exploration and development of passions and interests.
- The teacher understands the student and the content and encourages risk-taking while providing feedback and support to facilitate learning.
- The tasks are authentic, afford the opportunity for higher-order thinking, and intentionally build upon foundational knowledge to promote growth.

Figure 5.1 Portrait of a Graduate, Mansfield Public Schools

PORTRAIT OF THE GRADUATE MANSFIELD PUBLIC SCHOOLS

The Mansfield Public School student develops a love of learning rooted in a strong academic foundation. Students grow within a safe and respectful environment while contributing to the local and global community. This educational journey encourages risk taking, builds perseverance and resiliency, and celebrates individual growth. Skills and dispositions across five elements interact with each other and with content standards to support the development of a learner prepared to face future learning and career challenges.

If your POG does not specifically name self-direction (or a close synonym), you may find it elsewhere within your broader framework. For example, you may be leading in the direction of project-based learning or passion projects or having students create portfolios and lead conferences with their parents and teachers. These are examples of practices that elevate student voice and choice in learning and can be part of a transformation to more student-driven learning. The challenge isn't a lack of models or options; it's determining the right entry point and next steps for your school community.

What do you need to do to "take it seriously" when it comes to self-direction?

ASK YOURSELF

- *What do we mean in our school system when we talk about self-direction?*
- *How does our POG reflect our community's commitment to self-direction? Do we need to spend more time on this question with our stakeholders?*

TAKE IT DEEP

Schools that go deep with self-direction create multiple opportunities in the regular school day for students to discover their interests and set goals for the future they envision. Blue Valley Schools in Overland, Kansas, offers a good example. Its most recent strategic plan, developed in partnership with community stakeholders (including students), paints this picture:

> All students will engage in authentic, relevant, and personalized learning experiences—including experiences directly connected to community and industry—that develop students' competencies, activate their interests, and nourish their sense of purpose.

That goes well beyond giving students choices about their class assignments.

The next three field trips show what self-direction looks like in practice. As you consider these examples, be thinking about opportunities you may have overlooked to go deeper with self-direction within the classroom and curriculum.

Field Trip

Student-Led IEPs in Natick, Massachusetts

The Profile of a Graduate adopted by Natick Public Schools in Massachusetts defines six important qualities that contribute to students becoming Global Citizen Leaders. One of the six is initiative and self-direction.

What does this mean in practice? Natick High School Principal Brian Harrigan has worked with his staff to further define this goal, identifying specifics such as students setting goals, reflecting as learners, accepting both praise and constructive criticism, and persisting to overcome difficult tasks and overcome academic and personal barriers to meet goals. "We want to embed these strategies into everything," explained Tim Luff, assistant superintendent for student services, so that all students have practice applying them. That includes students with special needs.

To give special needs students a greater voice in their education, the Natick district encourages students to take a lead role in planning their Individualized Education Program. Tim led the district to try student-led IEPs after researching the idea and providing training for the district's special education teachers. "You can't just throw kids in front of an IEP meeting," Tim said. "This is about self-determination—a research-based way to have students assess their strengths, set goals, develop an action plan, and act on it." Since introducing student-led IEPs several years ago, he said, "100 percent of our [special needs] kids have engaged in the model somewhat. The IEP is no longer a piece of paper that adults fill out. Students are part of a meaningful process. They're engaged in what's happening in their own education." At times, students inspire even their parents with the learning goals they set. Tim recalls a special needs student who wanted to give a TED-style talk for a social studies project. "Here was a kid who was a self-directed learner who thought about his strengths. He developed a plan to give a talk and then acted on it." The parent at first expressed reservations, saying, "He wants to do *what*? On a *stage*?"

Social studies teacher Tracy Sockalosky facilitated that learning experience for a class of eighth-graders, including several special needs students. The experience not only aligned with the district vision but reflected her own values. As she explained, "A social studies class should be about developing empathy and understanding. If we eliminate a portion of the population of the school from these experiences, we're not having an inclusive conversation." When it was time for the TED-style event, the stage included "some of our most academically disabled students, discussing in depth sophisticated topics. They left that class with the sense that they were part of a bigger world," the teacher said. That's the kind of experience that brings to life the Profile of a Natick Graduate, showing what empathy, resilience, and self-direction look like when truly owned by students.

Field Trip

Developing Concrete Skills in Atlanta, Georgia

Hadley Lewis was about to enter her senior year of high school when she had an eye-opening moment. By traditional measures of success, she said, "I was a perfect student. I study hard. I attend class. I get As." What she lacked was a sense of direction. After eleven years of formal schooling, she realized, "I had no idea about my own interests."

After attending an open house at the Forest School, an innovative K–12 school in Atlanta that emphasizes self-directed learning, she decided to take a chance. "I knew I would be out of my comfort zone," she said later, "but I realized I could gain something that I didn't know I needed: life skills. I craved that challenge."

Fast forward a year and Hadley was an entering freshman at Auburn University. COVID-19 was still raging, disrupting campus routines and schedules. But from her first days of college, she realized she had the skills to adapt. Her final year of high school had taught her, in concrete ways, to set goals and manage her time, to advocate for herself as a learner, to question how potential majors would relate to her own interests. "I use those skills every day," she said. "I've learned to constantly ask questions, decrypt everything, and reflect."

Tyler Thigpen, founder of the Forest School, has set out to address a problem he cares about deeply. Traditional schools are graduating "a generation of learners who are dependent and not self-directed learners," he said. "Students are for years embedded in learning environments where they are following rules they didn't make and listening to answers to questions they didn't ask." His solution is a school that is small by design, with a maximum capacity of 150 students. Its mission couldn't be bigger: "Each person will find a calling that changes the world."

The intentionally diverse school is intended to be an incubator that larger systems can learn from. As a founding member of the Institute for Self-Directed Learning, the school is deeply invested in building the field and sharing best practices. Tyler also runs a design lab at the University of Pennsylvania Graduate School of Education, where school leaders develop their own blueprints for school transformation. A key question that leaders must answer: What do adults believe that young people are capable of handling, controlling, and leading? This is an invitation to "take it deep" when it comes to self-directed learning.

Wherever possible, the Forest School gives tasks and authority to students. Every public event is learner led. Yet students are not left on their own to succeed or fail. The school surrounds young people with multiple caring adults who serve as mentors and guides. Together with his staff, Tyler encourages students to shoulder the responsibility for their learning in countless concrete ways. "It looks like daily goal setting; flexible learning spaces; kids having autonomy and decision making to make rules for self-governance and to experience the natural consequences of that."

Field Trip

Learning Through Questioning in Encinitas, California

When the Encinitas Union School District in Southern California holds its regular meetings, board members expect to hear from students who bring their own agenda items. One month it's kindergarteners who have a plan to ban plastic straws from the cafeteria because of concerns about harm to sea turtles. Another month, it's fourth-graders reporting on their successful work as sustainability consultants for the local YMCA or sharing insights about how to improve remote learning during the COVID-19 pandemic. For former Superintendent Tim Baird, such moments show the power of entrusting students to direct their own learning. "Given the appropriate support and the right tools, you can turn a fourth-grader loose on anything," Tim said. "Kids will say, this isn't school. This is what I DO."

Superintendent Andrée Grey has continued to keep students at the center since taking the reins from Tim Baird in 2019. Students take a leading role in problem solving in the classroom, in the community, and often for the entire school system. "For every problem we're dealing with as adults," Andrée said, "how do we have students working to solve it? They're a tremendous asset." In this high-performing school system that serves 5,400 students in Grades K–6, the districtwide culture values students' questions as the most natural and engaging starting place for learning.

Concrete tools and resources sustain the culture and keep students at the center of learning. Students, teachers, and leaders use the same process for inquiry. They start with a question that's worth exploring, research the issue, and conclude with a well-researched solution that is shared with an authentic audience. "You can't just design from the seat of your pants," said Tim. He designed the inquiry protocol while superintendent and prototyped it with his leadership team before inviting teachers to bring it into their classrooms.

Fourth-graders recently used the inquiry protocol as part of a year-long project to serve as sustainability consultants for the YMCA in their community. Teacher Alice Larsen had no trouble connecting the project with learning goals in science, math,

(Continued)

(Continued)

and language arts. What's more, she saw this as an opportunity "to have my whole class contribute" and not limit learning only to students who volunteer to be part of environmental clubs. After considerable investigation, interviewing, and analysis, students were ready to present their final plan to the YMCA board. Alice used this as an opportunity to ensure that every learner had a voice in the project and engage "kids who don't always get chosen for these roles."

Another project began when students asked, "Why are we using plastic utensils in the cafeteria?" That became a districtwide opportunity for self-directed learning. "Instead of sitting around a cabinet table as adults, we put the challenge in front of students," recalled Andrée. Students conducted research, interviewed experts, designed experiments, gathered and analyzed data, and eventually presented their top solutions to the school board. When the board agreed to invest in metal silverware as a solution, it was up to students to plan assemblies and conduct public relations to ensure the success of the new approach.

During the COVID-19 crisis, the superintendent again turned to students to identify challenges with remote learning. "They didn't just tell us what the problems were—they created solutions," she says, such as student-created video tutorials for parents shared on the district website. When the district culture keeps students at the center, everyone benefits.

Take a moment to think about the examples you have encountered so far in this chapter.

ASK YOURSELF

- *Would you have recognized the "teachable moment" in each story?*
- *What support structures does your system need to develop to help all students become more confident as self-directed learners?*

TAKE IT WIDE

If students are going to become capable, self-directed people, they need experiences that build this capacity in their regular classes as well as outside the formal curriculum and beyond the official school day. That's why we also encourage you to "take it wide" when it comes to encouraging self-direction. Be rigorous about advocating for self-directed learning in class and recognize the rich potential of other school experiences and out-of-school opportunities to encourage self-direction.

From a young age, students need to practice advocating for what they want to accomplish and enlisting others to join them. Extracurricular activities can be a springboard for self-direction. This point is underscored by co-authors Jal Mehta and Sara Fine in *In Search of Deeper Learning* (2019). They describe high school students showing higher levels of motivation and taking more ownership in learning experiences at the periphery of school—including extracurriculars and electives—rather than in core subjects.

Along with giving students more voice in extracurricular options, you also need to commit to making these experiences accessible to all. Are high-interest activities available only after school, when some students have part-time jobs or responsibilities to care for younger siblings, or before school when transportation can be a challenge for some families? You may need to be creative about bringing these rich learning experiences into the school day so that all students can participate, such as scheduling time each week for clubs or other extracurriculars to meet.

The following field trips to diverse contexts show that this bold move doesn't require reinventing the entire curriculum but may well transform your school culture. By thinking about the role of students both in class and beyond the traditional school structure, you and your community may discover an antidote to disengagement and a powerful driver of equity.

To help you recognize opportunities within reach, let's consider four more ways to go wide with self-direction.

Field Trip

Students Leading in Makerspaces in Eminence, Kentucky

As a major commitment to 21st century learning, the rural community of Eminence, Kentucky, stepped up to invest in a $6 million, 30,000-square foot facility that features eight maker labs and a library where students can check out tools. Superintendent

(Continued)

(Continued)

Buddy Berry considers the facility the new heart of the school and trusts students to make it work. When students become experts in the use of specific technologies, they earn micro-credentials in skills like using 3D printers, laser cutters, or power saws. Credentialed students then teach their fellow classmates—and adults (Boss, 2017a).

These skills are not just extras for a few motivated Eminence students. They align with the district's graduate profile and are considered essential for college and career readiness. At student-led progress meetings, students share evidence of their proficiency not only with technology tools but also with competencies like public speaking and design thinking.

Programs like these create ongoing, structured opportunities to trust students with meaningful responsibilities. Students aren't left on their own to succeed or fail; mentoring and guidance from adults are embedded in the process.

Field Trip
Students Leading With Tech Support in Kettering, Ohio

At Dayton Regional STEM School in Kettering, Ohio, high school students work alongside IT experts to run a tech-support center for both staff and students. They gain hands-on experience with everything from cybersecurity to operating systems to laptop maintenance and apply their knowledge to earn industry certifications. "The school's mission is to prepare students with 21st century skills to enter the 21st century economy," explained Jordan Sloane, the school's IT director, in a video about the program. "Our goal is to send students out not only college ready but career ready" (Edutopia, 2020). Trusting students to be tech troubleshooters for your school system or to run "genius bars" that mimic Apple stores is a concrete way to develop those readiness skills.

Field Trip
Students Leading Extracurriculars in Perry Township, Indiana

When Jeff Spencer arrived as principal of Southport Elementary in Perry Township, Indiana, he knew he was assuming leadership of an already high-achieving Title I school. The community includes many Burmese Chin refugee families; about half the students are English learners.

Despite the academic strengths, Jeff realized that the school had few clubs or other extracurricular activities to tap into students' interests. Student voice was lacking. He worked with the PTA to support interest-driven opportunities outside regular class time. The school now offers more than a dozen clubs, focusing on robotics, gardening, American Sign Language, and more.

The principal could see that student voice was taking hold when a fifth-grader proposed a new coding club geared for girls. "I told her, OK, here's what you need to do," Jeff told her, outlining a few simple steps to develop her proposal. "She got it going, and now our girls' coding club meets every week." More students are stepping up to advocate for clubs that reflect their interests. "Student voice doesn't have to be only in academics," he reflected.

One of his favorite examples is the Eagle Action Network, the school's version of a daily announcement. Fifth-graders took on the challenge of revising what had been a rather dry recitation to incorporate more authentic student voice. They investigated how high schools and colleges run school news programs. They interviewed a speech teacher and broadcast reporter to learn more about effective programming. Some fifty students eventually joined the project, which happened outside regular classes. "It's been a powerful experience," Jeff said. "These students know that they have created an ongoing legacy."

Field Trip
Students Leading on Fundraising in Arvada, Colorado

While taking a STEAM elective designed around self-direction at North Arvada Middle School in the Jeffco District, Colorado, a student named Andrew Ellis decided to focus on addressing the school's lack of playground space. The well-scaffolded course taught him how to conduct an analysis of the problem; communicate with students, teachers, and administrators; design the success criteria; and manage time and budget. In researching possible sources of support, Andrew realized the school needed to partner with the city government to be eligible for a specific grant. So he worked to convince the city council to apply for the grant on the school's behalf.

Working alongside his fellow students and with the support of teacher Erin Fichtel, Andrew took the lead on completing the grant application, gaining student consensus, and designing a Ninja-Warrior-inspired playground design. Long story

(Continued)

(Continued)

short, the school won the $110,000 grant from GOCO (Great Outdoors Colorado), and the school and district added another $70,000. That's right: Andrew, a seventh grader, raised $180,000 for his school. The obstacle course was installed in the summer of 2019.

Andrew's teacher, Erin, explained that this project transformed Andrew, who had been an average student in reading and writing. Not only did Andrew learn important researching, writing, negotiating, and organizational skills, but he also developed a greater sense of confidence from a class project that allowed him to excel and make a much-needed difference for his school. "It makes me feel good to help other people. Now that my sister is in the school, she will get to use it [the playground]. That's pretty cool," Andrew explained proudly.

STUDENTS AS CHANGE AGENTS

Throughout this book, we have encouraged you to develop and implement your vision for student success by engaging with your community. The process must include student voices—not only to build students' success skills but also to reach better solutions. We hope the many examples in this chapter have expanded your thinking about how to amplify student voices so that students are true partners in the change process.

Even school systems that haven't planned for transformation are being forced to consider a new normal as a result of the pandemic and increased focus on racial and economic inequities. If self-directed learning is going to be part of that future, we need students to help design a better way forward.

Consider this compelling call-to-action from Brooklyn LAB Charter School, which has developed a *Learner Identity and Agency Guidebook* (2020) as part of its response to redefining education:

> This is a unique opportunity to shift the locus of control in schools and empower students to discover and affirm their authentic selves. . . .to become agents of change. . . . This is a moment of upheaval and uncertainty; however, it's also a

chance to help students learn how to navigate obstacles and personal challenges—skills that will set them up for success in school and beyond.

The survival skills of self-directed learners require time, support, and practice to take hold. "We can't wait until high school to start," said teacher Tracy Sockalosky from Natick, Massachusetts. "Students need to start developing these competencies by kindergarten and build their backpack of skills as they progress from K–12. It's not enough for teachers to teach these competencies," she insisted. "Students have to own it."

Let's close this chapter with the voices of students who are taking ownership of their own learning and, as a result, helping their schools and communities redefine student success. Merrit Jones, a current college student and senior adviser for a national youth-run advocacy group called Student Voice, encourages school leaders to think broadly about roles that students can take on. In student surveys and focus groups, her organization hears from students wanting to have more voice about everything from course offerings to scheduling to budgeting. "Schools can engage more deeply with students in the process of making decisions," she said. More pointedly, she added, "Schools continue to underutilize the creativity and courage of young people. There's so much untapped potential schools are missing by not engaging students as partners in governance, decision making, and so many aspects of the school experience."

Sixth-grader Drew Larsen shows us the contributions a self-directed learner can make. During her years at Ocean Knoll Elementary in the Encinitas district, she and her classmates have become adept at spotting environmental problems, enlisting adult allies, and advocating for solutions. She has learned that solutions often involve motivating people to change their behavior. For a veteran problem solver like Drew, that means creating public-service announcements or awareness-raising campaigns and then following up to see if campaigns result in real change. At times, her efforts have meant making presentations to the school board, city council, or other agency. Public speaking "can be scary at first, especially if there are a lot of people," she admits. "But you get the hang of it. And then it's cool, because the adults are asking *you* questions. It's like you're the adult!"

Enlisting students as allies to deal with controversies requires courage on the part of adults, but this is a bold leadership move worth making. Let's take one final field trip to see how empowered students are taking charge of change.

Field Trip

Addressing Racism in Charlottesville, Virginia

After the issue of racial injustice exploded in Charlottesville, Virginia, Matt Haas (who later became superintendent of Albemarle County Public Schools) entrusted students to run the task force on developing a new antiracism policy for the district. As part of that effort, the district was reviewing its dress code policy and had to decide whether to explicitly ban Confederate imagery.

Students started working on the policy before school started and did in-depth data work before they entered an intensive interview stage. They completed a draft policy in late 2018, and the new policy was later passed by the school board.

The antiracism policy is a general policy framework that will help push forward a path for more specific policies. One of the students describes it as a "first step" and said she was confident the policy would continue to receive adequate attention from the district and the school board. She also proudly explained that the policy creates an ongoing student review board to review the new data and believes the students will keep a continuing focus on issues of race (Kay, 2019).

In 2019, as part of its ongoing antiracism efforts, the board created the Student Equity Advisory Team (SEAT). This all-student team is an outgrowth of the recommendations made by the earlier student team, and ensures ongoing student input into this important work.

Along with broader benefits for their community, students benefited personally from their intense involvement in this work. One of the students recognized her own growth in public speaking and presentation skills, as well as her networking skills and her personal interest in public policy (Kay, 2019). Younger students in the group dramatically improved their communication and confidence skills throughout the six-month experience.

This story exemplifies what happens when we "take it wide," giving students significant responsibility while helping them build the competencies needed to navigate challenges. This is how school becomes a laboratory for leadership.

You've heard several examples of students tackling problems that extend well beyond the classroom. Take time to reflect on the many examples of self-directed learners that you have read about in this chapter.

ASK YOURSELF

- *What's your reaction to these stories? How would you have responded if the experiences had not gone so well?*

- *What more can you do as a leader to guide students to successful outcomes on self-directed experiences that "go wide"?*

Final Reflections
Green Light Culture for Students

After considering the many examples in this chapter, think about how you will pursue similar strategies in your own school system. It's not enough to emphasize self-direction in your POG or a broader framework for instruction. As a leader, you need to ensure that you are creating a green light culture for students to take more ownership of their learning.

- How will you determine whether students believe they have the green light to drive more of their learning? What evidence will you look for?

- What are your next steps to ensure that all students are developing a sense of agency as learners? What more can you do as a school leader to make sure that all students are welcome and valued as genuine partners in school change?

- What leadership challenges do you anticipate to support self-directed learning across your school system? What skills can you draw on? Who else might you enlist to support this important work?

RESOURCES FOR IMPLEMENTATION

Question Formulation Technique, developed by the Right Question Institute, promotes questioning strategies (for youth and adults) that build agency and promote democratic action. rightquestion.org/what-is-the-qft

(Continued)

(Continued)

Student agency rubrics, developed by the New Tech Network, promote a growth mindset and encourage learners to take more ownership of their learning. Search "agency rubrics" at newtechnetwork.org.

Student Voice, a nonprofit organization created by students for students, encourages students to take an active role in school transformation. www.stuvoice.org

Students at the Center, managed by KnowledgeWorks, provides resources, research, and a framework for student-centered learning. studentsatthecenterhub.org

Social and Emotional Learning: The concepts of self-advocacy for students are deeply rooted in the literature of social and emotional learning. Check out the resources created by the Collaborative for Academic, Social, and Emotional Learning (CASEL) at www.casel.org

For Your Bookshelf

Just Ask Us: Kids Speak Out on Student Engagement by Heather Wolpert-Gawron

Student Voice: The Instrument of Change by Russell Quaglia and Michael Corso

Students at the Center: Personalized Learning With Habits of Mind by Bena Kallick and Allison Zmuda

Action Steps

We hope the many field trips in this chapter have inspired your thinking about what self-direction learning looks like in practice. As you determine the next steps for your system, make sure that all students are developing the capacity to advocate for themselves. Self-direction should not be limited to students who fit a certain academic profile. Every student needs to improve their self-direction skills. Encourage students to create roles they can take on outside the classroom and trust them as valued partners in redefining student success.

Keep in mind our three suggestions for action:

1. **Take it seriously.** Clarify what self-directed learning means in your context and why this is an essential goal for student success. Determine how self-direction aligns with your POG goals and work with your team to define look-fors when it comes to students driving their own learning.

2. **Take it wide.** Consider opportunities your school system may have overlooked to go deeper with self-direction within the classroom and curriculum. Showcase effective practices and encourage teachers to support each other in developing new strategies to encourage self-direction.

3. **Take it deep.** Partner with students to improve your school system and entrust them to lead on everything from extracurriculars to governance to social change. Invite students to suggest new roles that align with their interests. Your students and your system will benefit.

To realize goals for self-directed learning across your system, you will need buy-in from your instructional staff as well as your broader community. As we move into Part III, we focus on strategies to lead your team in rethinking instruction and assessment to redefine student success and partnership strategies to build family and community support for changes in teaching and learning.

Building Your Vision

Your vision, described in Part I, is bold. Bringing that vision to life is inspiring, as you saw in Part II. Now we get to the hard part:

- Bringing the vision of self-directed problem solving to life in classrooms
- Bringing our schools and communities closer to identify real problems that exist in your community and giving students opportunities to have a real impact by working to solve those problems

We will introduce you in Chapters 6 and 7 to concepts and tools you can use in building your vision and bringing it to life:

- "Backward design" to fully implement your Portrait of a Graduate (POG)
- Student-led assessment
- Portfolio defenses and mastery learning strategies
- Community partnerships around creative problem solving

Taken together, these strategies will bring your POG to life and will tangibly transform pedagogy in your school or district. With support and collaboration, teachers will be making necessary shifts from a pedagogy that supports test taking to a pedagogy that supports creative problem solving.

By working together toward collective efficacy, you will be working as a team to attain the results for students that really matter. It's an exciting transformation.

This also means your community will shift from being bystanders or arms-length observers of education to being directly involved partners with your schools. Neighborhoods, communities, as well as many businesses, have challenges that students can engage with. These community partnerships help create opportunities for authentic, hands-on learning for your students.

This is the bold transition of education we hope that you will lead: from silos of test taking to interdisciplinary environments for real-world community problem solving.

What to Look For

"What would I tell my ninth-grade version of myself?"

"Proactively deciding who you are, what makes you happy, and who you want to be puts students in a powerful position. It makes us all supporting cast in their story, and I think that is a big part of the future of personalized education. If we can figure this out and find a way to capture the progress of each student on his or her path to achieving his or her goals and dreams and make that our assessment of our classrooms, campuses, feeder patterns, and districts, it seems we would have finally found the right path to demonstrating accountability at all levels. We could look at the data in 100 different ways—look for patterns of excellence and patterns of concern. And at the end of the day, if a student wants to be a marine and becomes a marine that, in my opinion, is success in PreK–12."

~Superintendent Elizabeth Fagen, Humble ISD, Texas

As you read Chapters 6 and 7, consider these questions:

- *Is our POG just a poster, or is it bringing meaningful change to our classrooms?*
- *How will changes in pedagogy benefit students who have been traditionally underserved?*
- *How will we engage our community in a real dialogue on creative problem solving for students and the role community partners can play in supporting those efforts?*

These provocations are important because, in Chapter 8, you will plan the next steps that will allow you to achieve the full potential of your POG. Your success will depend on your long-term commitment to transformed classroom practice and community partnerships. It's hard but exciting. Let's get to work!

CHAPTER 6

Be the Leader of Bold Learning

CHAPTER HIGHLIGHTS

Your Portrait of a Graduate (POG) makes clear what your community wants students to know and be able to do by the time they complete their K–12 education. Design backward from that vision to ensure that teaching and learning align with your goals. Systematically collect evidence that your students are growing in the POG competencies. Help teachers make necessary shifts in instruction and assessment by engaging them in high-quality, collaborative, professional learning. Manage the pace of change, but don't settle for incrementalism or pockets of success that reach only some students. Set challenges that are bold enough to redefine success so that all students become capable learners and effective problem solvers.

At the EdLeader21 national conference in 2019, twenty-one school districts were invited to share their learning about how they were putting their Portrait of a Graduate into practice. Trifold displays were set up science-fair style for the audience of eight hundred to explore.

Each school system's POG was displayed on the left panel, with the description of a key move to transform teaching and learning in the center and results for students on the right.

As Valerie Greenhill, co-founder of EdLeader21, explored the Portrait to Practice gallery, she was struck by "the diversity of how they told the story." There were common building blocks, in terms of effective instructional strategies, "but each district's context requires a unique path to implementation." What's more, the featured examples were not "jewel boxes"—classrooms or programs that are nice to show off to visitors but that don't reach every student across a system. Instead, districts highlighted key moves to scale progress toward their vision.

It was an apt reminder that, although there are guideposts, there's no one road map to help schools reach their North Star. Rethinking your district's approach to teaching and learning involves "a number of moving parts," Valerie acknowledged, including curriculum, instruction, assessment, and ongoing professional learning. The right lever for change in your context might be project-based learning (PBL), performance assessments, career pathways, portfolio defenses, or any number of effective strategies that build students' competencies as creative problem solvers. What's important is making sure there's coherence between leadership priorities and classroom instruction, with high-quality professional learning to support teachers in adopting new strategies. Across your entire system, Valerie advised, "you want vigorous agreement about what is good practice."

In previous chapters, you have heard dozens of examples of what learning can look like when students are creative problem solvers and self-directed learners. In this chapter, we encourage you to focus on the *how*. How are school systems rethinking instruction, assessment, and professional learning so that all students in a school system can have similarly rich experiences? How is your system closing the readiness gap to better serve students who have been underserved in the past?

To jumpstart your thinking, consider holding your own showcase modeled on the EdLeader21 Portrait to Practice event. What will you hope to see as evidence of your POG coming to life? You might start by asking every principal to hold a gallery at the building level to share with faculty, parents, and other interested community members. Then promote the best-of-building examples for a district showcase to share with your school board. Reflect on the story these events tell about your school system and what you value as good practice.

In this chapter, we suggest three more leadership moves to build and sustain momentum toward your vision: design backward from your POG; set an instructional challenge; focus on assessment.

DESIGN BACKWARD FROM YOUR POG

You are no doubt familiar with backward design as a sound approach to instructional planning. "Starting with the end in mind" is the *Understanding by Design* advice from Grant Wiggins and Jay McTighe (2005) that helps teachers plan effective instruction and assessment. The same kind of thinking will help you bring your POG to life across your school system.

As Jay McTighe told us, "If the Portrait of a Graduate defines the competencies for our 21st century students, *Understanding by Design* offers the framework to help us get there by design and in a systematic way. POG is the end, and UBD is the means to make it happen."

Let's hear how backward design has shifted practice in three very different contexts.

Leaders of Lindsay Unified School District can tell you exactly when their journey of transformation began. In 2007, the 4,200-student district in California's rural Central Valley was best known for its shortcomings. "We were failing learners, failing staff. We were the laughing stock of the county," admitted Barry Sommer, the district's director of advancement. Problems ranged from active gang membership to teen pregnancies to soaring dropout rates.

Barry recalled attending a conference with a cadre of district staff, school board members, and parents, when then-Superintendent Janet Kliegl said, "Why don't we just throw this whole thing out and do something radically different?" No one yet knew what "something different" might be, but everyone around the table nodded in agreement.

Thinking back on that moment, Barry said, "I don't know if we recognized how bold that was. We all knew that we had very little to lose. What motivated us? Pain. And the leadership to say, this is wrong. This is not why we're here. Let's come back to our core purpose, which is to prepare learners for their preferred future. And that's the path we've been on in a very focused way ever since."

Extensive community conversations led to adoption of a vision of lifelong learning and a strategic blueprint to make it a reality. More than a decade later, that vision continues to drive change. Demographics remain the same. Poverty is still pervasive. Average parent education still stops at fifth grade. But the culture has been transformed to emphasize highly personalized, competency-based, technology-enabled education. Each strategy that the district has implemented—including research-based instructional look-fors, community wi-fi that reaches every home, a pipeline to grow the teaching force, and competency-based transcripts—has been an outgrowth of the original vision. The school board assesses the performance of current Superintendent Thomas Rooney "based on his ability to make it [the vision] happen," Barry said.

*

Humble ISD is a diverse district serving 42,000 students in the suburbs of Houston, Texas. Under the leadership of Superintendent Liz Fagen, teachers and instructional leaders have done deep, thoughtful work to design backward from their POG. Thought leaders such as Jay McTighe, Bena Kallick, and Heidi Hayes Jacobs have shared insights to inform their journey. One key move has been for teachers and instructional leaders to identify learning progressions that build desired student outcomes from elementary through high school.

"Once you identify those learning progressions [aligned with the POG], that's where the magic happens," said Deborah Perez, director of contemporary instructional design and professional learning for the district. "Now as a teacher, I know what skills to nurture in the classroom. It's concrete."

Teachers can also see the connection between desired student outcomes and their own professional learning. Demand has skyrocketed for institutes facilitated by a growing cohort of teacher leaders. Elizabeth King from the district's Digital Learning Team describes teacher leaders as "our boots on the ground" for professional learning. The result is widespread adoption of authentic project-based learning, digital badging around technology integration, and other strategies that bring the POG to life in classrooms.

Equity goals have been embedded in the district's POG work. Luci Schulz, assistant superintendent for elementary, was inspired by her superintendent to make sure the POG was truly serving all children, especially those farthest from opportunity. That meant taking a fresh look at resource allocation. "We looked at all the research-based risk factors—economically disadvantaged, limited English proficient, homelessness or foster care—that show children are at a disadvantage of being able to read and perform at grade level by Grade 3 or 4. Then we assigned points to every student in K–3 across the district." Additional funding, plus a co-teacher, went to classrooms with the highest risk assessment scores. "All kinds of side benefits have come from this," she added, including job-embedded professional development and onboarding of new teachers. "When I walk into a classroom, I see children who are getting the attention they crave. Their needs are being met." She credits not only her innovative school leader but also the POG process for "giving us permission to do things we had not done before. This process repurposed our *'why?'*."

"It may sound simple," said Deborah Perez, "but one of the biggest shifts for our teaching and learning team was grounding everything we're doing in the *essential why*." The district's POG—developed with input from students, teachers, parents, and other community members—provides that *why* in clear language. "With that in place, we have a staff willing to take risks and try new strategies. It's not buy-in," she added. "It's believe-in."

*

Mansfield School District in Connecticut is a small and high-performing district, serving just over a thousand students from preK–8. Here, too, backward design is helping connect student learning with the district's POG. As one strategy, Superintendent Kelly Lyman enlisted teachers, instructional leaders, and other stakeholders to unpack what the vision means for the teacher, the student, and the learning task. They discovered that a definition alone—even one that drills down into clear "look-fors" across grade levels—doesn't automatically build POG competencies like critical thinking or being a citizen of the world.

Kaye Jakan, literacy specialist for the Mansfield district, knew there was more work to do when she listened to a teacher's conversation with seventh graders. The teacher asked: *"Why do readers read? Why do they write about their reading?"* Students answered with brutal honesty: *"We do it for the teacher." "We do it for the grade." "We do it because we're supposed to."* Nothing in their responses reflected the goals of the POG or the self-direction needed to reach them.

Kaye saw an opportunity to redesign the learning experience, and she was in the right position to help. She posed a coaching question to guide her collaboration with the teacher: "If students aren't taking ownership, if you don't see evidence of that, what can we do differently?" Together, Kaye and the teacher reimagined literature instruction so that students would be squarely at the center. Bottom line: "We knew that kids needed to find a reason to read—and not because we told you to!"

To launch the new unit, they started with a compelling book about violence and trauma (specifically, the award-winning young adult novel, *Long Way Down* by Jason Reynolds). Instead of doing a traditional read-aloud and plot summary, students were challenged to consider, "Why does this matter to *you*?" They quickly found their own reasons to analyze characters and dialogue, for example, because they wanted to figure out how people use language to influence others—to be change agents in the world.

Students learned new strategies for everything from having more productive discussions with peers to journaling (using drawing as well as writing) to track their own understanding. They eventually applied their learning to produce podcasts and other products of their choosing, focusing on issues of social justice that they cared about. Reflecting on what made the experience successful, Kaye said, "Students had to own it. The goal shouldn't be, *I covered this* [as a teacher]. Instead, it should be, *What did you learn? Why does it matter to you? How do you know you learned that?*" Those questions keep the focus on student progress toward POG goals.

*

When it comes to demographics and geography, the three districts you just heard about vary dramatically when it comes to socioeconomics, size, and populations. Yet each has made significant progress by designing backward from its POG to reimagine teaching and learning strategies. Each has developed its own metrics to track progress toward redefined outcomes for student success.

Think about your own context as you reflect on the following suggested questions.

ASK YOURSELF

- *How are you encouraging your instructional staff to design backward from your POG?*
- *How are you capturing key moves that teachers and instructional leaders are making to shift their practice toward creative problem solving?*
- *What are the outcomes for students, and how do you measure and communicate them?*

SET AN INSTRUCTIONAL CHALLENGE

During the past two decades, school systems typically began their journey toward 21st century learning by embedding the 4 Cs within core content areas. That's a reasonable strategy, but the pace of school change has been slow. Breakthroughs have happened in pockets and pilots more often than across entire systems, leaving many students without the essential skills they need to thrive. It's going to take bolder leadership to transform teaching and learning to truly align with your POG goals.

In diverse contexts, leaders are now making progress toward their POGs by setting instructional challenges that catalyze significant changes in teaching and learning. These aren't scattershot strategies that reach only a few or short-term projects that risk initiative overload. Many districts launch pilots, but the real goal is to establish bold instructional challenges that set a new normal across your entire system so that every student benefits.

> Many districts launch pilots, but the real goal is to establish bold instructional challenges that set a new normal across your entire system so that every student benefits.

Mike Duncan, veteran superintendent in Pike County, Georgia, can recall the exact day he decided to upend the status quo in his district. A German exchange student was about to head home after her year in Pike County Schools when she stopped by the superintendent's office. Mike couldn't resist the opportunity to ask her, "What was the difference, from Germany to the U.S.?" She replied without hesitation: "In Germany, we are presented with content and have to use it to solve problems. In the United States, the answers are given to you—you just have to pick the right one. You never really learn."

Mike credits that conversation as a turning point for his district. Instead of continuing to focus on traditional achievement scores and graduation rates, he started asking parents, "After your kids have been with us for thirteen years, what in the world do you want them to be able to *do*?" Parents named competencies like collaboration, critical thinking, personal responsibility, and digital fluency—all aspects of creative problem solving. "This is what our community wants," the superintendent realized.

The superintendent set an instructional challenge to focus on more authentic, deeper learning that would foster those desired competencies (Hewlett Foundation, 2013; National Research Council, 2012; Newman, Carmichael, & King, 2016). He recognized that this would be "a 180-degree pivot" from test prep, and he knew that it would take time and resources to accomplish. As part of his challenge, Mike reached out to each teacher individually. He told them, "I want us to focus on the 4 Cs and deeper learning. I'm asking you to trust me. If our test scores go down, if our graduation rates plummet, I'll take full responsibility."

To support teachers in adopting new practices, the superintendent convinced his school board to reduce instructional days so that he could double the time allotted for professional learning. To make effective use of that time, the district partnered with Bruce King from the Center for Authentic Intellectual Work at the University of Wisconsin. Bruce King and his colleagues provided a research-based framework for authentic intellectual work, calling for *"construction of knowledge*, through the use of *disciplined inquiry*, to produce discourse, products, or performances that have *value beyond school"* (Newman, Carmichael, & King, 2016, p. 8). Once Pike County teachers unpacked and embraced that description, "it became our definition of rigor," the superintendent said.

The next challenge was creating authentic performance tasks in every content area that would challenge students to apply their learning. Using the collaborative structure of professional learning communities (PLCs), teachers evaluated each other's performance tasks before giving them to students. "Having an English teacher review an AP calculus task had such power," Mike said. The PLC structure transformed the teaching culture to be more collaborative and reflective (DuFour & Eaker, 1998).

As teachers continued to fine-tune instruction, they layered on practices like instructional rounds to see each other in action, using protocols to provide collegial feedback. They collaborated on unit planning that organized learning around big ideas. Gradually, teachers added human-centered design and project-based learning to their toolkit. Each new strategy related directly to the initial challenge of providing students with more authentic learning experiences. By fall 2020, teachers were ready to launch an innovative high school pathway called "Imagineology" that ties interdisciplinary learning goals to global problem solving.

Aligned with changes in instruction, Pike County educators are also developing new methods to measure and document outcomes and track student growth. The current goal is for each student to maintain a digital portfolio where they curate their best work toward mastery of POG competencies—including performance tasks tied to content standards and competencies, with capstone experiences at transitional grades.

While the sustained focus on authentic learning has shifted classroom practice across Pike County Schools, other school systems have had their own breakthroughs by focusing on practices such as mastery learning and student-led conferences. There's not one best solution to transform teaching and learning; the right challenge for your context should create a cascade of benefits across your entire system, aligning what happens in classrooms with your POG goals.

In Chapter 3, you heard how Frederick County Middle School in Virginia changed its schedule so that every student would have more time to participate in Innovation Hour. Recognizing time as the unit of change, Principal Jerry Putt works with his team to rebuild the master schedule every year. "We believe the master schedule is the foundation for instructional changes," he explained. Revisiting the schedule "forces us to reflect on what's working and where we can make improvements."

Are you choosing an instructional challenge that will create change across your school system? For example, if you are committed to students developing their capacity as creative problem solvers, can you commit to providing every student with interdisciplinary project-based learning experiences at least once in every grade level? Will you also commit to the professional learning and collaborative structures teachers need to be successful with high-quality PBL (Larmer, Mergendoller, & Boss, 2015)?

Margaret Honey, president and CEO of the New York Hall of Science, describes the leadership challenge this way: "We have treated education as a gatekeeper as opposed to a focus on engaging every kid. Whether it's in school or at a museum, how do you build or create really meaningful points of connection so kids are inspired and motivated?"

Let's consider how another school leader has tackled this challenge.

When Jason Glass was superintendent of Jeffco Public Schools in Colorado, he brought a singular focus to "the task as the unit of change." His leadership challenge was to find a strategy that would be relevant across the large district, serving 86,000 students in more than two hundred facilities. A tradition of local control meant that a wide range of instructional models was in place across the district, including STEM, PBL, Advanced Placement, International Baccalaureate, and career and technical education. They needed a unit of change that would impact all of these diverse delivery systems. The task as a unit of change fit the bill.

Matthew Flores, chief academic officer for Jeffco, explained, "When students engage with content and are challenged to create a product or artifact to apply their learning, that's what we identify as the task. Focusing on the task brings all our conversations about teaching and learning back to the student experience. What formative data does the teacher collect throughout a learning experience? How do teachers help students get to that deep level of understanding?" Improving the task improves the student learning experience.

To help teachers improve tasks, Jeffco invites teachers to participate in learning labs for collaborative professional development. "Teachers push each other with questions around their practice," Matt Flores said. For example, middle school engineering teachers have formed one learning lab. A teacher might ask the group: "How can I pair the engineering process with the science curriculum?" Others in the group offer suggestions, and then teachers take turns rotating through each other's classroom as observers and coaches. A debrief and reflection follows the observations. For participants, said Matt, "it pushes their learning, and it pushes the learning of every other teacher in the process. Teachers are driving the inquiry process." By working collaboratively to improve instruction, teachers become creative problem solvers themselves.

The district reinforces its commitment to learning labs by budgeting for release time and substitutes and documenting the professional learning that results. "From the central office perspective," Matt added, "we can see that this moves the dial." Units that are created and improved in learning labs are uploaded to the curriculum database so that others can benefit. He added, "This is the kind of professional development that transforms the task."

As you consider the right instructional challenge for your district, make sure that teachers are part of the design team. As you move forward with implementation, do so in partnership with teachers. Their buy-in is essential. In previous examples, you heard how PLCs helped to transform the teaching culture in Pike County. Learning labs have improved teacher practice in Jeffco. Both examples reflect the advice we heard from Ann Johnson, chief academic officer in Humble ISD: "Trust your teachers. They truly are the experts when it comes to learning."

In Shelby County, Kentucky, each instructional strategy that the district implements is introduced using the workshop model. "That's our delivery model. No matter what we're doing next," said Susan Dugle, "it happens within the workshop." Even new teacher induction happens within workshops. Early in the district's transformation, teachers and leaders invested time and resources to learn how to use the workshop structure effectively. Teams traveled to Colorado to take part in training with PEBC (Public Education and Business Coalition, www.pebc.org/) and eventually created their own lab classrooms back in Kentucky to demonstrate effective workshop practices. Having that structure in place has enabled the district to move forward with next steps on its POG journey, with teachers as willing and capable partners.

Whatever you decide to focus on as an instructional challenge, successful implementation will depend on your ability to manage the timing and pace of change. Several superintendents identified timing as critical to success with their bold challenges. David James in Akron tried to initiate career academies in 2011, then realized that the timing was wrong. He showed patience and perseverance by tabling the idea until 2016 when he recognized that the timing was right. Steve Holmes, superintendent of Sunnyside School District in Tucson, Arizona, made the point this way: "Leaders often don't think about, 'What are the pivotal moments to change the system?' When they don't, they will create a Profile of a Graduate without any idea of how to implement it."

Keep in mind the saying, "Go slow to go faster." Helping teachers take on this work in stages and not all at once can help them to adjust to the new system that they are creating with you. Leaders who see this as a long-term commitment and not a quick fix will fare better. As you consider an ambitious instructional challenge that will bring your POG competencies to life for students, think about the following questions.

ASK YOURSELF

- *How will you communicate a clear message about the challenge and your reason for promoting it?*
- *How will you give your teachers the green light to co-design and implement the challenge?*
- *How will you manage the pace of change?*

FOCUS ON ASSESSMENT

It's hard to imagine a school system making progress toward its POG without tackling the big topic of assessment. "No matter where you sit in the system, you've got skin in that game," said Valerie Greenhill, vice president of Battelle for Kids. "Assessment is consequential for everyone."

That includes students themselves. Ironically, students are too often left out of the conversation when schools start to rethink assessment. Throughout this book, we have highlighted examples of student work to show how education is changing. You have heard students reflecting on their growth as 21st century learners. For transformation to truly take hold, these can't be isolated experiences of creative problem solving. They need to be core to teaching and learning across grade levels and content areas. When aligned with instruction that emphasizes student-centered learning, assessment becomes an integral part of the solution, not a barrier to innovative practices.

Ron Berger, senior advisor for teaching and learning of EL Education, describes the power of student-engaged assessment this way: "It changes the primary role of assessment from evaluating and ranking students to motivating them to learn. It builds the independence, critical thinking skills, perseverance, and self-reflective understanding students need for college and careers" (Berger, Rugen, & Woodfin, 2014, p. 5).

Stillwater Area Public Schools in Minnesota offers a good example. Early in its POG journey, the district reached out to students to help define a new vision for teaching and learning. Students were recruited to serve alongside adults on district committees and learned to use design thinking protocols for creative problem solving. A key priority that emerged was to focus less on content-heavy Advanced Placement courses and more on learning experiences that would develop skills such as financial literacy and collaboration, as well as career pathways.

To bring this vision to life, tests that emphasized content recall had to be replaced with more appropriate assessment strategies. Rachel Larson, director of learning and student engagement, heard a clear theme in students' comments: "Students told us that grades are important, but they don't find a lot of meaning in the work they're doing. They wanted different opportunities to demonstrate their learning and show their growth."

To convince teachers that traditional assessment practices needed a makeover, students volunteered to be part of a provocative event. In front of the entire high school faculty, students stood ready to respond to questions about instruction and assessment. Each time a question was asked, students held up cards that read either, "Works for me," "Doesn't work for me," or "Neutral."

"The overwhelming message was that we're not meeting the mark [with assessment]," Rachel said. "What students told us they want most is feedback." The experience "transformed our staff," she added, and led to productive conversations about better ways to engage students in assessment.

To help students become "leaders of their own learning," as Ron Berger advocates, school systems can leverage a number of entry points and practices—from how teachers check for understanding in daily lessons to how students experience rites of passage at important milestones. Let's take a closer look at approaches in school systems that are putting their POG into practice. Here are three strategies that school leaders recommend to elevate student voice in assessment practices. Each one requires collaboration with your teachers as co-designers and professional learning to help them succeed with new practices.

1. **Plan projects and performance-based assessments that incorporate POG goals.**

Earlier, you heard Mike Duncan from Pike County, Georgia, describe how his teachers worked together to design authentic tasks and performance-based assessments across content areas. This was an essential step in the shift to more authentic learning for students and an invaluable professional-learning experience for teachers.

"Good assessments can be powerful drivers of instruction," agrees Bruce King from University of Wisconsin-Madison. Well-designed assessments make clear what students need to know or be able to do by the end of a learning experience. That clarity enables teachers to plan backward to help students reach those goals through project-based learning and other instructional strategies that amplify student voice and choice.

Although many teachers are familiar with backward design to address content goals, they may need to unpack the POG competencies, come to an agreement about what "success" looks like at different grade levels, and plan learning experiences that integrate POGs with academics. As a leader, it requires a commitment to providing the necessary time and resources for those conversations to happen.

When teachers have the necessary support to develop performance assessments aligned to POG goals, students experience expanded opportunities to demonstrate deeper learning competencies—including improved communication and presentation skills; greater confidence in college and career preparation; and growth in social-emotional skills (Maier et al., 2020).

Justin Wells, executive director of Envision Learning Partners, works with districts across the country that are redesigning assessment systems to better align with their POG. He cautions schools against moving too fast on assessment without first ensuring that students are getting frequent opportunities to practice and improve on desired skills. Student work should be "the constant barometer for how we're doing and where we need to go next," he said. In a blog post about fulfilling the promise of POGs, he advised: "Answer the practice question, and the measurement answer comes easily. It's not so easy the other way around" (Wells, 2020).

2.   **Map sets of assessments across grades and collect evidence of students' growth in the POG competencies over time.**

Assessment expert Jay McTighe recommends "mapping" sets of authentic assessments across grades and subject areas. This becomes your road map to building the POG competencies over time. Bring more student voice into assessment by having students themselves curate evidence of their growth as learners (McTighe, Doubet, & Carbauch, 2020; McTighe & Silver, 2020).

In previous chapters, we have suggested using portfolios to gather evidence of students' creative problem-solving efforts. Portfolio defenses build on this idea and have the potential to be the cornerstone of high-quality assessment systems. To create portfolios, students must curate and reflect on evidence of their learning over time. They share that evidence with panelists (including teachers, parents, and other community members) who evaluate their readiness to move on to the next stage of their education.

The practice not only amplifies student voice in assessment but also provides motivation to improve instruction. Adopting portfolio defenses for assessment "makes it incumbent on a learning organization to give kids rich experiences so they have something worthy of reflection. Four years of worksheets and multiple-choice tests will not produce meaningful portfolio defenses," said Justin Wells.

His own classroom experience shows how the goal of engaging students in portfolio defenses raises expectations for teachers. Justin started his career teaching English in what was then a brand-new high school in the Envision Schools network in California. The model, as designed by co-founder Bob Lenz, included instructional practices such as interdisciplinary project-based learning, arts integration, and advisories to foster strong teacher–student relationships.

By the time the first class reached their senior year, students were expected to present portfolios as evidence of their learning. This was always part of the master plan, "but it was an abstraction to me for four years," Justin said. "We didn't have any seniors yet!" When that first class of seniors reached their final semester, it was showtime. As students prepared for the experience, it turns out they had plenty of compelling evidence to discuss as a result of four years of challenging project experiences.

"That first set of defenses was so powerful," Justin reflected, "I've devoted my career to spreading the practice." That has included working with researchers at the Stanford Center for Assessment, Learning, and Equity (SCALE) to make the portfolio defense process more rigorous and replicable. In his current role at Envision Learning Partners, Justin helps district partners move forward with their own versions of portfolio defense.

Districts that are making progress with this practice describe key strategies, including the following:

- **Allow time for design and improvement:** Schools need to invest adequate time to prepare for their first student defenses and then to continue improving the practice based on lessons learned.
- **Help students learn from failure:** More than 90 percent of students will likely pass their portfolio defense by the end of high school but not all on their first try. "Students who have to resubmit—after getting feedback— are the lucky ones," Justin Wells suggests. "They go on to college with a powerful experience of what it means to fail and then succeed. This is about preparing them to do something very challenging and ultimately to succeed." Plan for how you will help students recover from failure and use feedback to improve.
- **Align portfolio defense with your theory of action:** Portfolio defense is not a stand-alone practice. Instead, it should fit coherently within your overall framework for teaching and learning. If you apply backward planning to portfolio defense, you will see the need for classroom and community experiences that generate evidence of deep learning. Helping your students prepare for portfolio defense means encouraging them to reflect on their learning and hone their presentation skills. That may mean introducing student-led conferences or project exhibitions in earlier grades. Gibson Ek High School in Issaquah, Washington, part of the Big Picture network, emphasizes internships, project-based learning, and exhibitions where

students present evidence of learning. Over four years, those experiences enable students to build a rich portfolio using the Mastery Transcript (which you will hear about more at the end of this chapter).

- **Make it your own:** Each school system that adopts portfolio defense as part of its assessment system has to customize the experience to reflect local context, including POG goals. Some schools that emphasize college and career readiness, such as the Linked Learning network (www.linkedlearning.org), have adopted portfolio defenses because the assessment practice aligns with their career pathways approach.

With any approach to student-engaged assessment, Justin Wells advises, "the goal needs to be kids using the terms of the graduate profile in their own unscripted language to talk about their growth."

3.   **Engage students in assessment**

When students are directing more of their own learning, they set goals, seek feedback, make adjustments, and reflect on their growth. The right kind of assessment supports their journey, putting students on what assessment expert Rick Stiggins has described as "winning streaks" (2007).

As a leader, create opportunities for teachers to get comfortable with assessment practices that engage students. You might encourage learning walks, for example, so that teachers can watch as a colleague guides students in co-creating a rubric for an upcoming project or observe a peer feedback protocol in action.

In the San Francisco Unified School District, the lesson study approach provides a more formal framework for teachers to think deeply—and collaboratively—about assessment. One cohort of teachers, for example, focuses on project-based learning. Nora Houseman and Nolberto Camarena, with the district's professional learning and leadership team, support the PBL Teacher Leader Fellowship. "Teachers apply, and then recruit and lead a lesson study team. They choose their focus question," Nora explained. Facilitators model effective practice by providing guiding documents and modeling the use of tools like critical friends protocols for peer feedback. "We're trying to create the same thing we want to see in the classroom," Nolberto said. "Then we build in time for teachers to think: How might you modify what we've done here in your own context? When wouldn't this work? Why?"

As you lead your staff in the direction of more student-engaged assessment, showcase positive results. Remember the insight you heard from Principal David Johnson in Chapter 4. He encouraged his middle school faculty to attend an exhibition at the end of a capstone project. He asked them, "Isn't this what education is all about?" The event generated staff buy-in by putting student learning on display.

COMPETENCY-BASED LEARNING

Some school leaders are taking a more systemwide approach to student-engaged assessment. Competency-based learning (also known as mastery learning) is one example.

When school leader and author Brian Stack explains why assessment needs to be redesigned, he often uses the analogy of a driver's license. Learning to drive involves not just knowing the rules of the road but, more importantly, mastering a number of practical skills. A multiple-choice test alone won't show if you can safely navigate highway traffic or park a car. That requires behind-the-wheel demonstration of proficiency measured against defined standards of success. New drivers develop those skills with practice and feedback, moving toward that driver's license at the speed of their own learning.

In more than a decade as principal of Sanborn Regional High School in New Hampshire, Brian has been guiding his community in the direction of mastery rather than memorization as the goal of education. He also consults with other districts that are making a similar transformation.

The work can be transformative, indeed, based on what we have heard from several districts that are on the path to mastery. Lindsay Unified, which you read about earlier in this chapter, has developed its own, highly personalized approach as a cornerstone of its ambitious reform effort. Learners set individual goals and use a digital dashboard to track their progress against performance assessments. Teachers (called facilitators across the district) create playlists of learning activities to support each student's success. To graduate from high school, learners must achieve at least a 3.0 (on a 4-point scale) on each major competency; they have multiple opportunities to succeed.

Unlike Lindsay, Farmington Public Schools in Connecticut was already a high-performing district when it began to rethink its approach to instruction and assessment. The catalyst for change was adoption of its POG, highlighting new indicators of student success that are not well-served by traditional teaching and assessment methods. Motivated by their shared reading of Ron Berger's *Leaders of Their Own Learning*, district leaders began to consider strategies for more student-engaged assessment. They learned from other districts that were doing similar work. Their progress over a decade has meant rethinking everything from lesson planning to rubrics to report cards to parent engagement. To shift from traditional academics to mastery learning aligned to the POG, "everything has to change," said Veronica Ruzek, director of curriculum and instruction.

What have school systems learned along the way to mastery? Let's consider some key takeaways.

Partner With Teachers

When Brian Stack, a former math teacher, became principal in 2010, he was already convinced that assessment practices needed to change. "The way we were instructing and assessing and reporting progress on learning for kids was haphazard at best. There was not a lot of calibration from teacher to teacher or grade level to grade level. I had no confidence that an A in science class in Grade 9 would have the same meaning as an A in Grade 12 English."

Rather than demanding top-down change, he engaged teachers in conversation about how to define more consistent learning goals and support students in reaching them. "We're all here to help kids. Let's talk about what learning looks like and what mastery looks like for the different skills we have deemed important. That gave us purpose as educators," he said. "Once you have a better understanding of what you want students to learn and how you're going to assess them, now you get into bigger discussions. How will you support each student? How will you change the instructional model to meet kids' needs?"

The adoption of PLCs proved to be a key factor in the school's progress, as teachers worked together to design performance tasks that were assessed against rubrics. "We had a collaborative model where teachers had an investment in what was happening and an opportunity to hold each other accountable. If you're not inviting teachers to the table to be part of the work," the principal added, "it won't be successful."

Control the Pace of Change

Moving toward mastery takes time; there are no shortcuts. In Farmington, Connecticut, early wins happened in the elementary grades. As young learners learned to assess their own growth against learning targets, parents could appreciate the benefits. "When you hear kids talk about themselves as learners, they're impressive. Parents are thrilled," said Assistant Superintendent Kim Wynne. Parents of high schoolers, however, may push back if traditional grading practices get a sudden makeover. "You have to make this transformation understandable to parents," she added, "and you can't start with high school juniors or seniors. Kids need time to grow up with it."

At Sanborn Regional High School, Brian Stack and team were strategic about introducing competency-based learning in the self-contained ninth-grade academy. As students moved into upper grades, new assessment practices moved with them. "We were careful to phase things in and never change too much in any one year," he added.

Mastery Transcript

The Mastery Transcript is another vehicle for change. Unlike traditional transcripts, which show credits and grades earned, this is a digital portfolio that conveys a more holistic view of a student's strengths, accomplishments, and reflections. It is being used across the United States and internationally by both independent and public schools.

Hadley Lewis, who graduated from the Forest School in Georgia in 2020, was among the first students in the country to apply to college using the reimagined transcript. She appreciated being able to share reflections about what she learned through apprenticeships and service learning, along with her growth as a leader. Through this new version of a transcript, she said, "colleges see what I bring—my optimism, how I give back, all of me. It's not just numbers." She applied to five colleges and was accepted by all of them.

You have heard a number of strategies that school systems are using to rethink traditional assessment to align with redefined goals for student success. Reflect on how these questions apply to your context.

ASK YOURSELF

- *To what extent are students currently engaged in the assessment process? How could you find out which assessment practices are most valuable for them as 21st century learners and effective problem solvers?*

- *Are you (the system and teachers) currently assessing everything that you value (including POG competencies) or only those things that are easiest to test and grade?*

- *How will you help parents understand why assessment needs to change and how they can support their children with new assessment practices?*

If there is a silver lining to COVID-19 and the world of education, it's been the opportunity to imagine a new normal for teaching and learning. Even school systems that have been resistant to change have had to pivot overnight because of this unforeseen challenge. Online learning has forced conversations about how to engage students, how to support them in managing their time, and how to help them assess their growth as learners.

During conference calls with other school leaders who were wrestling with the pandemic, Brian Stack was struck by what he heard: "Schools in a more traditional model were struggling with teaching and learning in ways that competency-based schools were not. We had already calibrated what success looks like. Our teachers had worked together to create performance tasks. Our students knew exactly where they were and where they needed to go next."

Post-pandemic education "won't be traditional school," he predicted. "It's going to be more competency based, more student centered, more flexible. All the best ideas about teaching and learning," he added, "will help us create a new normal."

Final Reflections

The power of the POG depends on your ability to bring it to life in as many aspects of your district operation as possible. In Part I, we showed how your POG work affects human resources, hiring, evaluation, orientation, strategic planning, and budgeting. In this chapter, we have connected your POG work to curriculum and instruction, assessment, and professional learning. Imagine how far you will have come if your POG is embedded across all these parts of your system.

Let's close this chapter with these final questions for reflection:

- How will you operationalize the POG across your entire school system?

- As you work with your instructional team to bring your POG to life, how will you make sure that teachers know they have the green light to try new strategies and learn from setbacks?
- How will you draw on your own experiences as an educator and lifelong learner to guide the work?
- How will you help all students become more active participants in their own education, including assessment practices?
- How will you capture and share stories of diverse students making progress toward POG goals?

RESOURCES FOR IMPLEMENTATION

Cultures of Thinking, from Project Zero at Harvard Graduate School of Education, aims to improve learning and collaboration with the use of structured protocols and routines. www.pz.harvard.edu/projects/cultures-of-thinking

Edutopia, published by the George Lucas Educational Foundation, produces videos, practitioner stories, and research about school transformation, documenting the benefits of project-based learning, social and emotional learning, and comprehensive assessment. edutopia.org

Getting Smart showcases innovations in education and curates resources on emerging topics about teaching and learning. gettingsmart.com

Learner Variability Navigator from Digital Promise is an online platform to support the development of instruction and technology tools that meet the needs of individual learners. lvp.digitalpromiseglobal.org

Jay McTighe, co-author of *Understanding by Design*, shares a wealth of free resources for curriculum design, assessment, and technology integration. jaymctighe.com/resources

For Your Bookshelf

Authentic Intellectual Work by Fred M. Newmann, Dana L. Carmichael, and M. Bruce King.

Breaking with Tradition: The Shift to Competency-Based Learning in PLCs at Work by Brian M. Stack and Jonathan G. Vander Els.

Creating Cultures of Thinking: 8 Forces We Must Master to Truly Transform Our Schools by Ron Ritchhart.

Leaders of Their Own Learning: Transforming Schools Through Student-Engaged Assessment by Ron Berger, Leah Rugen, and Libby Woodfin.

(Continued)

(Continued)

Leader's Guide to 21st Century Skills: 7 Steps for Schools and Districts by Ken Kay and Valerie Greenhill.

Project Based Teaching: How to Create Rigorous and Engaging Learning Experiences by Suzie Boss with John Larmer.

Resolved: Debate Can Revolutionize Education and Help Save Our Democracy by Robert E. Litan.

Teaching for Deeper Learning: Tools to Engage Students in Meaning Making by Jay McTighe and Harvey F. Silver.

Action Steps

Bringing your POG to life for students will require you and your team to make decisions about instruction and assessment, taking into consideration both timing and capacity. Leverage the advice in this chapter to help you plan next steps.

1. **Design backward—and consistently—from your POG.** As you move from vision to implementation, you will be required to make crisp decisions about initiatives, programs, and requests that are inconsistent with the POG goals and implementation. Be transparent and consistent in your decision making. Be willing to say "no" when needed so that your system stays focused on your POG goals.

2. **Maintain your focus on equity**. Make sure that new initiatives help to close the readiness gap so that all students are prepared to tackle future challenges. When you find evidence of success, spotlight the strategies that are leading to transformation, especially for diverse learners.

3. **Create a bold instructional challenge.** Focus on an instructional challenge that's bold enough to create a cascade of benefits across your system, such as portfolio defenses, competency-based learning, or widespread implementation of project-based learning. Manage the pace and timing of instructional challenges, and invest resources in professional development needed to achieve desired results.

4. **Be bold when it comes to assessment.** As you redefine student success, you will need to look beyond standardized assessments to measure the outcomes that your community values. Work with your instructional team to develop assessments that align with changes in pedagogy. Look for opportunities to amplify student engagement in the assessment process.

One of your most important jobs as a leader is to help your team feel safe as you work together on change. This work is not for the faint of heart, and it takes courage to persevere—both your own personal courage and that of each team member. As you tackle the challenges we have discussed in this chapter, rely on your team-building abilities. Collaboration will be a cornerstone of the new normal you are creating. Partnering with teachers is essential but not enough. You will also need to reach beyond school to build partnerships with your wider community. That's the focus of the next chapter.

CHAPTER 7

Be the Leader of Strong Partnerships

CHAPTER HIGHLIGHTS

All the stakeholders who have been instrumental in shaping your community's vision of education have a continuing role to play as you bring your Portrait of a Graduate (POG) to life. Apply your networking skills to expand the conversation and enlist more allies to support student success, especially for students who have been underserved in the past. Help potential partners think more creatively about the roles they can play, including identifying problems that students can help to solve. Communicate concrete progress toward shared goals. Engagement with partners is not just an important catalyst for change; it's an essential component of how you will grow and sustain transformation.

Who do you turn to first to help you realize the vision of your POG?

No doubt, teachers and instructional leaders are at the top of your partnership list. Examples in previous chapters have highlighted how school leaders are collaborating with staff members in creative ways to improve instruction and assessment. We have shared examples of progress achieved with the involvement of professional learning communities (PLCs), teacher leaders, instructional coaches, and professional development by teachers for teachers. When teachers are your partners in change efforts, you show that you value their wisdom. By working together, you build a collaborative culture that ultimately leads to better results for students.

Students themselves are another key constituency. Throughout the book, we have highlighted examples of students taking ownership of their learning and contributing to their schools and communities in the process. When students are trusted partners in school change, they have a greater role in decision making. They have a voice in setting their own learning goals and assessing growth. They identify and solve worthy problems, leveraging these experiences to build knowledge and develop competencies. (See Appendix B for student resources.)

Without the strong engagement of both students and teachers, your POG is unlikely to come to life in the classroom. But it will take more than these important stakeholders to grow and sustain change. In this chapter, we focus on three additional partnership strategies to help you achieve your vision: partner with families; enlist business and community allies; leverage networks. Each strategy depends on your ability to form strong relationships and be an effective communicator and storyteller.

PARTNER WITH FAMILIES

Although decades of research underscore the importance of family engagement for student success, the pandemic has put a spotlight on the essential role of parents as school partners. During the shift to remote learning, many parents found themselves in unfamiliar roles as tech troubleshooters, time managers, and content experts. Memes about teacher appreciation went viral as families got a first-hand look at the challenges of 21st century education, including tending to students' social and emotional wellness along with their academic growth. Some families with financial resources hired tutors or formed small learning "pods." As learning from home stretched from weeks to months, more inequities became apparent—from uneven technology access to economic hardship to inadequate access to medical care in communities of color.

In school systems that had made progress on change efforts before the pandemic hit, a more hopeful story emerged. In Lindsay, California, discussed in the previous chapter, high school senior Alexis Leon said she and her younger sister "kept moving at our own pace during the shutdown." The district's personalized, competency-based system "lets me take learning into my own hands." The girls' mother could monitor their progress on the digital learning platform. "They can tell me which learning target they are working on and how they plan to meet it. They're motivated to set their own goals. They know right where they're at—and so do I," said Lorena Leon.

In Pike County, Georgia, Superintendent Mike Duncan used the early days of the pandemic as an opportunity for parent education. "Let's have parents experience the authentic learning their children are engaged with every day," he told site leaders. Principals and assistant principals designed performance tasks for parents and their children to tackle together, aligned to POG goals around collaboration, creativity, communication, critical thinking, and responsibility. Parent feedback was overwhelmingly positive, showing a new depth of understanding of the district vision.

To help parents get more comfortable with digital tools used for online learning, Encinitas Union School District in California enlisted students to create video tutorials, which were posted on the district website. It was a practical strategy that also reflected the district's emphasis on students as problem solvers.

Beyond the pandemic, how else are school systems engaging families as partners in school transformation? Two strategies stand out in our interviews with school leaders. (See Appendix C for parent resources.)

Continue to Reinforce Your "Why" Ideally, you engaged parents in community conversations that led to the creation of your POG. Keep parents connected to this "why" as you continue to work together toward shared goals, and be creative about engaging a wide swath of parents—not just the same small (and sometimes vocal) group that reliably shows up.

When Eric Eshbach was superintendent of Northern York County School District in Pennsylvania, he used a technology tool called ThoughtExchange (thoughtexchange.com) to generate conversation among parents to inform development of the district's Portrait of a Graduate. More robust than a simple survey tool, the platform enabled parents to dialogue with each other and with the school leader about the knowledge, skills, and dispositions they wanted to see in their children. A diverse group of students, teachers, businesses, and parents then met in person to analyze the data, find patterns, and identify key concepts. "We could start to visualize from those comments what's important to our community," Eshbach said. Once the POG was created, parents "could see how their input had shaped the profile," creating more buy-in for the next steps to transform teaching and learning.

In Farmington, Connecticut, parents were quick to endorse POG goals "as the promise we are making," said Kim Wynne, assistant superintendent. "It was all great on paper." When it came to changing sacred cows like grading as part of a shift to mastery learning, however, it was a different story. She recalled one particularly tense board meeting when dozens of angry parents arrived to complain about new high school homework policies that they didn't understand.

Rather than giving up on mastery learning as an instructional challenge for the district (discussed in Chapter 6), the Farmington team doubled down on parent engagement. At parent forums, they offered analogies to help parents understand the value of assessing mastery instead of rewarding effort or compliance. For example: "Which pilot do you want flying your plane: the one who passed because of extra credit? Or the one who passed a mastery-based assessment based on demonstrated proficiency?" Veronica Ruzek, director of curriculum and instruction, used a medical analogy to help parents understand the importance of assessing and reporting on growth toward competencies. "If the doctor tells you that your checkup is a C+, what do you do with that information? Isn't it better to get more specific information so that you know what to pay attention to?"

One of their best strategies to reinforce the "why" was to turn the microphone over to students. "When students understand and exemplify what we want them to know and do," Veronica Ruzek said, "parents are amazed. Then their anxiety lowers."

To help parents understand changing assessment practices, Jeffco Public Schools in Colorado has held community events to help parents understand changes in instruction and assessment practices. The result is better appreciation for standards-based grading and the role of rubrics in supporting student growth as learners. "Our community is eager to have those conversations and be more informed," said Matt Flores, chief academic officer.

Jeff Spencer, principal of Southport Elementary in Indianapolis, Indiana, uses a variety of communication strategies to keep his diverse parent community connected to the "why." Many families at the Title I school are immigrants who are accustomed to more traditional, teacher-driven instruction. During his first year at the school, he used a weekly newsletter to educate families about the need for more student-centered learning as preparation for the 21st century workplace. Two years later, he and his staff had built a foundation to move forward with project-based learning (PBL) as a schoolwide instructional challenge. Spencer helped each teacher develop an elevator speech to explain PBL to parents. Teachers also created materials about helping your child succeed in a PBL environment; materials were translated into the three major languages spoken by families. At frequent events to showcase student learning, Jeff added, "we do a lot of intentional talk with our families about what we're doing and why."

Creating new metrics to measure your redefined goals is essential to tracking your progress. Just as important is communicating progress to your stakeholders.

Bellingham School District in Washington has created a collective commitment to the community's children called the Bellingham Promise. Equity is at the heart of the Promise, which Superintendent Greg Baker considers to be a moral imperative. The district uses data to analyze past inequities, inform programming, and keep the community informed of progress. For example, a hard look at early childhood programs revealed that access to full-day kindergarten was an equity issue, favoring families with financial resources to pay for extended learning time. That drove the decision to provide full-day kindergarten for all students. Another initiative, Project Free Education, ended the practice of charging families for extracurriculars or asking them to pay for their children's school supplies. Why? Data analysis showed that out-of-pocket expenses were not only unequal from one school to the next, but highest in the highest-poverty schools. By eliminating out-of-pockets costs, the district has saved families an estimated $1 million—a measurable outcome that's shared in district communications (Our Kids, Our Future, 2019). Regular progress reports keep community members updated about students' growth in academics, social and emotional learning, and indicators such as whether students are able to persevere through failure.

Invite Parents to Take on New Roles When you set an instructional challenge to move toward POG goals, think about the role parents can play to support student success. If your schools are implementing project-based learning, for example, students and teachers will likely need access to content experts. Parents in careers related to student projects can share their insights about specialized topics and offer helpful, informed feedback on student work. Just as importantly, parents may be able to provide firsthand insight into the challenges that students are investigating—such as managing household budgets, reducing their family's carbon footprint, or finding a path to citizenship. Recruiting family members for these roles not only supports student learning but gives parents a window into how and why instruction is changing.

If student-engaged assessment is part of your plan, get parents ready for their role in student-led conferences, project exhibitions, or portfolio defenses. These experiences will likely be unfamiliar at first for many families. Prepare them to be active listeners and good questioners by sharing videos of previous events, having veteran parents describe their experiences, and providing them with sample questions. "Student-led conferences run into trouble when adults take over or dominate during the conference," caution the authors of *Leaders of Their Own Learning* (Berger, Rugen, & Woodfin, 2014, p. 208). Logistics matter, too. Schedule events so that all families can participate, and provide translation if needed.

As you think about your strategies for enlisting parents and extended family members as partners, consider the following.

ASK YOURSELF

- *How effective are your communication strategies for reaching all families across your school system? How can you connect with families you are not yet reaching?*
- *How do you document and celebrate students' growth and share stories that demonstrate their progress toward POG goals?*

ENLIST BUSINESS AND COMMUNITY ALLIES

In previous chapters, you have heard many stories of students tackling real-world problems in their communities. If learning beyond the classroom is going to be the norm in your school system and if you are going to overcome inevitable challenges, you will need to engage diverse community members as ready and willing partners.

When Talisa Dixon became superintendent of Columbus City Schools in Ohio, she knew that the challenges ahead were too big to tackle alone. The district was facing its second "F" grade from the state. "I had a sense of urgency about how I had to change the narrative," she said, "and I wanted all the business and nonprofit leaders—the benefactors—at the table. I wanted us to work together in a way we had not worked before."

The results were eye-opening. "There were people at the table who had not had conversations together about the district's overall mission or about the collective impact of all of us working together." Stakeholders were just starting to come to a consensus about aspirations for students when the difficult summer of 2020 arrived. "That made us reflect even more deeply on the importance of the competencies we were considering," the superintendent said. "Would the POG we were contemplating give students the tools they needed to deal with the most complex and challenging of crises, like the civil unrest in Columbus that followed in the wake of the murder of George Floyd?" That became the lens for evaluating their proposed POG.

Since that summer, the district has adopted the POG and is now working on a POG diploma. Talisa sees the diploma as a tangible outcome of the collaboration. "It will show the progress students have made that we can report to our partners and to the community."

School leaders emphasize the following strategies as essential for building strong partnerships.

Help Partners See Students as Problem Solvers When the community is the curriculum, students learn by tackling challenges close to home. Parents and businesses are in a great position to help you identify community challenges for students to tackle. Help community partners recognize that their support of these experiences can advance their own agendas while building students' problem-solving skills.

> When the community is the curriculum, students learn by tackling challenges close to home. Parents and businesses are in a great position to help you identify community challenges for students to tackle.

Iowa BIG, a project-based high school in Cedar Rapids that serves students from three public districts, uses community-based problem solving as its core instructional strategy. To move forward, a project must have both student interest and a committed partner. As the school explains to interested partners, "This goes beyond having an evening where students show off their work or having a professional Skype in for a class period. Our partners fully integrate with our students as they work on authentic, contextually rich projects" (Iowa BIG, n.d.).

Benefits extend in both directions, as a corporate executive from a communications company explained about a project to provide free wi-fi to families unable to afford it (Kazimour, 2019): "As a company, this project wasn't mission critical and wasn't moving forward. We thought bringing in actual students' perspectives would benefit us and add a spin to our project. They helped us figure out what those families need and what would be best for the students. Their input and ideas were extremely valuable and real to us."

In the Encinitas district, community partners have become accustomed to elementary students tackling projects alongside them. Fourth graders spent an entire school year as sustainability consultants for the local YMCA. Teacher Alice Larsen knew her students would be up to the challenge. "By this age, they're more aware, more vocal, and they deeply care about things. They authentically gravitate toward solving real-world problems," she said. From past experience, she knew how to align the project to important learning goals. She also knew she could count on community allies to support student efforts. YMCA staff welcomed students on repeat visits to conduct surveys, gather data, and educate adults. After students presented their final recommendations to the board, the organization moved forward on implementation and put up signs to recognize student-led improvements around the building.

In Granville Exempted Village Schools in Ohio, a 98-acre biodiversity project called the Land Lab has resulted from a combination of student initiative and community partnerships. In 2012, students in an Advanced Placement Environmental Science class had the idea to create a living laboratory for scientific research and community enhancement. Students recruited a biologist from the U.S. Fish and Wildlife Service to help them restore five acres of wetland near Granville Middle School. "Five acres turned into forty-three, and today it's almost at 100," said a student who helped launch the project. "While the initial project was ambitious, what it has become is incredible," added another student.

Partnerships with a wide range of stakeholders have been key to the success of the Land Lab. Experts in native prairies, agroforestry, vernal pools, waterfowl, bees, and other specialties have mentored students on ambitious research projects. Individuals and service groups from the community have donated labor and resources to help students add features such as a weather station, hiking trails, and an observation deck. The project is a tangible reminder of what students and communities can accomplish by working together, as one student explained: "As each group of students adds their mark to the Land Lab, they own the project and continue to leave their legacy on Granville. It is and will always be a reminder that they can change the world."

Jeff Spencer, the Indiana principal mentioned earlier, relies on partners themselves to help recruit others in the community. For one recruiting event, he invited the owner of a local art gallery to speak. The gallery employs adults with developmental disabilities, many of whom create original artwork. To raise awareness of this community asset, third graders interviewed gallery staff and made their own artwork to contribute. "When the gallery owner shared this story [with potential partners], who could say no?" the principal said. He had a recruiting brochure ready, outlining specific ways that partners could work with students on upcoming projects.

Create Menus of Engagement Potential partners are likely to have varying comfort levels when it comes to working directly with students. Make it easier for partners to engage by creating multiple opportunities and providing resources or training they need to be effective.

In Anaheim Union High School District, students participate in a range of experiences that relate to career exploration and workplace readiness, from one-time field trips to extended internships to career pathways. These require active participation from business, nonprofit, and civic organizations across the community.

Scott Reindl, program administrator for career education, uses a variety of strategies to make it easy for partners to engage. Partners can choose from a menu of options, ranging from career days for middle school students to mentorships that help high school students prepare for college and careers. The district takes care of logistics, such as transportation. "Partners just need to provide their talent," he added.

Partnerships with the business community and the City of Anaheim are part of a larger initiative called the Anaheim Educational Pledge. The pledge formalizes the efforts of local school districts and two- and four-year colleges and universities to prepare all students for college, careers, and engaged citizenship. Instead of leaving collaboration to chance, the pledge formalizes partner commitments around the shared goal of redefining student success.

Connect to Workforce Development Help potential partners see how engaging with students supports workforce development. For school leaders, this means building strong relationships with local employers and staying alert for changing industry trends.

Val Verde Public Schools in California uses career pathways as a strategy to reach its POG goals. In defining the focus areas of more than forty pathways at different high schools, "we want to be sure we are connecting to what our community needs," said Aimee Garcia, director of education services, "and what our kids will experience once they leave us." That requires ongoing dialogue with the business community. Doug Henderson, director of STEAM and career and technical education (CTE) for the district, has seen attitudes change with the expansion of career pathways into high-demand fields like advanced manufacturing, engineering, video production, and medicine. "It used to be, you were either a college kid or a CTE kid. But every kid needs a career," he emphasized. The new goal is for every student to take part in a pathway.

To initiate ambitious programs like this, says Val Verde Superintendent Mike McCormick, "you have to come up with a way to unify your community—teachers, administrators, students, board, and business. You need to do that around what is good for kids. The POG is a great mechanism to make this happen. This will help you lead your community in a straightforward manner and create the mental model community members need to make sense of all the moving parts of education."

Workforce development is happening globally, as well. For example, Singapore American School connects high school juniors and seniors with industry partners through an elective program called Quest. Students work with professionals on research projects that relate to their interests and career aspirations.

Streamline Connections For many teachers, the biggest barrier to making learning more authentic is figuring out how to find willing partners and experts beyond the campus. "Educators aren't necessarily taught networking skills," acknowledged Jeff Spencer. As a principal, he streamlines the process by bringing potential partners into the school and teaching students how to be greeters and guides. He even coaches students on how to make small talk to put adult visitors at ease.

Encinitas Unified Schools maintains a "human digital library" to smooth the matchmaking process. Glen Warren, director of literacies, outreach, and libraries, maintains the database to support students on their path of self-directed learning or what he prefers to call "the world of wonder. Libraries aren't about just choosing a book to read. They should help you go after the things you want to learn. Who are the experts who know the subject you want to learn about?"

Glen has curated the digital library with local contacts, including family volunteers and staff within the school system who are potential partners for students' investigations. After the director of nutrition collaborated with students, for example, her name was added to the database. Students themselves are added once they become experts in a topic as a result of their learning. The result is a hyper-local platform for connecting industry professionals with teachers and students.

Think about how community partnerships can help you achieve your POG goals by asking the following questions.

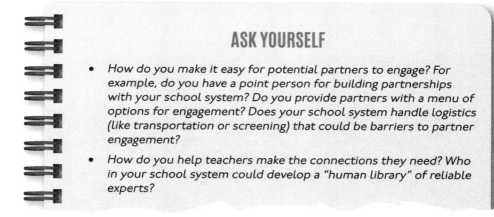

ASK YOURSELF

- *How do you make it easy for potential partners to engage? For example, do you have a point person for building partnerships with your school system? Do you provide partners with a menu of options for engagement? Does your school system handle logistics (like transportation or screening) that could be barriers to partner engagement?*

- *How do you help teachers make the connections they need? Who in your school system could develop a "human library" of reliable experts?*

LEVERAGE NETWORKS

Many of the school systems described in previous chapters have looked beyond their own communities to learn about strategies that will help them achieve their goals. David James, Akron Superintendent, took business and community leaders from Ohio on a field trip to Nashville to garner enthusiasm for career academies. A leadership team from Stillwater Schools in Minnesota spent time at the Stanford d.school to build their understanding of design thinking, which has become embedded in the district culture. When Shelby County Public Schools in Kentucky was preparing to adopt mastery learning, the district sent teams to other communities that had already moved in this direction.

"We learned early on [in our transformation] that we need to reach out to different people along the way," said Susan Dugle, chief academic officer for Shelby County. "We'll get to a certain spot and ask ourselves, who's the partner to move us forward in that learning? Then we take the learning we gain from external partners and make it our own."

Both formally and informally, savvy school leaders leverage networks to accelerate change. "Being part of a community of practice exposes you to so many more examples," said Valerie Greenhill of Battelle for Kids, who directs EdLeader21, a national network of districts that are implementing 21st century learning. The organization provides professional learning opportunities, resources, and conferences to bring members together in person. Many of the school leaders interviewed for this book are from EdLeader21 member districts.

Statewide PLCs are also being formed to support districts that are collaborating on POG implementation. In Ohio, the state PLC is SOAR; in Virginia, it is the Virginia School Consortium for Learning, and in California, a recently formed PLC is Scaling Student Success (see Resources to learn more). All of these networks are good organizations for you and the members of your community who either need to be convinced of the value of a POG or are interested in deepening their understanding of how to implement your POG.

Networking can also advance research into the effectiveness of school transformation strategies. Digital Promise League of Innovative Schools engages educators to work with researchers on specific challenges, such as developing and prototyping tools and strategies to accelerate real-world learning. Several of the districts highlighted in this book are members who showcase specific strategies through the network.

Some communities are forging their own local or regional networks to support 21st century learning goals. This strategy builds a community-based approach to youth development, harnessing the resources of all the organizations that share a commitment to the healthy development of young people.

Remake Learning in Pittsburgh, Pennsylvania, is a prime example. It brings together stakeholders from K–12 and higher education, libraries, museums, industry, churches, community centers, and others who support student-centered learning in both formal and informal settings. The result has been increased collaboration among diverse stakeholders and rapid dissemination of effective strategies, including an open-source digital "playbook" and shared understanding of key competencies for 21st century success (Boss, 2017b).

Another robust network to support school transformation is emerging in the Kansas City area. Across six counties in Kansas and Missouri, alliances between employers and school systems are creating new learning opportunities that will better prepare some 100,000 students for college and careers.

The Real World Learning network grew out of research by the Kauffman Foundation. An analysis of career education opportunities revealed a wide range of activity but little coordination across the region. "Every district was doing something of high quality," said Miles Sandler, the foundation's director of engagement for education, "but it was disparate and not connected." What's more, career-related education offerings were only reaching about 15 percent of students across the region. In some districts the percentage was much lower, revealing an equity challenge.

A working group of about fifty—including representatives from K–12 districts, higher education, business, parents, and civic leadership—crafted a Portrait of a Graduate for the entire region. As a backward design strategy, the group then mapped out career-related learning experiences that would lead to the desired outcomes captured in the regional POG.

Through that collaborative design work, the network has formalized ambitious and equitable goals to build the competencies of every student. By the time students across the network finish high school, they now need to have earned a diploma plus *at least one* of these in-depth experiences:

- Work experience, which could be an internship of at least 120 hours with a business or nonprofit organization or a client-connected project addressing a real-world problem that a business or nonprofit partner identifies
- College credits, with at least nine credits in an area of focus
- Industry-recognized credential
- Entrepreneurial experience, such as developing a workable business plan for a start-up

By 2020, the network had grown to include more than thirty school districts and charter schools and their existing business partners, along with more than fifty business and civic partners that had not previously been active in K–12 education. The Kauffman Foundation continues to grow the network with grants for design and implementation, technology pilots, and regular convenings of members. When school systems join Real World Learning, superintendents gain access to a network of thought partners. They also agree to assign a staff person as their "B2E" (business to education) point person. This person within the school system helps potential partners choose from a menu of options for engagement.

The network's ongoing dialogue between education and industry has helped to keep educational offerings in sync with changing trends. For example, many of the industry credentials and certifications offered in schools across the region were outdated. The Mid-American Regional Council helped to vet the list so that certifications students were earning in high school would be valued by regional industries.

Real World Learning network is still relatively young, but leaders are already seeing the benefits. "There's a lot of learning as we build this," Miles Sandler said. "The way superintendents have come together to learn from each other has been huge."

Networks will offer you multiple benefits, but the value proposition clusters around the following:

- Validating what you're doing
- Pushing you to go farther by seeing what's possible
- Providing feedback on your work
- Providing a platform to share your best practices and inspire others

As you consider the benefits of networking to help achieve your shared vision of student success, ask yourself the following questions.

ASK YOURSELF

- *Where do you turn now, outside of your own school system, to deepen your learning, troubleshoot common challenges, and share your own insights? Who are your thought partners? Think about both formal and informal networking that strengthens your leadership.*
- *What steps will you take to learn about best practices around the country and also create local or regional networks with other organizations committed to healthy youth development or workforce development?*

Final Reflections

As we near the end of our shared journey, take time to reflect on how your commitment to partnerships will help move your vision forward.

Here are final reflections to consider:

- What are your leadership strengths when it comes to building effective partnerships? What are your areas for growth? If you aren't strong on building partnerships, who will you identify on your team who has that strength?
- As you form partnerships to help achieve your vision, how will you ensure that all students will benefit from these new opportunities to redefine success?
- How will you communicate progress toward POG outcomes so that your stakeholders stay engaged and connected to your shared "why?"

RESOURCES FOR IMPLEMENTATION

EdLeader2I, a national network of Battelle for Kids, promotes connections among district leaders and collaborative professional learning to support districts in the design and implementation of their POGs. battelleforkids .org/networks/edleader2I

Iowa BIG is an innovative public high school model that combines project-based learning with community partnerships. iowabig.org/about/model

Nepris is an online platform to connect educators and students with industry professionals to bring real-world expertise into the classroom. nepris.com

Real World Learning, a project of the Kauffman Foundation and community partners across the Kansas City region, connects students with projects, internships, and opportunities for entrepreneurial experiences while in high school. kauffman.org/real-world-learning

ThoughtExchange is a technology tool to engage stakeholders in virtual conversations and bring more voices into community decision making. thoughtexchange.com

To learn more about states with PLCs of schools and districts focusing on Portrait of a Graduate, see

- Scaling Student Success in California, scalingstudentsuccess.org

- SOAR network in Ohio, battelleforkids.org/networks/soar

- Virginia School Consortium for Learning, vascl.org

For Your Bookshelf

All Together Now: How to Engage Your Stakeholders in Reimagining School, by Suzie Boss

An Intro to Project Based Learning for Parents, by John Larmer, available in both English and Spanish from PBLWorks

Parent Voice: Being in Tune With Your Kids and Their School, by Russell Quaglia, Kristine Fox, and Deborah Young

Action Steps

Just as diverse stakeholders helped to shape your new vision of student success, they remain critical partners as you work toward realizing your POG. Be intentional about leading strong partnerships with these action steps:

1. **Expand family outreach.** Think beyond traditional family engagement strategies as you work toward POG goals. Introduce new roles for parents that support student success. Investigate barriers that might be preventing some families from taking a more active role in their children's education, and then be creative about seeking solutions (such as providing translation, offering flexible scheduling for parent conferences, providing learning opportunities for parents, or using social media or technology platforms). Keep families informed of progress toward POG goals.

2. **Get creative about engaging community allies.** Reduce barriers to business and community partnerships by offering a menu of ways that allies can support student success. Help partners recognize students as capable problem solvers. Once you do, encourage them to provide challenges for students to work on. Look across your region for potential partners who share your school system's commitment to healthy youth development.

3. **Leverage the power of networks.** Validate the work you are doing and spur your team to tackle new goals by taking part in professional networks focused on redefining student success. Rely on these relationships as sources of wisdom when you encounter barriers and bumps in the road.

We hope you have gained ideas and inspiration about leveraging partnerships to support the work ahead. As we move on to the final chapter, be ready to turn to your networks and partners to support you with the next steps in your journey as a bold leader.

CHAPTER 8

Your Next Steps as a Bold Leader

Redefining student success is the great issue of the moment for K–12 education. We hope you are inspired by the potential of creating this vision of transformation for your school or district. Clearly the work is hard, but now at the end of our journey together, we want to leave you with a sense of optimism. We have shared powerful and inspiring examples of

- Communities and educators partnering to redefine student success as a vision for the future of education
- Students solving real-world, challenging problems
- Education leaders like yourself helping to lead the transformation process

You should be encouraged by these examples. They show evidence of substantial progress as this work continues to gain momentum.

Before moving forward with next steps, let's take time to look back. Throughout the book, we have asked what you saw as the "through lines" in the stories we shared. As a summary, we want to share the three major themes that capture our attention and encourage you to connect them to your context.

FOCUS ON YOUR STUDENTS

Your role is to keep the focus on your students' best interests. This means focusing on outcomes that matter to prepare them for the future. If you focus only on the achievement gap, you will not close the *readiness gap*. Pay particular attention to self-direction as the mode by which students can navigate their own learning. Cultivate a green light culture for students to be creative problem solvers in meaningful contexts. To help you in your dialogue with students, Appendix B includes information to download a free companion booklet, *The Student's Guide to 21st Century Learning*, available in English and Spanish.

Looking back at the many field trips in the book, you may be struck, as we are, by what students are capable of achieving given the opportunity and guidance by their teachers. Too often we underestimate students' abilities. We hope this book will dispel that attitude with the display of impressive student work. *Recall the examples of students making big differences by changing state policy to remediate mold in their school ["Removing Mushrooms (and Mold) in Alexandria, Virginia" in Chapter 3]. Think about the team of students who developed a patented breathalyzer bracelet ("Inventing a Breathalyzer Bracelet in Lancaster, California," also in Chapter 3).*

ASK YOURSELF

- *What are the best examples today in our school or district of students engaged in creative problem solving?*
- *What are the content or interdisciplinary areas where creative problem solving is currently thriving in our system?*

FOCUS ON YOUR COMMUNITY

As a society, we are facing extraordinary, unsolved challenges. Here's the thing—the challenges confronting your community, our nation, and beyond present a major opportunity:

- We need students' help in addressing these challenges.
- When students are engaged in helping, they are developing the competencies they need to solve their own personal challenges and their community's collective challenges of the future.

To succeed with school transformation, you need to define community in the broadest sense. By co-creating your vision and your Portrait of a Graduate (POG) with diverse stakeholders, you ensure that the POG will have durability because it has emerged from your own context.

Embrace your teachers and your administrators, co-creating implementation plans with them. Remember that redefining student success also means redefining educator and leader success.

Pay special attention to parents. Involve families from the beginning and keep communicating with them about the changes and progress you are making. To help in this relationship, Appendix C includes information to download a free companion booklet, *The Parent's Guide to 21st Century Learning,* available in English and Spanish.

Understand that your implementation plans, including development of creative problem solvers, depend in good measure on your ability to partner with your community. *Remember how business leaders in Akron worked with the school district to develop career academies (described in Chapter 1) and how leaders in Kansas City collaborated on creating opportunities for students to have real-world learning experiences (described in Chapter 7).*

ASK YOURSELF

- *Who are currently my most effective partners?*
- *Which of these partnerships are focused on helping my students prepare for their future?*

FOCUS ON YOUR GREEN LIGHT CULTURE

As we have emphasized, creating a green light culture for your school system will enable and support the innovation and experimentation necessary to change the status quo and to respond to challenges. Green light culture sends a clear message to students, teachers, and building leaders that their ideas are worth pursuing—and that you will have their backs. Building this culture will be a critical element of your transformation. *Remember the Colorado teacher who knew her principal would give her a green light for the Lake Arbor science project in their community—and the principal, in turn, knew that the superintendent encouraged such innovation ("Contributing as Citizen Scientists in Arvada, Colorado," in Chapter 3). Remember, too, how educators in West Bloomfield, Michigan, were able to adapt quickly during the COVID-19 crisis because their culture valued experimentation and collaboration (described in Chapter 2).*

ASK YOURSELF

- *To whom have I and my team attempted to give a green light for an innovative idea or project?*
- *Who in my district currently understands that they have a green light?*

YOUR SIX NEXT STEPS AS A BOLD LEADER

We have asked you to look back and assess where you are. Now we want you to determine your next steps. Much of our advice has been built on the premise that incrementalism is not the solution to close the readiness gap. The work of transformation runs up against the intransigence of current practices and policy. We have recommended bold moves to help create the necessary momentum to overcome the status quo and make the shift from addressing the achievement gap to focusing on the readiness gap. At the end of each chapter, we identified action steps you can take to bring the focus of that chapter to your context. Now we consolidate these into six bold moves to help you to realize the vision that you and your community share.

1. **Focus on bold challenges.**

Incremental steps may have a place on occasion, but the premise of this book is that we are at a moment that demands bold action. You will need bold leadership skills in imagining and then co-creating your vision. Two tools will support your work. Your POG defines the competencies that students need for future success. Your Portrait of an Educator (POE) defines the competencies teachers need to be successful in helping students reach their goals. Don't stop at developing these visions; continue to use them as your North Star to guide implementation. Your bold leadership will articulate and follow through on the development of your green light culture. You also can set challenges for your school or district around creative problem solving, civic engagement, and self-direction. Addressing these challenges will require rethinking pedagogy and assessment. *Be inspired by the story from Anaheim, California (at the start of Chapter 5), where students were entrusted to lead their community through a racial controversy with the support of teachers who had been trained in a methodology to teach critical thinking and build students' citizenship skills.*

It will take bold leadership to successfully implement creative problem solving through interdisciplinary learning. You can expect resistance, but you must overcome it. In the next decade, we predict that the rise in interdisciplinary learning and creative problem solving will be the biggest shift in education.

Keep the focus on your students and the problems they want to solve rather than the heavy content burdens imposed by outdated standards.

ASK YOURSELF

- *How can I work with students to identify challenges in the school or community that they want to help solve?*
- *How will I and my team reach out to community partners to help students take on the challenges that they care about solving?*

2. **Green light your priorities.**

The green light culture is critical to building and sustaining momentum for this work. Remember, however, as Jason Glass, Kentucky commissioner of education, points out in Chapter 2, you need to determine exactly what it is that you are going to green light.

Throughout the book, we have shared examples of specific strategies and initiatives that have catalyzed significant improvements for students and communities. Do your own green light assessment using Figure 8.1 to identify which of these bold moves will be most urgent for your school system. Figure 8.1 is also available for download on this book's companion website at https://resources.corwin.com/redefiningstudentsuccess.

Figure 8.1   Assessing Your Green Light Priorities

Which of these components need to be given a green light in the next phase of your work? Use the table to make notes about your top priorities and what you hope to accomplish as a result. Which ones stand out as most urgent or potentially transformative for your school system?

BOLD MOVE	YOUR PRIORITIES
Portrait of a Graduate (POG)	
Community advisory board for POG	
Portrait of an Educator (POE)	
Green light culture for adults	
Creative problem-solving challenge	
Sustainability challenge	
Innovation, invention, and entrepreneurship challenge	
Civic engagement challenge	
Green light culture for students	
Instructional challenge	
Assessment challenge	
Community partnerships	

As you identify the components you want to focus on in the next phase of your work, remember the advice you have heard about pacing and timing. Your priorities will depend on where you are in the transformation process.

Once you have identified your own bold moves, ask your leadership team to go through the same exercise. (They may want to discuss the book first to understand the concepts—see Appendix A for a Discussion Guide.) The goal is to reach a consensus on the next steps for all of you to move forward with the transformation of your system. Your next steps must be based on the co-created priorities of your team. Focus on the elements you want to prioritize in the coming three to five years and include them in your strategic planning process.

To fine-tune your leadership message as you move forward, pay attention to the tight–loose leadership continuum we discussed in Chapter 2.

ASK YOURSELF

- When you are in a tight phase, focus on, *How can I be clear that this is something we absolutely need to do for every child?*
- If it's a loose phase, focus on, *How do we make clear that principals and their teachers need to find their own way to best implement the overall goal?*
- *Which of the strategies in Figure 8.1 will be the best levers for moving my system forward from where it is today?*

3. **Lead through the continuums of change.**

Developing your green light culture is not a matter of just flipping a switch. There is a tendency to think that the light is either "on" or "off." In reality, these elements are on a continuum of development when it comes to culture. Your role is to help your system navigate the continuums of change we have described:

Figure 8.2   Continuums of Change

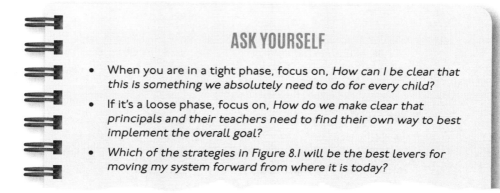

Achievement Gap	⟶	Readiness Gap
State Policy	⟶	POG
Incrementalism	⟶	Bold Leadership
4 Cs in Silos	⟶	Interdisciplinary Problem Solving
Teacher-Driven Instruction	⟶	Self-Directed Learning
Top-Down Culture	⟶	Green Light Culture
Isolation	⟶	Collective Efficacy and Partnerships

Reflect on where you and your system are on each of these continuums. Identify these continuums to your team and then lead them in thoughtful, collaborative work on how to move forward on the element you are focusing on together. Visualizing, articulating, and coaching your team along the continuums is a central part of your work as a transformation leader.

Managing the continuum between state policy and your POG can be particularly challenging. As we discussed in Chapter 1, there is an inherent tension between current state policy focused on traditional achievement metrics and the vision of your POG.

Rich Fry, superintendent in Big Spring, Pennsylvania, describes the tension this way: "The leadership challenge of this work is finding out how to balance between conviction and compliance. The superintendent must take care of the compliance side while lighting the fire for what kids truly need."

Phil Downs, superintendent in Southwest Allen, Indiana, poses these essential questions to keep his team focused on their shared vision: "What do your kids need to take away from their K–12 experience? How do you balance this broader view with what the state is asking for? My job as a leader is to give my team the authority to pursue the broader view."

Convince your team to trust that you and your board really want them to teach toward the outcomes of the POG. This aspect of your work will require backbone and courage on your part and on the part of your team. If you want your team to be responsive to your POG, they must be assured that you will run interference and that they won't be chastised or penalized for committing to your new collective vision.

ASK YOURSELF

- *Which of these continuums do we need to prioritize for the next phase of our work?*
- *How will I help educators move along the continuums that we identify as top priorities?*

4. **Focus on equity.**

Another area that requires bold leadership is equity. As you lead this work, you and your team must keep your focus on equity. The effects of COVID-19 on people of color and the issues raised by the

Black Lives Matter movement have made clear how extensive these equity challenges are. Seize this opportunity to address not only a new model of change but also insist that the broader issue of equity be addressed at the same time. Remember, if you attempt to redefine student success without addressing equity, you will be building upon and likely exacerbating the inequities of the past.

Now is the time to take on the challenges of equity and equitable access in every aspect of your work.

Aaron Spence, superintendent in Virginia Beach, Virginia, explains how the POG process connects to equity. "One of the biggest impacts of our POG was that it pushed us to define what we mean by success and pushed us to personalize those outcomes for *every* student."

ASK YOURSELF AND YOUR TEAM THESE CRITICAL QUESTIONS

- *What kind of leadership do I need to provide so that the POG competencies are truly available to each and every child?*
- *What will be our strategy to ensure that the POG competencies reach those students farthest from opportunity?*

5. **Emphasize collective efficacy.**

You may recall that in Chapter 2, Mike Duncan, superintendent in Pike County, Georgia, talked about "collective efficacy." He used this term in the context of his teachers recognizing that they had to improve their performance "together," thus replacing the traditional isolation of the past. We want to underline the importance of this and expand its application.

The concept of collective efficacy is crucial going forward. It is not only crucial for your teachers, but it is crucial for your students, as well. The term "collaboration" can seem like a "nice to have." Wouldn't it be better if we all got along? Collective efficacy makes it clear that we must collaborate to improve our collective performance. There isn't a business or nonprofit today that isn't reliant on collective efficacy. It is a requirement of every successful enterprise or organization. The same requirement applies to education.

Think about your school or district governance and the governance of your community. Collective efficacy is an essential element of your system's success.

We acknowledge (and many of you are painfully aware) that many school boards and local governments are wracked with dysfunction. And while we have tried to avoid politics in this book, there's no question that the 2016 and 2020 national elections have underscored the political divisiveness in the United States and around the world. These developments cry out for the prioritization of collective efficacy by our educational systems. Our local communities are the best place to model collective efficacy and civility. This is where we can create the future of education by redefining student success. If our communities, nation, and society will survive and thrive, restoring a sense of collective efficacy and civility will be crucial.

In this book, we have gone to great lengths to emphasize the importance of creative problem solving. If we can combine collective efficacy and creative problem solving, we will be well on our way toward addressing the challenges facing our communities and society at large.

We want you as a leader to reflect deeply on the union of "creative problem solving" and "collective efficacy" and hope you and your team will realize the importance of embracing them both—for the well-being of each of your students and the communities, organizations, and cultures that they will be part of in the future.

ASK YOURSELF

- *How will I motivate my team to move beyond collaboration as a "nice to have" and embrace collective efficacy of students and educators as essential for transforming our system?*
- *How can we specifically embrace collective efficacy and creative problem solving in addressing the challenges of our community?*

6. **Embrace resilience.**

COVID-19 shined a bright light on issues of equity and also illuminated the relationship between crisis and resilience. Too often, headlines concerning COVID-19 and education have focused on disruption. We suggest more positive possibilities:

- COVID-19 has spurred innovation by exposing the needs of the system requiring attention.
- Transformational leaders have used the pandemic to more deeply embed some of the innovation practices already underway.

There will be crises in the future, always. If not a pandemic, then a budget crisis, or a major weather disaster, or . . . The question for you as a leader is whether you allow a crisis to delay or disrupt your vision or whether you use the crisis as an opportunity to deepen your commitment to your vision.

Resilience is not about merely surviving a crisis. It is about using the crisis to drive toward your ideal vision. It's about moving toward an even better future. *Remember the example in Chapter 4 about Humble ISD in Texas, where the school community came together to recover from Hurricane Harvey.*

During the pandemic, Kelly Lyman, superintendent in Mansfield, Connecticut, worried that the crisis "would take us off track with respect to implementation of our POG. The opposite occurred. We doubled down on our commitment, and we saw examples of POG teaching and learning in all three modes of our COVID-19 existence: physical presence learning, hybrid learning, and online learning. As a result, I am now convinced this work will live in our community for a long time."

School leaders would be wise to take to heart this advice from Lee Fisher, dean of the Cleveland State University Cleveland-Marshall College of Law, when it comes to leading through times of crisis (Fisher, 2020):

> If COVID-19 has taught us anything, failure is not only an option, it's a requirement. Leaders must give permission to themselves and to those with whom they work to experiment, innovate, and take risks. With that approach comes permission to fail along the way to finding the things that work and make a difference.
>
> Beware of leaders who say they know the answer. The single most important leadership quality in a crisis is knowing what you don't know and having the humility to admit it . . . Leading in the pandemic is what I call Corona Leadership—it's about leaning into uncertainty and ambiguity, embracing some inevitable failures along the way, and working together to find the best winding, crooked path forward.

What we have found during the writing of this book is that transformational leaders and their teams showed incredible resilience during COVID. Not only did they get through the crisis, but they were also able to leverage it to advance their vision.

You should do the same. Whether you are still dealing with the aftermath of COVID-19 or if you are on to your next crisis, use the opportunity to advance the work of redefining student success.

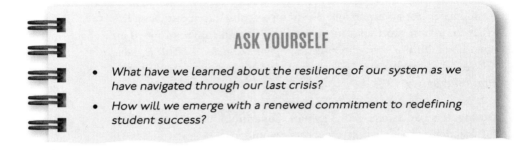

ASK YOURSELF

- What have we learned about the resilience of our system as we have navigated through our last crisis?
- How will we emerge with a renewed commitment to redefining student success?

Figure 8.3   Redefining Student Success: 6 Steps as a Bold Leader

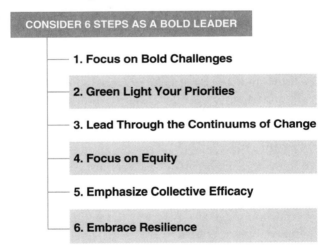

CONSIDER 6 STEPS AS A BOLD LEADER

1. Focus on Bold Challenges

2. Green Light Your Priorities

3. Lead Through the Continuums of Change

4. Focus on Equity

5. Emphasize Collective Efficacy

6. Embrace Resilience

MOMENTUM IS GROWING

The stories of students and educators featured in previous chapters offer inspiring evidence that change is indeed possible. Another encouraging trend is the coalescing of broad-based community support around a powerful new model of education. Leaders and their communities working together to forge new visions will be the foundation of the future of education. To reinforce our message that you have allies to support your work, we highlight five trends.

National Organization Momentum There is evidence of growing support for the work that communities like yours are undertaking. Organizations in education working on diverse areas— including project-based learning, competency-based education, entrepreneurship, and career academies—confirm that their own efforts at improvement in institutions are vastly enhanced when the school or system has already adopted a set of student competencies.

Cheryl Carrier, executive director of Ford Next Generation Learning, describes the essential relationship between the POG and new school models: "The career academy is a transformation model for high school. You can't start the model without a POG. Once you develop your POG, everything is built around it. It becomes their guiding star. The POG helps us take the career academy model from a workforce development strategy to a personalized learning strategy for each student."

Bob Lenz, CEO of PBLWorks, confirms this perspective, saying, "If you don't have a POG, you are going to need to create one. Our work on PBL makes more sense if the district has already defined the 'why.' The POG is critical and should be the driver for everything the district does."

The POG has also picked up momentum from some accreditation groups. The New England Association of Schools and Colleges has included a requirement that schools and districts adopt a "Vision of a Graduate." To harness the full potential of the POG and get to the real and deep implementation we describe in Chapter 6, these new requirements must not be treated as a superficial "check the box."

State Momentum A growing group of allies for the POG has emerged in state government. Several states have adopted or are in the process of developing their own POG. One of the early states to adopt a POG was South Carolina. The SC POG sprang from a dialogue between a group of local school district superintendents and members of the state business leader community at a meeting hosted by Molly Spearman, then executive director of the South Carolina Association of School Administrators. That dialogue led to the proposal of a POG that was subsequently adopted by the SC Superintendent Roundtable and the South Carolina Chamber of Commerce. Today, as South Carolina state education commissioner, Molly is working to embed the state POG in state policies.

The adoption of a POG in Virginia came after many individual districts in the state had adopted their own POGs. James Lane, Virginia superintendent of public instruction, notes, "The best way to get a state to support the POG is for key districts to adopt their own POGs and then urge the state to support that innovative direction. The POG is such a big piece of where we are now. I think we have institutionalized it in the right way. We chose guidance and capacity building over reporting, regulations, and codification. Also, the POG has become an essential component of our equity work. We have fused them together. We believe we are putting in place a structure where a student's race or socioeconomic background will no longer be a predictor of their outcomes." Lane underscores the importance of this work when he says, "Every student highly engaged every day will eradicate the readiness gap."

Utah has begun its POG journey more recently. Sydnee Dickson, state commissioner of education, comments, "We have been driven for a long time by the 3 Bs—Bells, Buses, and Butts [seat-time]. Here is what I want our direction to be: When our students graduate from our system, can they be articulate about their future and what they are taking into their future?"

Jason Glass, state commissioner of education in Kentucky, will be launching extensive statewide conversations in 2021, which will lead to the adoption of a Kentucky POG.

These four states are just at the beginning of what we see as a broad consideration of the "readiness gap" by state governors and legislatures. "The key is to make sure that states understand that the POG will become part of the personalization not the standardization of education," emphasizes Tom Vander Ark, CEO of Getting Smart. "We need to get states to create a climate in which communities will create their own POG. We want to encourage the POG, not mandate the specific skills."

Urban District Momentum States must encourage and support their urban districts in redefining student success. We are pleased that we could include some urban examples in this book (including Akron and Columbus, Ohio, and the greater Kansas City area). Not enough urban districts have taken on the challenge of redefining student success. We hope that more urban districts will pursue this path.

David James, superintendent in Akron, reflects on why urban districts have been slower to adopt a POG for their students: "I am afraid that in most urban districts the central conversation focuses on how to maintain the interests of the adults in the system. If those districts keep asking themselves, 'What is in the best interests of the kids?'

they won't be stuck in a system that simply perpetuates old policies and practices that don't serve kids well. I suggest they focus less on the problems of adults and more on the dreams and aspirations that kids have for themselves."

Talisa Dixon, superintendent in Columbus, Ohio, thinks some urban districts have shied away from this work out of a concern for what a dialogue with their community might entail. She observes: "Community conversations can be scary. You have to be open to being vulnerable with your stakeholders. We were fortunate to have a local not-for-profit with experience in hosting these community conversations. It may be viewed in some communities that these conversations are too hard, but you can't expect the kinds of partnerships you need to forge without these conversations. Our POG process allowed us to expand and strengthen our partnerships, and the process put our district on a much more solid foundation."

Wendy Kopp, former CEO of Teach For America and current CEO of Teach For All, has pointed out, "In the U.S., we feel so pressured by the current disparities of traditional academic outcomes that many urban districts, in particular, can't think bigger. We are too focused on 'catching up' kids to a narrow range of outdated outcomes."

More urban districts need to begin this journey. Their students need the 21st century competencies as much as or more than any other group of students in the country.

Federal Momentum There is reason for optimism in this country with the advent of a new administration. A new president, first lady, and secretary of education who are focused on the future of U.S. education should be open to redefining student success as a fundamental strategy to prepare young people for their future challenges. We call on them to use their bully pulpits to urge communities around the country to begin the dialogue on how to redefine student success.

Global Momentum International comparisons show that 21st century competencies are further along around the globe than in the United States (Taylor, Fadel, Kim, & Care, 2020). The work of Fernando Reimers, Ford Foundation Professor of Practice in International Education, Harvard University, has documented well the global interest in 21st century competencies (Reimers & Chung, 2016; Reimers, 2021).

In Chapter 4, you heard from Wendy Kopp about the work of her organization to develop young education leaders globally. She explained how, five years ago, Teach For All stepped back as a global network to articulate a twenty-five-year vision. She said, "We reflected on where the world would be in the year 2040 and recognized the incredible challenges we would face in navigating a changing economy, geopolitical conflicts, and challenges around inclusiveness and sustainability. We saw all the more clearly that we need to develop the students in classrooms today as leaders who can shape a better future for themselves and all of us. In fact, countries in many parts of the globe are reaching consensus on this purpose for education."

We are hopeful the momentum we see in communities, education organizations, states, and globally will continue and grow. We share this momentum so you can see you aren't alone as you take on the challenge of redefining student success. The reality is that every school and district needs to address the readiness gap. All students need 21st century competencies, no matter where they live.

In the end, you and your community can make a firm stand for change and transformation in the best interests of your students. You and your community, along with others following this course of action, will serve as beacons for all communities in your state and beyond. You will be part of the growing momentum for this work in the United States and around the globe.

Final Reflections
Inspiration From the Field

For us as authors, one of the most fulfilling aspects of this project has been talking with the people you have met and many others you haven't. We want to thank all of them. Because of their willingness to talk about their efforts to shape the future of education, we have been able to include the perspectives of teachers, superintendents, union leaders, business owners, state education commissioners, entrepreneurs, nonprofit leaders, principals, and—most importantly—students. Their voices will help us end the book with a message of inspiration.

- Karen Garza has worked with many districts on the

challenges we have discussed, and she is hopeful. "The POG work I did with my district in Virginia was the most inspiring work of my professional life. Today I work with hundreds of districts around the country and several dozen leaders in Ohio very intensely. I am heartened by the dynamic leadership I am seeing and the amazing support for transformation that these leaders provide for each other. Courageous leaders working together can ensure that this vision for students becomes reality."

- A student from Tucson, Arizona, told us how much she appreciated being taken seriously in a civic engagement program. "You come out of it knowing that you learned something. You can talk about issues in our world. You can apply what you know to the real world."

- Rick Robins, former superintendent of Juab, Utah, school district, fully implemented their POG. Rick is now superintendent in the Canyons School District, Utah. He is emphatic about this work as well, saying, "We are trying to get systems to move on from a 1900 factory-based model of educating the masses, teaching to the middle, and fitting square pegs into round holes. The challenge is to get leaders to determine what could be, to be the experts, to look forward. Locking ourselves into the status quo is such a disservice to our students

and community. I have come to really believe in the power of a community-based POG. I am an optimist and I will carry this vision until my last breath."

- David James, Akron superintendent, describes the goal this way, "We need to prepare our students for what they are going to face beyond the K–12 environment. Our POG is critical because it is our vision of where students need to be when they leave us."

- For Karen Cheser, superintendent in Fort Thomas, Kentucky, the promise of this work is for students "to realize their passions and have a viable career. We want their sweet spot to be at the intersection of their interests and talents and the needs of the community and the world. Our POG defines what skills our students will need to find their sweet spot. That is the destination for education that inspires me."

We hope you, too, have been inspired by the great work we have described. If you commit to creating your vision and start to implement it, we predict you will also understand that the process itself will take you in the right direction. The best thing to do is simple: Get started.

As you go forward with creating your vision for redefining student success, wear your leadership mantle humbly and with empathy. Keep in mind the message of this book: BE BOLD. Your students deserve nothing less.

Appendix

INTRODUCTION

The book opens with stories of two young adults who used their skills to tackle difficult challenges. Do you agree with the authors' argument that every student needs to be ready to tackle similar challenges? Can you share more examples involving students from your school system who have tackled their own challenges? What skills and competencies did they harness? (For example: Communication skills to be effective in online and in-person advocacy? Collaboration skills to lead and contribute to teams? Digital skills to create or leverage technology tools to meet their goals? Others?) How might your shared reading of this book help you bring these critical skills to all students?

CHAPTER 1: BE THE LEADER OF A BOLD VISION

Early in this chapter, you were introduced to leaders who encountered crossroads at different phases in their careers. Discuss where you are on your individual leadership journeys. What has shaped your core beliefs about the purposes of education? How would you describe the gap between what each of you wants for your students and what your current system is accomplishing? When you think about redefining student success, what comes to mind? As you think about engaging your community to adopt a bold vision, have you considered developing a Portrait of a Graduate (POG)? How will you convene a diverse group of stakeholders to shape your POG? How will you engage community members (including students) whose voices have not been heard in the past? How will you ensure that you view this work through an equity lens?

CHAPTER 2: BE THE LEADER OF A GREEN LIGHT CULTURE

This chapter introduces the concept of a green light culture. Does this concept cause you to think differently about culture? Discuss how each of you nurtures a green light culture with the people around you. What next steps will you take to assess and nurture your system's green light culture? What have you done as a system to embed your Portrait of a Graduate and Portrait of an Educator (POE) deeply into your system, including policies for hiring, professional development, and teacher evaluation? Are there other aspects of your system that should be anchored in your POG/POE?

CHAPTER 3: BE THE LEADER OF CREATIVE PROBLEM SOLVERS

What is your reaction to the authors' suggestion that creative problem solving is the "first among equals" when it comes to core competencies that students need to develop? Author Daniel Pink asserts that problem *seeking* is even more important than problem solving. He also advocates viewing the world through a wide aperture rather than in content silos, to find connections between disparate topics. How does your system give students the green light to identify problems they want to solve? How do you help your students engage in interdisciplinary problem solving? What success stories can you share about your students tackling sustainability challenges? What benefits have resulted for your school or system? After exploring the "field trips" to see innovation, invention, and entrepreneurship education in action, what new ideas do you want to bring to your schools? Teacher Rachel Thibault described her successful student inventors as "the most unlikely of student teams." What more could you do to promote creative problem solving by students in your system who are not already STEM superstars or advanced academically? Later in the chapter, both Ayele Shakur and Tom Vander Ark argue that every student needs an entrepreneurial mindset and skillset. What are you doing already to develop these qualities for every student? How can you build on existing efforts?

CHAPTER 4: BE THE LEADER OF ENGAGED CITIZENS

This chapter acknowledges the leadership challenges of preparing students to be active citizens. Discuss your reactions to the opening story from Anaheim (or student involvement in more recent events, such as Black Lives Matter). How would you have responded to these community challenges? Do your stakeholders understand that effective civic education includes both building knowledge and taking informed action? How do you celebrate and showcase your students' efforts to make the world a better place? As you consider bold citizenship challenges for your community, discuss your strategies for the following:

- Staffing: If you're designing new courses or adopting new programs, how will you ensure an interdisciplinary focus? Who will teach them? How will you ensure that teachers have the time and professional development they need to be successful?
- Assessment: How will you evaluate students' civic development? How will students document their growth in both content knowledge and civic engagement?
- Community buy-in: How will you enlist community partners who are willing to collaborate with students on civic problem solving?

CHAPTER 5: BE THE LEADER OF SELF-DIRECTED YOUNG PEOPLE

This chapter summarizes several competing terms for students owning their learning. Does your system have more work to do to clarify the language in your POG about self-direction? Has your team identified practical look-fors that describe evidence of students becoming self-directed? What support structures do your students need to take more ownership of their learning? How do you encourage students to take advantage of opportunities outside the classroom to develop their skills as self-directed people? How will you know if a green light culture that encourages students to innovate and experiment is taking hold across your system?

CHAPTER 6: BE THE LEADER OF BOLD LEARNING

If you were participating in an event like the Portrait to Practice example described at the start of this chapter, what would you showcase from your school system? Why? How would you utilize a Portrait to Practice exercise in your district or school? How are you encouraging your instructional staff to design backward from your POG? Who in your district can coach and support teachers as they rethink instruction? How are you capturing key moves that teachers and instructional leaders are making to shift their practice toward creative problem solving? How might you enlist external partners or consultants as thought leaders to launch or support your instructional challenge? What structures for adult learning (such as instructional coaching, professional learning communities, classroom walks, or learning labs) will help your teaching team adopt and sustain new classroom practices? How can you allocate resources to support these structures? What is the right entry point to introduce student-engaged assessment?

CHAPTER 7: BE THE LEADER OF STRONG PARTNERSHIPS

How can you encourage parents and community partners to take on new roles to support student learning, especially around neighborhood and community problem solving? How can you help parents prepare for these roles, especially those who have not traditionally been active participants in their children's education? How can you encourage partners to recognize the benefits of supporting student success? How will you access best practices from around the country and globe to help you with this work? How might your school system build a local or regional network with other organizations committed to your POG competencies and healthy youth development? What would you hope to gain? Who could help you launch an effort like this? What would it take to grow and sustain this network?

CHAPTER 8: YOUR NEXT STEPS AS A BOLD LEADER

The final chapter challenges you to focus on six bold moves to realize the vision that you have created in collaboration with your community. As you review the second bold move that uses the green light tool, what are you going to green light? What will your team prioritize, and how will you support them as a leader? Discuss which specific actions each of you is willing to commit to now and also in the longer term. Consider planning a follow-up discussion to share your progress and support each other's efforts. How will you use Figure 8.2 in this chapter to assess where you are now and how you will lead your team to make progress on the continuum items you have prioritized? Where are your educators on the continuum between isolation and collective efficacy? How can you help them move? As you move ahead with your vision, how will you keep equity at the heart of the work you are doing so that students who have been farthest from opportunity develop the skills they need to survive and thrive? Keep in mind this key leadership question: "Which of the strategies will be the best levers for moving my system forward from where it is today?"

This Discussion Guide can also be found on the book's companion website at **https://resources.corwin.com/redefiningstudentsuccess**.

Appendix B: Help Students Develop Their Competencies

How are you helping students gain experience as creative problem solvers and engaged citizens? Are you encouraging them to look for opportunities outside of school as well as during class time to tackle challenges, build their competencies, and reflect on their growth?

To support this important work, we have developed a free resource, available in both English and Spanish. Download *The Student's Guide to 21st Century Learning* from the companion website at **https://resources.corwin.com/redefiningstudentsuccess** You will also find a downloadable poster that highlights six success skills students need for the future.

Here are suggestions for sharing these resources with your students.

- Download, print, and share copies of the guide as discussion starters with students, teachers, parents, and other community members
- Share on your school or district website
- Share with your school board
- Use in presentations to parents and community groups
- Encourage counselors and career counselors to share with students
- Encourage teachers to use these resources to encourage students to set goals and assess their own progress toward the competencies they want to develop, both for individual projects and for learning in general

For *The Student's Guide to 21st Century Learning*, *The Parent's Guide to 21st Century Learning* (both available in English and Spanish), and other materials, please visit the book's companion website at https://resources.corwin.com/redefiningstudentsuccess

Appendix C: Engage Parents as Partners

Parents and other family members are essential partners when it comes to school success. That's especially true when schools pursue new visions to better prepare students for today's challenges.

To help parents understand how the changing landscape of education will support their children's success, we have developed a free resource in both English and Spanish. Download *The Parent's Guide to 21st Century Learning* from the companion website at **https://resources. corwin.com/redefiningstudentsuccess.**

Here are suggestions for sharing this resource with your community.

- Download, print, and share copies of the guide as a discussion starter with your parent association or other interested parent groups
- Share on your school or district website
- Share with your school board
- Share in presentations to parents, community groups, and business partners
- Encourage teachers to share copies with families at back-to-school nights and during parent conferences.
- Use as a resource to generate interest in developing a Portrait of a Graduate with your community

For *The Student's Guide to 21st Century Learning, The Parent's Guide to 21st Century Learning* (both available in English and Spanish), and other materials, please visit the book's companion website at https://resources.corwin.com/ redefiningstudentsuccess

Appendix D: List of Interviewees

Many people contributed time, ideas, and research to help us create this book.

State Superintendents of Education

Kentucky State Education Commissioner Jason Glass

Virginia Superintendent of Public Instruction James Lane

Utah State Superintendent of Public Instruction Sydnee Dickson

South Carolina State Superintendent of Education Molly Spearman

Additional State-Level Leaders

North Dakota Department of Corrections and Rehabilitation: Penny Hetletved, director of education

South Carolina Department of Education: Stephanie DiStasio, director of personalized learning

Utah State Higher Education Commissioner Dave Woolstenhulme

Utah State Board of Education: Sarah Young, director of strategic initiatives

District and Instructional Leaders, Teachers, Parents, and Students

Akron Public School (OH): Superintendent David James; Rachel Tecca, director of college and career academies

Albemarle County Public Schools (VA): Superintendent Matt Haas and leadership team

Alexander Dawson School (NV): Brandon Wiley, chief academic officer

Alexandria City Public Schools (VA): Mary Breslin, teacher; Bridget and Benjamin, students

Anaheim Union High School District (CA): Superintendent Michael Matsuda; Carlos Hernandez, director of curriculum and instruction; Jackie Counts, director of innovative programs; Scott Reindl, career education program administrator

Andover Public Schools (MA): Superintendent Sheldon Berman

Antelope Valley Union High School District (CA): Rachel Thibault, teacher

Bellingham Public Schools (WA): Superintendent Greg Baker; Mike Copland, deputy superintendent

Belpre City Schools (OH): Superintendent Jeff Greenley

Big Spring School District (PA): Superintendent Rich Fry; Crystal Header and Leslie Locy, teachers

Boston Public Schools (MA): Allison Hramiec, head of school, Boston Day and Evening Academy

Canyons School District (UT): Superintendent Rick Robins

Columbus City Schools (OH): Superintendent Talisa Dixon

Cumberland County Public Schools (VA): Superintendent (retired) Amy Griffin, teacher Sherri Almond

Davis Joint USD (CA): Associate Superintendent Rody Boonchouy

Encinitas Union SD (CA): Superintendent Andrée Grey; Tim Baird, former superintendent; Alice Larsen, teacher and parent; Drew Larsen, student; Glen Warren, director of literacy, outreach, and libraries

Environmental Charter Schools (CA): Alison Diaz, founder

Ephrata Area School District (PA): Superintendent Brian Troop

Farmington Public Schools (CT): Superintendent Kathy Greider, Kim Wynne, assistant superintendent; Veronica Ruzek, director of curriculum and instruction

The Forest School (GA): Co-founder Tyler Thigpen

Fort Thomas Independent Schools (KY): Superintendent Karen Cheser; Elizabeth Koch, teacher

Frederick County Public Schools (VA): Superintendent Dave Sovine; Jerry Putt, principal

Glenbard High School District 87 (IL): Superintendent David Larson

Granville Exempted Village Schools (OH): Superintendent Jeff Brown and students

Humble ISD (TX): Superintendent Elizabeth Fagen; Luci Schulz, assistant superintendent for elementary; Ann Johnson, chief academic officer; Deborah Perez, director of contemporary instructional design; Elizabeth King, professional learning coordinator

Hyde Park Central School District (NY): Superintendent Aviva Kafka and Superintendent (retired) Greer Rychcik; Mary Beth Scattergood, NYSUT Hyde Park Local president

International School of Prague: Director Chip Kimball

Jeffco Public Schools (CO): Matthew Flores, chief academic officer; Brenda Fletcher, principal; Alicia Asmus and Erin Fichtel, teachers; Andrew Ellis and Zach Ford, students; John Ford, parent and past president of Jefferson County Education Association

Juab School District (UT): Assistant Superintendent Royd Darrington

Lincoln-Sudbury Regional High School (MA): Superintendent Bella Wong

Lindsay Unified SD (CA): Barry Sommer, director of advancement; Alexis and Gaby Leon, students; Lorena Leon, parent

Mansfield School District (CT): Superintendent Kelly Lyman; Kaye Jakan, district literacy consultant; Mike Seal, principal; Melissa DeLoreto and Catherine Hain, teachers; Oliver Smithson, student

Mechanicsburg Exempted Village Schools (OH): Superintendent Danielle Prohaska

Napa Valley Unified School District (CA): Superintendent Rosanna Mucetti

Natick Public Schools (MA): Superintendent Anna Nolin; Tim Luff, assistant superintendent for student services; Brian Harrigan, principal; Tracy Sockalosky, Stacy Gauthier, and Grace Magley, teachers; Jefferson Wood, co-president, Education Association of Natick

Needles USD (CA): Superintendent Mary McNeil

New Tech Network (CA): Jim May, former chief schools officer

Newington Public Schools (CT): Superintendent Maureen Brammett, Director of Secondary Education Kristen Freeman, teachers Ashley Klopfer, Jennifer Freese, Nate Emerson, Matt Zitney

North Salem Central School District (NY): Julio Vazquez, director of instruction and human resources

Nyack (NY): Superintendent James Montesano; David Johnson, principal; Tom DiLeo, assistant principal

Oak Park USD (CA): Jay Greenlinger, director of curriculum and instruction; Brendan Callahan, director of bond programs and sustainability; Winnie Sloan, teacher

Pequea Valley School District (PA): Superintendent Erik Orndorff, Director of Technology Ashley Rednak, Assistant Superintendent Rich Eby

Pike County Schools (GA): Superintendent Mike Duncan

Pomperaug High School, Region 15 (CT): teacher Lois de Gregory

Portland Public Schools (OR): Nichole Berg, program manager for Climate Change and Climate Justice; Yena Perice and Sriya Chinnam, students

Reynoldsburg City Schools (OH): Superintendent Melvin Brown

Saline Area Schools (MI): Superintendent (retired) Scot Graden; Superintendent Steve Laatsch

Salt Lake City Public Schools (UT): Dessie Olson, education specialist-social studies

Sanborn Regional High School (NH): Principal Brian Stack

San Francisco USD (CA): Nora Houseman and Nolberto Camarena, Department of Professional Growth and Development

Schalmont Central SD (NY): Superintendent (retired) Carol Pallas and student Mariana Riccio

School of Environmental Studies (MN): Principal Lauren Trainer

Shelby County Public Schools (KY): Susan Dugle, chief academic officer

Southwest Allen County Public Schools (IN): Superintendent Phil Downs; Luann Erickson; Park Ginder, principal; Adam Schenkel, Homestead High School radio and television director; students Ashton Hackman and Chris Wang

Stillwater Area Public Schools (MN): Superintendent (retired) Denise Pontrelli; Rachel Larson, director of learning and student engagement; Rob Bach, principal

Sunnyside (AZ): Superintendent Steve Holmes; Steven Ujeda and Norma Higuera-Trask, teachers; Yaxiri Ortiz, Monique Trujillo, Patrick Robles, and other students

Tiverton Public Schools (RI): Superintendent Peter Sanchioni

Val Verde USD (CA): Superintendent Michael McCormick; Aimee Garcia, director of K–12 education; Jennifer Gronotte, teacher; and Doug Henderson, director of STEAM and CTE

Virginia Beach City Public Schools (VA): Superintendent Aaron Spence; Tim Cole, sustainability officer; Chris Freeman environmental studies program coordinator; Kelly Hedrick, principal; Melissa Follin, teacher

West Bloomfield (MI): Superintendent Gerald Hill; Kimberly Abel, president of West Bloomfield Education Association

West High School (UT): Suzanne Arthur and Holly Reynolds, teachers

Whitefish School District (MT): Ryder Delaloye, director of curriculum and instruction

Additionally, We Wish to Acknowledge the Following:

Juan Manuel Gonzalez Barajas, Teach For All Mexico

Carole Basile, dean, Mary Fulton Teachers College, Arizona State University

Phoebe Beierle, Green Schools Fellowship manager, Center for Green Schools

Tracy Benson, president, Waters Center for Systems Thinking

Tony Bent, leadership consultant and former local superintendent in Massachusetts

Anirban Bhattacharyya, partner, Transcend Education

Veronica Boix-Mansilla, principal investigator, Project Zero, Harvard Graduate School of Education

Cheryl Carrier, executive director, Ford Next Generation Learning

Ruiz Clarke, interim CEO, Teach For All Armenia

Jaimie Cloud, founder and president, The Cloud Institute for Sustainability Education

Laura Cole, assistant professor, architectural studies, University of Missouri

Bill Considine, CEO emeritus, Akron Children's Hospital

Jon Corippo, chief learning officer, CUE

Stephanie Couch, executive director, Lemelson-MIT Program

Andre Daughty, urban educator and consultant

Kristin de Vivo, director, Lucas Education Research

Ted Dintersmith, author and education change agent

Joe Dragone, senior executive officer, Capitol Region BOCES (NY)

Nadine Eckstom, president, Academic Discoveries LLC

Heather Ehlers, freelance editor

Eric Eshbach, assistant executive director, Pennsylvania Principals Association

Steve Farr, Teach For All Global Learning Lab

Lee Fisher, dean, Cleveland-Marshall College of Law

Peggy Zone Fisher, president, The Diversity Center of Northeast Ohio

Cindy Meyers Foley, executive assistant director, Columbus Museum of Art

Nancy Ford, council member, City of Arvada (CO)

Erica Fortescue, creativity architect and consultant

Karen Garza, president and CEO, Battelle for Kids

Brian Greenberg, CEO, Silicon Schools Fund

Valerie Greenhill, vice president, Battelle for Kids

Cindy Gutierrez, director of partnerships, Urban Community Teacher Education, University of Colorado-Denver

Elaine Gurian, senior museum consultant

Richard Haass, president, Council on Foreign Relations

Virgel Hammonds, chief learning officer, KnowledgeWorks

Anisa Heming, director, Center for Green Schools

John Henry, STEAM and Sustainable Schools Specialist New Jersey School Boards Association

Margaret Honey, president and CEO, New York Hall of Science

Gretchen Hooker, senior program manager, Biomimicry Institute

Kathy Hurley, education consultant

Archana Iyer, Teach For All Global Learning Lab

Cindy Johanson, executive director, Edutopia

Merrit Jones, senior adviser, Student Voice

Braden Kay, sustainability director, City of Tempe, Arizona

Dan Keenan Jr., executive director, Martha Holding Jennings Foundation

Lisa Kensler, associate professor of education leadership, Auburn University College of Education

Bruce King, University of Wisconsin-Madison, Center for Authentic Intellectual Work

Christine Lawlor-King, professional development coordinator, Lemelson-MIT Program

Wendy Kopp, CEO, Teach For All

Rick Lear, education strategist

Hadley Lewis, student, Auburn University

Brent Maddin, executive director for education workforce initiatives, Mary Lou Fulton Teachers College, Arizona State University

Michael Manore, president and founder, Vispective LLC

Michael Marks, CEO (retired), Flextronics and Katerra; adjunct faculty, Stanford Business School

Sheri Marlin, chief learning officer, Waters Center for Systems Thinking

Donna McDaniel, educator-in-residence, Ewing Marion Kaufman Foundation

Scott McLeod, associate professor of education leadership, University of Colorado-Denver

Jay McTighe, education consultant and author

Vince Meldrum, president and CEO, Earth Force

Matt Mervis, director, Skills21

Amy Meuers, CEO, National Youth Leadership Council

Ann Millner, Utah State Senator

Pam Moran, executive director, Virginia School Consortium for Learning

Alyson Nielson, vice president, Battelle for Kids

Aaron North, vice president of education, Ewing Marion Kauffman Foundation

Scott Palmer, community coach, Ford Next Generation Learning

Walter Parker, professor emeritus of social studies education and political science, University of Washington

Bob Pearlman, education strategy consultant

Jim Phillips, president and CEO, Azomite Mineral Products

Daniel Pink, author

Sandeep Rai, Teach For India

Fernando Reimers, Ford Foundation Professor of International Education, Harvard Graduate School of Education

Miles Sandler, director of engagement-education, The Kauffman Foundation

Sam Seidel, director of K–12 strategy and research, Hasso Plattner Institute of Design at Stanford University ("the d.school")

Jenny Seydel, executive director, Green Schools National Network

Ayele Shakur, CEO, BUILD

Roman Stearns, founder and executive director, Scaling Student Success

Betty Sternberg, commissioner emerita and director, Teacher Leader Fellowship Program, Central Connecticut State University

Kylie Stupka, president, Youth Entrepreneurs

Tom Vander Ark, CEO and partner, Getting Smart

Pat Wasley, CEO (retired), The Teaching Channel

Justin Wells, executive director, Envision Learning Partners

Don Wettrick, CEO and co-founder, StartEdUp

Jeremy Wickenheiser, executive director, Watson Institute

Matt Williams, executive vice president and chief strategy officer, KnowledgeWorks

Julie (Wilson) Jungalwala, founder and executive director, Institute for the Future of Learning

April Wright, senior product manager, Buddy Technologies

David Young, CEO, Participate Learning

Mi Zhenhua, Teach For All Global Learning Lab

References

Ban Ki-moon. (2012). Global Education First initiative: Statement from the Secretary-General. Retrieved from http://www.unesco.org/new/en/gefi/about/an-initiative-of-the-sg/

Berger, R., Rugen, L., & Woodfin, L. (2014). *Leaders of their own learning: Transforming schools through student-engaged assessment.* San Francisco, CA: Jossey-Bass.

Boss, S. (2017a, Dec. 7). A small town school embraces a big vision. *Edutopia.* Retrieved from https://www.edutopia.org/article/small-town-school-embraces-big-vision

Boss, S. (2017b). *All together now: How to engage your stakeholders in reimagining school.* Thousand Oaks, CA: Corwin.

Boss, S., & Krauss, J. (2018). *Reinventing project-based learning: Your field guide to real-world projects in the digital age* (3rd ed.). Portland, OR: ISTE.

Boss, S., with Larmer, J. (2018). *Project based teaching: How to create rigorous and engaging learning experiences.* Alexandria, VA: ASCD.

Brooklyn Lab Charter School. (2020). *Learner identity and agency guidebook.* New York: Author. Retrieved from https://e82589a9-6281-40c3-81a5-087eb2ac5db9.filesusr.com/ugd/e57059_0bb757de108b4d8595bb324e22348bf3.pdf

Carnegie Corporation of New York & CIRCLE. (2003). *The civic mission of schools.* New York: Author. Retrieved from https://www.carnegie.org/publications/the-civic-mission-of-schools/

Choi, Y. (2019, June 24). Oakland's graduate profile: A spotlight on what matters most. Retrieved from https://www.nextgenlearning.org/articles/oaklands-graduate-profile-a-spotlight-on-what-matters-most#:~:text=A%20graduate%20profile%20can%20help,toward%20the%20vision%20it%20set

CivXNow. (2019). *Coalition policy menu: A guide for state and local policymakers with options to strengthen and improve civic learning for all students.* Washington, DC: iCivics. Retrieved from https://civxnow.org/sites/default/files/basic_page/CivXNow%20Policy%20Menu%20-%20FINAL.pdf

Dintersmith, T. (2019). *What school could be: Insights and inspiration from teachers across America.* Boston, MA: Edu21c Foundation.

DuFour, R. (2007). In praise of top-down leadership. *School Administrator, 64*(10), 38–42. Retrieved from https://aasa.org/schooladministratorarticle.aspx? id=6498

DuFour, R., & Eaker, R. (1998). *Professional learning communities at work: Best practices for enhancing student achievement.* Bloomington, IN: National Educational Service.

Edutopia. (2020, July 10). A tech support center run by students. *Edutopia.* Retrieved from https://www.edutopia.org/video/tech-support-center-run-students

EL Education. (2020, Feb. 3). *A reason to believe: Stories of literacy impact.* Retrieved from https://eleducation.org/news/a-reason-to-believe-all-students-can-reclaim-their-right-to-literacy

Fisher, L. (2020, May 1). Lee Fisher's take on leading in a crisis. *Cleveland Magazine.* Retrieved from https://clevelandmagazine.com/cleader/community/articles/lee-fisher-s-take-on-leading-in-a-crisis

Folkman, J. (2015, June 18). Bold leadership: The 4 steps that take leaders to another level. *Forbes.* Retrieved from www.forbes.com/sites/joefolkman/2015/06/18/bold-leadership-the-4-steps-that-take-leaders-to-another-level/? sh=49fb6e245cfa

Frederick County Public Schools (FCPS) Media Network. (2019). *Student innovation and creativity* [video]. Available online at https://www.youtube.com/watch? v=AhYsZXIxbYA&feature=youtu.be

Fullan, M., Quinn, J., & McEachen, J. (2017). *Deep learning: Engage the world, change the world.* Thousand Oaks, CA: Corwin.

Gallup. (2016). *The Gallup-HOPE Index: Quantifying the economic energy of America's youth.* Washington, DC: Gallup Inc. and Operation HOPE. Downloaded from https://news.gallup.com/reports/207899/2016-gallup-hope-index-report-download.aspx

Glass, J. (2020, Sept.). On civility: Five rules for engagement. *School Administrator 8*(77), 35–37.

Green, D. (2021). *One school's commitment to equity using student-centered learning.* Retrieved from https://studentsatthecenterhub.org/resource/one-schools-commitment-equity-student-centered-learning/

Greenberg, B. (2020, June 2). What we've learned from distance learning, and what it means for the future. *Education Next.* Retrieved from https://www.educationnext.org/what-weve-learned-from-distance-learning-what-it-means-for-future-improving-online-education/

Haass, R. (2020). *The world: A brief introduction.* New York: Penguin Press.

Hewlett Foundation. (2013, April 13). *Deeper learning defined.* Menlo Park, CA: Author. Retrieved from https://hewlett.org/library/deeper-learning-defined/

Hodgin, E., & Choi, Y. (2016, Sept. 30). Educating for democracy in the digital age [Tchers' Voice Blog]. Retrieved from https://www.teachingchannel. com/blog/educating-for-democracy-in-the-digital-age

Iowa BIG. (n.d.). *The Iowa BIG model.* Retrieved from https://iowabig .org/about/model/

ISTE (International Society for Technology in Education). (2016). *ISTE standards for students.* Portland, OR: Author. Retrieved from https://www.iste.org/standards/for-students

Kahne, J., & Middaugh, E. (2008). *Democracy for some: The civic opportunity gap in high school* (CIRCLE Working Paper 59). Medford, MA: Center for Information and Research on Civic Learning & Engagement. Retrieved from https://circle.tufts.edu/sites/default/files/2019-12/ WP59_TheCivicOpportunityGapinHighSchool_2008.pdf

Kallick, B., & Zmuda, A. (2017). *Students at the center: Personalized learning and habits of mind.* Alexandria, VA: ASCD.

Kawashima-Ginsberg, K., & Sullivan, F. (2017, March 26). Study: 60 percent of rural millennials lack access to a political life. *The Conversation.* Retrieved from https://theconversation.com/study-60-percent-of-rural-millennials-lack-access-to-a-political-life-74513

Kay, K. (2019, Sept. 16). "The power of student-led learning." *Battelle for Kids Learning Hub.* Retrieved from https://www.battelleforkids.org/ learning-hub/learning-hub-item/the-power-of-student-led-learning

Kay, K., & Greenhill, V. (2012). *The leader's guide to 21st century education: 7 steps for schools and districts.* New York: Pearson.

Kazimour, K. (2019, June 24). #MeetAPartnerMonday—Meet Bernard Dutchik. Retrieved from https://iowabig.org/2019/06/24/imon/

Klingel, S. (2003). *Interest-based bargaining in education.* Washington, DC: National Education Association. Retrieved from https:// ecommons.cornell.edu/handle/1813/74328

Kundu, A. (2020). The power of student agency to combat educational inequity. *Learner Agency and Identity Handbook.* New York: Brooklyn Lab Charter School. Retrieved from https:// e82589a9-6281-40c3-81a5-087eb2ac5db9.filesusr.com/ugd/ e57059_0bb757de108b4d8595bb324e22348bf3.pdf

Larmer, J., Mergendoller, J., & Boss, S. (2015). *Setting the standard for project based learning: A proven approach to rigorous classroom instruction.* Alexandria, VA: ASCD.

Maier, A., Adams, J., Burns, D., Kaul, M., Saunders, M., & Thompson, C. (2020). *Using performance assessments to support student learning: How district initiatives can make a difference.* Palo Alto, CA: Learning Policy Institute. Retrieved from https://learningpolicyinstitute .org/product/cpac-district-initiatives-assess-student-learning

McTighe, J., & Silver, H. (2020). *Teaching for deeper learning: Tools to engage students in meaning making.* Alexandria, VA: ASCD.

McTighe, J., Doubet, K., & Carbauch, E. (2020). *Designing authentic performance tasks and projects: Tools for meaningful learning and assessment.* Alexandria, VA: ASCD.

Mehta, J., & Fine, S. (2019). *In search of deeper learning: The quest to remake the American high school.* Cambridge, MA: Harvard University Press.

National Center for Learning Disabilities. (2018). *Agents of their own success: Self-advocacy skills and self-determination for students with disabilities in the era of personalized learning.* Washington, DC: Author. Retrieved from https://www.ncld.org/wp-content/uploads/2018/03/Agents-of-Their-Own-Success_Final.pdf

National Council for the Social Studies. (2013). *Career, college, and civic life: C3 framework for social studies state standards.* Silver Spring, MD: Author. Retrieved from https://www.socialstudies.org/sites/default/files/c3/c3-framework-for-social-studies-rev0617.pdf

National Education Association. (n.d.). *Preparing 21st century students for a global society: An educator's guide to the "Four Cs."* Washington, DC: Author. Retrieved from http://dl.icdst.org/pdfs/files3/0d3e72e9b873e0ef2ed780bf53a347b4.pdf

Newman, F., Carmichael, D., & King, M. (2016). *Authentic intellectual work: Improving teaching for rigorous learning.* Thousand Oaks, CA: Corwin.

Niehof, J. (2020, Aug. 5). The virtuous cycle of student agency [CompetencyWorks Blog]. Retrieved from https://aurora-institute.org/cw_post/the-virtuous-cycle-of-student-agency/

Our Kids, Our Future. (2019). *All kids should be loved: A glimpse at Bellingham's approach to equity, diveristy and inclusion.* Retrieved from https://www.ourkidswa.com/all-kids-should-be-loved-a-glimpse-at-bellinghams-approach-to-equity-diversity-and-inclusion/

Pelligrino, J. W., Hilton, M. L. (Eds.), National Research Council (NRC) Committee on Defining Deeper Learning and 21st Century Skills (2012). *Education for life and work: Developing transferable knowledge and skills in the 21st century.* Washington, DC: National Academies Press.

Pink, D. (2006). *A whole new mind.* New York, NY: Riverhead Books.

Poon, J. (2018, Sept.). Part 1: What do you mean when you say 'student agency'? *Education Reimagined.* Retrieved from https://education-reimagined.org/what-do-you-mean-when-you-say-student-agency/

Portland Public Schools. (2019). *Portland Public Schools reimagined: Preparing our students to lead change and improve the world.* Portland, OR: Author. Retrieved from https://www.pps.net/cms/lib/OR01913224/Centricity/Domain/219/PPS_Vision_Final.pdf

Reimers, F. (Ed.). (2021). *Leading educational change during a pandemic: Reflections of hope and possibility.* Cambridge, MA: Fernando Reimers.

Reimers, F., & Chung, C., Eds. (2016). *Teaching and learning for the twenty-first century: Educational goals, policies, and curricula from six nations.* Cambridge, MA: Harvard University Press.

Rogers, J., & Kahne, J. (2021, Feb. 11). Leading for democracy: A vital agenda for public school principals. *ASCD Express 16*(11). Retrieved from http://www.ascd.org/ascd-express/vol16/num11/leading-for-democracy-a-vital-agenda-for-public-school-principals.aspx

Rose, T. (2013). *The myth of average.* TEDxSonomaCounty [video]. Retrieved from https://www.youtube.com/watch?v=4eBmyttcfU4&feature=emb_title

Schwab, K. (2016, Jan. 14). "The fourth industrial revolution: what it means, how to respond." [World Economic Forum Global Agenda Blog]. Retrieved from https://www.weforum.org/agenda/2016/01/the-fourth-industrial-revolution-what-it-means-and-how-to-respond/

Slocum, N. (2016, Feb. 17). What is personalized learning? [Education Domain Blog]. Retrieved from https://aurora-institute.org/blog/what-is-personalized-learning/

Stiggins, R. (2007, May). Assessment through the student's eyes. *Educational Leadership, 64*(8), 22–26. Retrieved from http://www.ascd.org/publications/educational-leadership/may07/vol64/num08/Assessment-Through-the-Student's-Eyes.aspx

Taylor, R., Fadel, C., Kim, H., & Care, E. (2020, Oct.). *Competencies for the 21st century: Jurisdictional progress.* Center for Curriculum Redesign and Brookings Institution. Retrieved from https://www.brookings.edu/research/competencies-for-the-21st-century-jurisdictional-progress/

Trilling, B., & Fadel, C. (2012). *21st century skills: Learning for life in our times.* San Francisco, CA: Jossey-Bass.

Wagner, T. (2008). *The global achievement gap: Why even our best schools don't teach the new survival skills our children need—and what we can do about it.* New York: Basic Books.

Wagner, T., & Dintersmith, T. (2016). *Most likely to succeed: Preparing our kids for the innovation era.* New York: Scribner. New York: Basic Books.

Wells, J. (2020, Oct. 1). From poster to practice: How to fulfill the promise of graduate profiles [PBLWorks blog]. Retrieved from https://www.pblworks.org/blog/poster-practice-how-fulfill-promise-graduate-profiles

Wiggins, G., & McTighe, J. (2005). *Understanding by design* (2nd expanded ed.). Alexandria, VA: ASCD.

Winthrop, R. (2020, June 4). The need for civic education in 21st century schools. *Policy 2020 Brookings*. Retrieved from https://www.brookings.edu/policy2020/bigideas/the-need-for-civic-education-in-21st-century-schools/

YouthTruth. (2017). *Learning from student voice: Are students engaged?* San Francisco, CA: Author. Retrieved from https://youthtruthsurvey.org/student-engagement/#section1

Zhao, Y. (2012). *World class learners: Educating creative and entrepreneurial students*. Thousand Oaks, CA: Corwin.

Index

Leadership That Makes an Impact

MICHAEL FULLAN & MARY JEAN GALLAGHER

With the goal of transforming the culture of learning to develop greater equity, excellence, and student well-being, this book will help you liberate the system and maintain focus.

PETER M. DEWITT

This step-by-step how-to guide presents the six driving forces of instructional leadership within a multistage model for implementation, delivering lasting improvement through small collaborative changes.

BRYAN GOODWIN

If you've ever wondered anything, really—just out of curiosity—then you have what it takes to lead your school to restored curiosity and your students to well-being and success.

JOHN HATTIE & RAYMOND L. SMITH

Based on the most current Visible Learning® research with contributions from education thought leaders around the world, this book includes practical ideas for leaders to implement high-impact strategies to strengthen entire school cultures and advocate for all students.

DAVIS CAMPBELL & MICHAEL FULLAN

The model outlined in this book develops a systems approach to governing local schools collaboratively to become exemplars of highly effective decision-making, leadership, and action.

MICHAEL FULLAN, JOANNE QUINN, & JOANNE MCEACHEN

The comprehensive strategy of deep learning incorporates practical tools and processes to engage educational stakeholders in new partnerships, mobilize whole-system change, and transform learning for all students.

JOANNE QUINN, JOANNE MCEACHEN, MICHAEL FULLAN, MAG GARDNER, & MAX DRUMMY

Dive into deep learning with this hands-on guide to creating learning experiences that give purpose, unleash student potential, and transform not only learning, but life itself.

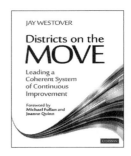

JAY WESTOVER

The transformative framework outlined in this book creates a districtwide approach for changing the culture of learning and creating a coherent system of continuous improvement.

Also Available

**ANTHONY KIM,
KEARA MASCARENAZ,
& KAWAI LAI**

This guide provides battle-tested practices to help leaders build better habits for team learning, meetings, and projects, to achieve a more responsive, innovative organization.

EVAN ROBB

Build the foundations of effective leadership despite daily distractions. Learn how to intentionally use ten-minute opportunities to consider and execute your vision.

**AMY TEPPER &
PATRICK FLYNN**

Nineteen strategies help leaders, coaches, and teachers improve their ability to identify desired outcomes, recognize learning in action, collect relevant evidence, and develop effective feedback.

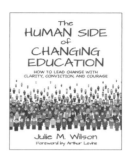

JULIE M. WILSON

Learn to make sense of challenging change journeys and accelerate implementation with this practical framework that includes human-centered tools, resources, and mini case studies.

GRANT LICHTMAN

Our rapidly evolving world is dramatically impacting how we view schools. *Thrive* shows educators how they can help their schools not only survive but thrive during rapid change.

ERIC SHENINGER

The future-forward framework in this book prepares leaders to harness the power of innovative ideas and digital strategies to create relevant, engaging, and intuitive school cultures.

**CHRISTINE MASON,
PAUL LIABENOW, &
MELISSA PATSCHKE**

Envision and enact transformative change with an iterative visioning process, thought-provoking vignettes, case studies from exemplary schools, key strategies and tools, and practical implementation ideas.

**KIRSTEN RICHERT,
JEFFREY IKLER, &
MARGARET ZACCHEI**

Shifting empowers educational change leaders to proactively and coherently navigate complex, unprecedented change in schools and establish a school culture in which changemakers can thrive.

LDN20264

CORWIN
A SAGE Publishing Company

Helping educators make the greatest impact

CORWIN HAS ONE MISSION: to enhance education through intentional professional learning.

We build long-term relationships with our authors, educators, clients, and associations who partner with us to develop and continuously improve the best evidence-based practices that establish and support lifelong learning.